At David C Cook, we equip the local church around
the corner and around the globe to make disciples.
Come see how we are working together—go to
www.davidccook.org. Thank you!

DAVID **C** COOK
transforming lives together

What people are saying about …

The Fresh Life Series

"I'm touched and blessed by Lenya's heart for His kingdom."

—**Kay Arthur**, Bible teacher and author of many bestselling Bible studies

"What a great way for women to learn to study the Bible: interesting stories, thought-provoking questions, and a life-changing approach to applying Scripture. Lenya provides a great method so women can succeed and grow spiritually in a short period of time. Kudos!"

—**Franklin Graham**, president and CEO of Billy Graham Evangelistic Association and Samaritan's Purse

"Skip and Lenya Heitzig have been friends of my wife, Cathe, and I for more than twenty years. Lenya loves to study God's Word and teach it to women in a way that is both exciting and accessible. I trust her latest book will be a blessing to you."

—**Greg Laurie**, pastor and evangelist of Harvest Ministries

"Lenya's love for the Lord and knowledge of His Word uniquely equips her to help other women discover the pathway to God through these in-depth Bible studies."

—**Kay Smith**, wife of Chuck Smith (Calvary Chapel)

"The Fresh Life Series is an insightful and in-depth look at God's Word. Through these Bible studies, Lenya Heitzig leads women to deeper intimacy with God."

—**K. P. Yohannan**, president of Gospel for Asia

"Lenya has created another wonderful Bible study series that invites participants to spend time in God's Word and then see the Word come to fruition in their lives. What a blessing! These studies are perfect for small groups or personal daily devotions."

—**Robin Lee Hatcher**, women's event speaker and award-winning author

Live Hopefully

The Fresh Life Series

Live Hopefully

A Study in the Book of Nehemiah

Lenya Heitzig

DAVID C COOK

transforming lives together

LIVE HOPEFULLY
Published by David C Cook
4050 Lee Vance Drive

Colorado Springs, CO 80918 U.S.A.
David C Cook U.K., Kingsway Communications

Eastbourne, East Sussex BN23 6NT, England

The graphic circle C logo is a registered trademark of David C Cook.

The website addresses recommended throughout this book are offered as a resource to you. These websites are not intended in any way to be or imply an endorsement on the part of David C Cook, nor do we vouch for their content.

Unless otherwise noted, all Scripture quotations are taken from the New King James Version®. Copyright © 1982 by Thomas Nelson. Used by permission. All rights reserved. Scripture quotations marked NIV84 are taken from the Holy Bible, New International Version®, NIV®. Copyright © 1973, 1984 by Biblica, Inc.™ Used by permission of Zondervan. All rights reserved worldwide. www.zondervan.com. Scripture quotations marked NIV are taken from the Holy Bible, NEW INTERNATIONAL VERSION®, NIV®. Copyright © 1973, 2011 by Biblica, Inc.® Used by permission. All rights reserved worldwide. NEW INTERNATIONAL VERSION® and NIV® are registered trademarks of Biblica, Inc. Use of either trademark for the offering of goods or services requires the prior written consent of Biblica, Inc. Scripture quotations marked NLT are taken from the *Holy Bible, New Living Translation*, copyright © 1996, 2007 by Tyndale House Foundation. Used by permission of Tyndale House Publishers, Inc., Carol Stream, Illinois 60188. All rights reserved.

LCCN 2017946245
ISBN 978-1-4347-1247-9
eISBN 978-0-8307-7257-5

Published in association with William K. Jensen Literary Agency, 119 Bampton Ct., Eugene, OR 97404.

The Team: Alice Crider, Amy Konyndyk, Rachael Stevenson, Heather Gemmen Wilson, Susan Murdock
Cover Design: Nick Lee and Ashley Ward
Cover Photo: Getty Images

Contributors: Misty Foster, Maria Guy, Vicki Perrigo, Trisha Petero, Laura Sowers, Christy Willis
Printed in the United States of America

First Edition 2018

1 2 3 4 5 6 7 8 9 10

102717

Contents

Introduction

Why Nehemiah? Why Now?

If you are unfamiliar with the Old Testament book of Nehemiah, you may wonder how an ancient book could possibly be relevant to your twenty-first-century life. How could a story about a man who had a passion to rebuild the wall around Jerusalem help you in your job, in your relationships with family and friends—and enemies—and in your spiritual life? You won't have to look far to find principles and examples that transcend time and space to speak to your life right here, right now.

Renovate Your Life

Most people are captivated with the idea of renovation and restoration. In the year 2000, a program called *Trading Spaces* popped up on American TV. The cast included two couples who were neighbors, their designer, and a carpenter. Their mission was to trade houses for a few days and renovate a room in each other's homes. That show was met with such enthusiasm that today there are eighty-nine renovation-style programs on HGTV alone.

We can't seem to get enough of watching something in disrepair be transformed into a vision of beauty and function. Nehemiah had this kind of vision. Living a privileged life in the palace of King Artaxerxes, Nehemiah became aware that Jerusalem was in a dilapidated condition. His heart broke when he heard the accounts of crumbling walls, burned gates, and the shattered spirits of his fellow Jews.

Key Verse: And I told them of the hand of my God which had been good upon me, and also of the king's words that he had spoken to me. So they said, "Let us rise up and build." Then they set their hands to this good work. Nehemiah 2:18

Author: Ezra. Most scholars agree that Ezra wrote the book of Nehemiah based on Nehemiah's diaries, which is why it is written in the first-person (Nehemiah's) perspective. Originally, the books of Ezra and Nehemiah were one book in the Hebrew canon.

Themes: Obedience, prayer, restoration, and the good hand of God

Date: 445 BC, during the twentieth year of the Persian king Artaxerxes

Setting: Judah and Israel had persisted in stubborn unfaithfulness to the Lord. Following seventy years of captivity in Babylon, it was time for Judah's restoration. At this politically delicate and critical time, God placed Nehemiah in a position of trust and influence in the palace of the most powerful king in the Near East: Artaxerxes.

Think about your own life. Is there an area that is in disrepair? A relationship that is crumbling? A wall of protection that needs to be raised? A barrier of misunderstanding that needs to come down? A pile of rubble that is cluttering your focus? If so, Nehemiah is the book for you. You'll learn the basics of serving, leading, motivating others, overcoming adversity, praying and planning, and doing it all to the glory of God. Along the way, we'll find templates in Nehemiah's actions that work just as well today as they did three thousand years ago.

For instance …

Tune In

In the business world, one of the guiding principles of leadership is, "People don't care what you know until they know that you care." Nehemiah cared. When he heard about the situation in Jerusalem, he cared so much that it drove him to his knees in prayer. He mourned and he wept. Already, God had given Nehemiah a heart for His people and His city. And because Nehemiah cared passionately, he knew that God's reputation was at stake. Nehemiah tuned in to the problem and prayed to be part of the solution.

Pray Constantly

It would have been easy for Nehemiah to hear the sad news of the Jews, pray about it, and continue on with his daily life, unaffected by the conditions in far-away Jerusalem. Yet this truth did not slide off his heart. Instead, his prayers kept him focused on the matter and receptive to God's leading. He stuck with the hard work of constant prayer until he knew God's will.

Wait for God's "Go-Ahead"

Nehemiah didn't seek the opinions of others or rush to his own initial conclusions. He waited to hear from God. It was months before God gave Nehemiah the go-ahead to set his plan in motion. If we are not following God, our first step may be in the wrong direction.

Be Prepared

Have you ever launched into a situation and realized you had not considered all that was involved? The result can be embarrassment or, worse, failure. "Ready! Fire! Aim!" rarely results in hitting the mark. Nehemiah prayed before starting the work of rebuilding. It was a good thing, because he was immediately faced with challenges that required diplomacy and preparedness.

Expect Obstacles

How can you know that you are in the midst of a good work that glorifies God? You will experience resistance. Are you surprised? Dismayed? Don't be! The Devil doesn't bother with efforts that have no impact on the kingdom of God. Will you experience ridicule? Maybe. Hostility? Possibly. Jealousy? Likely. While the barriers might seem overwhelming, when you, like Nehemiah, are in God's will, you will encounter great mercy and great power and great goodness from your great God.

Stand Up for What Is Right

It's one thing to recognize when something is wrong, but it's quite another to stand up for what is right. Henry Blackaby said that leadership is the process of moving people to God's agenda. Nehemiah did just that. He stood before the Jews, pointed out the distress of their Jerusalem, and invited them to join in his mission to rebuild the wall so they would no longer be a reproach to themselves and to God. The first question to ask yourself when you set out to do something is, "Is this *right* in God's eyes?"

Fasten Your Seat Belts

Have you ever wondered why God placed you here in the world right now? Of all the centuries past and all the times future, this is the time in which God has placed you in order to fulfill His divine purposes. Wouldn't it be awful to reach the end of your life and find that you missed your opportunity to impact God's people, accomplish a meaningful work, or experience the joy of risking your comfort for a God-inspired work?

You don't have to rebuild a city wall to be involved in a God-glorifying work: "And whatever you do in word or deed, do all in the name of the Lord Jesus, giving thanks to God the Father through Him" (Col. 3:17). Sometimes you needn't look any further than your home, work, or church to find your place of renovation.

Are you engaged in a godly battle? "Wherever you hear the sound of the trumpet, rally to us there. Our God will fight for us" (Neh. 4:20). If the battle is to do a godly work, rejoice. If it's not, search your heart, and ask God to lead you to peace.

Don't let fear, opposition, obstacles, ridicule, complacency, jealousy, statistics, comfort, or skeptics be the walls that keep you from being the woman God has called you to be. Don't neglect the work He has laid out for you since the very foundation of the world! Don't let the mundane demands of daily life blind you to the eternal vision God has set before you.

As you study Nehemiah, be prepared to have your world rocked. This is *your* time to be used for God's purpose. This is your call to action. Be strong, faithful, prayerful, determined, and delighted to do the work God sets before you.

You can live with confidence in an unpredictable world. You can accomplish great things in your immediate surroundings. You can look forward to the future. You can *live hopefully*!

How to Get the Most out of This Study

Each week of this study is divided into five days for your personal time with God. There are five elements to each day's lesson. They are designed to help you fully live as you apply the truths you learn to your life:

1. Lift Up … Here we ask you to "Lift Up" prayers to God, asking Him to give you spiritual insight for the day.

2. Look At … This portion of the study asks you to "Look At" the Scripture text, using inductive questions. These questions help you to discover *What are the facts?* You'll learn the basic who-what-when-where-how aspects of the passage as well as some of the important background material.

3. Learn About … The "Learn About" sidebars correlate to specific questions in order to help you understand *What does this text mean?* These sidebar elements offer cultural insight, linguistic definitions, and biblical commentary.

4. Live Out … These questions and exercises are designed to help you investigate *How should this change my life?* Here you are challenged to personally apply the lessons you have learned as you "Live Out" God's principles in a practical way. I recommend that you write out your answers to all of the questions in this study—especially those for

personal application—in a journal. By writing your insights from God day by day, you'll have a record of your relationship with Him that you can look back on when you need a faith boost.

5. Listen To … The study ends with inspiring quotes from authors, speakers, and writers. You'll be able to "Listen To" the wisdom they've gleaned in their lives and relate it to your own.

Live Hopefully is ideal for discussion in a small-group setting as well as for individual study. The following suggestions will help you and your group get the most out of your study time:

Personal Checklist

- Be determined. Examine your daily schedule, then set aside a consistent time for this study.
- Be prepared. Gather the materials you'll need: a Bible, this workbook, a journal in which to write your thoughts, and a pen.
- Be inspired. Begin each day with prayer, asking the Holy Spirit to be your teacher and to illuminate your mind.
- Be complete. Read the suggested Bible passage and finish the homework each day.
- Be persistent. Answer each question as fully as possible. If you're unable to answer a question, move forward to the next question or read the explanation in the "Learn To …" question and allow the Lord to search your heart and transform your life. Take time to reflect honestly about your feelings, experiences, sins, goals, and responses to God.
- Be blessed. Enjoy your daily study time as God speaks to you through His Word.

Small-Group Checklist

- Be prayerful. Pray before you begin your time together.
- Be biblical. Keep all answers in line with God's Word; avoid personal opinion.
- Be confidential. Keep all sharing within your small group confidential.
- Be respectful. Listen without interrupting. Keep comments on track and to the point so that all can share.
- Be discreet. In some cases, you need not share more than absolutely necessary. Some things are between you and God.
- Be kind. Reply to the comments of others lovingly and courteously.
- Be mindful. Remember your group members in prayer throughout the week.

Small-Group Leader Checklist

- Be prayerful. Pray that the Holy Spirit will "guide you into truth" so that your leadership will guide others.
- Be faithful. Prepare by reading the Bible passage and studying the lesson ahead of time, highlighting truths and applying them personally.
- Be prompt. Begin and end the study on time.
- Be thorough. For optimum benefit, allot one hour for small-group discussion. This should allow plenty of time to cover all of the questions and exercises for each lesson.
- Be selective. If you have less than an hour, you should carefully choose which questions you will address and summarize the edited information for your group. In this way, you can focus on the more thought-provoking questions. Be sure to grant enough time to address pertinent "Live Out …" exercises, as this is where you and the women will clearly see God at work in your lives.

- Be sensitive. Some of the "Live Out …" exercises are very personal and may not be appropriate to discuss in a small group. If you sense that this is the case, feel free to move to another question.

- Be flexible. If the questions in the study seem unclear, reword them for your group. Feel free to add your own questions to bring out the meaning of the verse.

- Be inclusive. Encourage each member to participate in the discussion. You may have to draw some out or tone some down so that all have the opportunity to participate.

- Be honest. Don't be afraid to admit that you don't have all the answers! When in doubt, encourage the women in your small group to take difficult questions to their church leadership for clarification.

- Be focused. Keep the discussion on tempo and on target. Learn to pace your small group so that you complete a lesson on time. When participants get sidetracked, redirect the discussion to the passage at hand.

- Be patient. Realize that not all people are at the same place spiritually or socially. Wait for the members of your group to answer the questions rather than jumping in and answering them yourself.

Trust, Pray, and Wait

Nehemiah 1

On August 12, 1961, while East Berlin slept, an army of trucks and men surrounded the city, tore up the streets, dug holes for concrete posts, and strung barbed wire across the border dividing East and West Berlin. The citizens awoke to a new reality: they could no longer cross the border to work, go to school, or visit family and friends—they were captive. Eventually, the wall of barbed wire was replaced with concrete that stretched over a hundred miles. For decades, the wall served as a grim reminder of the constraints of communism, the failing economy, and shrinking personal freedoms.[1]

Walls have purpose. They are built to protect, establish territory, or contain people or things. The wall dividing East and West Berlin was a barrier to keep people from escaping the oppressive communist rule for the freedoms of a democratic society.

In the ancient city of Jerusalem, however, the wall was just the opposite. This magnificent wall was built for the purpose of protecting the borders from invaders and setting God's chosen people apart. The wall must have been a symbol of strength, security, pride, and freedom. What a different perspective from that of the wall that divided Berlin.

When the Jerusalem wall fell into disrepair, it reflected the crumbling and neglected relationship of the Jews with their God.

In the first chapter of the book of Nehemiah, we follow Nehemiah through his journey of prayer, planning, purpose, and the steadfast promises of God.

Day 1: Nehemiah 1:1–3   **Broken Lives and Burned Walls**

Day 2: Nehemiah 1:4–6   **Deep Grief and Passionate Prayer**

Day 3: Nehemiah 1:6–7   **Honest Confession and Merciful Love**

Day 4: Nehemiah 1:8–10   **Reliable Promise and Faithful Redeemer**

Day 5: Nehemiah 1:11   **Humble Servant and Royal Cupbearer**

DAY 1

Broken Lives and Burned Walls

Lift Up ...

Lord, I pray for an open heart and mind as I read this ancient account of Nehemiah. Help me learn the lessons that are mortared within these sacred words. I want to be a good steward of my life and to keep always in good repair. In Jesus' name. Amen.

Look At ...

In this first lesson we meet Nehemiah, the author of the memoir that inspired Ezra to pen this book of the Bible. Nehemiah wrote his account in the first-person point of view, so we see the events unfold through his loving eyes and his Jewish heart. He devotedly chronicled his own thoughts and actions in the context of this significant time. Although Nehemiah was a Jew, he was living and serving the king of Persia in his luxurious palace. Nehemiah demonstrated his deep concern and love for Jerusalem by taking advantage of the opportunity to talk to someone who knew the conditions of the exiles. Regardless of the consequences, he wanted to learn the absolute truth. In reading this very personal book, we find a man whose faith was neither passive nor impetuous. He sought the Lord's will and followed through with his actions.

Read Nehemiah 1:1–3.

The words of Nehemiah the son of Hachaliah. It came to pass in the month of Chislev, in the twentieth year, as I was in Shushan the citadel, that Hanani one of my brethren came with men from Judah; and I asked them concerning the Jews who had escaped, who had survived the captivity, and concerning Jerusalem. And they said to me, "The survivors who are left from the captivity in the

1 A Man of Comfort

Nehemiah's father is mentioned here to distinguish Nehemiah from other Jews of the same name. The name *Nehemiah* means Jehovah consoles. The definition of his name is especially meaningful in light of the comfort and consolation Nehemiah brought to the Jews. He cared deeply for them and followed God's leading.

2 A Time of Need

Chislev corresponds to our months of November/ December. "The twentieth year" indicates the length of King Artaxerxes' reign. In 538 BC Zerubbabel led the Jews' return to Jerusalem. Ezra led the second return in 458 BC, and in 445 BC a third and final group returned with Nehemiah.[2]

3 A Place of Grandeur

Shushan was located about 150 miles north of the Persian Gulf, in present-day Iran. As a citadel, it was fortified to protect the king from enemy attacks. Built on the acropolis, it served as the Persian monarch's winter palace.

province are there in great distress and reproach. The wall of Jerusalem is also broken down, and its gates are burned with fire." Nehemiah 1:1–3

1. Whose words are written in this book, and how is he identified?

2. In what month and year did Nehemiah begin recording his thoughts and actions?

3. According to verse one, where was Nehemiah residing?

4. Why do you think the men visiting the palace from Jerusalem were of particular interest to Nehemiah?

5. What grievous details did Hanani and the men from Judah give about the people living there?

6. Describe the condition of Jerusalem's walls and gates according to the visiting men.

Live Out ...

7. Do you believe the old adages, "What you don't know won't hurt you" and "Ignorance is bliss"? Why or why not? (Support your answer with examples.)

8. Recognizing the needs of others should do more than evoke our sympathy. There is a difference between a casual concern and a deep care that prompts us to respond.

   a. Read Matthew 14:15. Briefly describe the disciples' response to the needs of the hungry multitudes.

b. Describe how Jesus responded to the multitudes' need for food in verse 16.

9. What walls have been destroyed in your life?
   - ❏ Relationship with God
   - ❏ Finances
   - ❏ Family
   - ❏ Health
   - ❏ Friendships
   - ❏ Other: _____

10. Is God prompting you to take action regarding something you care deeply about? Pray and write about your impressions.

_____

The wall surrounding Berlin was constructed not for the purposes of protection and preservation but for the purposes of imprisonment and control over human hearts and will.

There are times when we must construct walls and other times when we must tear them down. This was the case in Berlin in November 1989. After years of separation and deprivation, the East German Communist Party announced that citizens could once again cross the borders.

The party's attempts to stop the hemorrhaging of the best and brightest people in their city to the democratic West came to an end. Over the years, the citizens never gave up their efforts to escape the tyranny and restrictions imposed on them. At least 171 people were killed trying to escape. Early on, the wall was rebuilt to make it even higher and wider, but people still tried every way imaginable to reach freedom. They dug under it, climbed over it, drove vehicles through the weak sections, and even crossed over in hot air balloons.[4]

6 A State of Disrepair

The people in Jerusalem felt a sense of reproach: scorned, rebuked, and ashamed. Without walls and gates to protect it, Jerusalem was easy prey for attacking enemies and roaming animals. The rubble was a continual source of humiliation to the Jews who loved their city.[3]

7 Open Eyes

Paul the apostle told the Corinthians that he did not want them to be ignorant of his trials. He gave them details that were designed to move them to compassion and prayer. In doing so, the people saw God's glory in the provision for and deliverance of their fellow believers (see 2 Cor. 1:10–11).

8 Open Ears

It's easy to close our hearts to people in need. Yet when we hear about the plight of someone in need, God often prompts us to action. That was the case for Nehemiah. He could not ignore God's prompting to respond to the needs of His exiled people and the fallen walls of his homeland.

What effort and determination! Does it make you wonder how you would respond to such a challenge? The story of Nehemiah's pilgrimage to deal with the Jerusalem wall has lasting lessons for us all.

Listen To ...

Involuntary ignorance is not charged against you as a fault; but your fault is this—you neglect to inquire into the things you are ignorant of.

—*Augustine*

Deep Grief and Passionate Prayer

It had been three and a half years since America joined with the Allies in the war to stop the aggressions of the Axis powers of Germany, Italy, and Japan.

On June 6, 1944, 160,000 Allied troops landed along the highly fortified French coastline to fight. Nine thousand men were killed or wounded; yet the remaining soldiers marched across Europe, determined to defeat Hitler and claim victory.[5] In these dark times, the country looked to President Franklin D. Roosevelt for leadership and direction. On D-day, he led the nation in this prayer:

> Almighty God: Our sons, pride of our nation, this day have set upon a mighty endeavor, a struggle to preserve our Republic, our religion and our civilization, and to set free a suffering humanity.... Lead them straight and true; give strength to their arms, stoutness to their hearts, steadfastness in their faith. They will need Thy blessings. Their road will be long and hard. For the enemy is strong.... Success may not come with rushing speed, but we shall return again and again; and we know by Thy grace, and by the righteousness of our cause, our sons will triumph.... Amen.[6]

With the nation in tears and on its knees, we looked to God for the strength and determination we needed to face a monumental task and prevail. Nehemiah did the same. Nehemiah's private prayers yielded public results and glory to God.

Lift Up ...

Dear Lord, make me mindful of the great privilege and power of prayer. No matter how daunting or frightening the task, my tears should always bring me to You in prayer. Help me remember You are my very first resort. In Jesus' name. Amen.

Look At ...

Yesterday we met Nehemiah. He was neither a prophet nor royalty but a man with a listening ear and a heart burning with love for his homeland and his fellow Jews. His concern propelled him to prayer and action. He actively looked for God's will. The description of God's city, Jerusalem, fallen into ruin and disrepair, fell like stones on his heart.

Today we find the newly informed Nehemiah weeping, fasting, and praying for the Jews and Jerusalem. The grim news struck him deeply. He didn't rush his time before the Lord or begin a dialog with anyone else. Instead, he grieved and waited, prayed and praised his great God. This news was weighty and sobering but physically far removed from Nehemiah's comfortable life. Yet that didn't stop him from his sincere appeal to the One who watched Nehemiah and heard his prayer.

Read Nehemiah 1:4–6.

So it was, when I heard these words, that I sat down and wept, and mourned for many days; I was fasting and praying before the God of heaven. And I said: "I pray, LORD God of heaven, O great and awesome God, You who keep Your covenant and mercy with those who love You and observe Your commandments, please let Your ear be attentive and Your eyes open, that You may hear the prayer of Your servant which I pray before You now, day and night, for the children of Israel Your servants." Nehemiah 1:4–6

1. a. What was Nehemiah's first response to the news of the state of Jerusalem?
    b. What does that tell you about his character?

2. Nehemiah was burdened with the condition of the Jewish exiles and the city of Jerusalem, yet what did the first words of his prayer reveal about his faith?

3. According to verse 4, Nehemiah engaged in prayer. What else was he doing, and what does this course of action indicate?

4. What two adjectives did Nehemiah use to acknowledge God as a compassionate, merciful promise keeper?

    1.

    2.

5.   a. What did Nehemiah ask God to do?

    b. What did he want God to hear?

Live Out ...

6. In his prayer, Nehemiah included four basic elements that form the acronym ACTS—Acknowledgement, Confession, Thanksgiving, and Supplication.

Take a moment to write a prayer to God that includes each of these elements. Have you honored the covenants in your life? (Think of your spoken and unspoken agreements: marriage, friendships, business, and family.)

7. Prayer is a useless pursuit without the acknowledgement of who God is.

    a. When you pray, are you actively aware that a sovereign God is listening to your words as well as your heart?

    b. Does that change your attitude about prayer?

1 Tears of Strength

Weeping can be a sign of weakness or it can be a sign of strength and compassion. Throughout the Bible, we see that the people who cared deeply about a situation were often brought to tears. Jesus wept at the tomb of His dear friend Lazarus, even knowing He would momentarily restore his life (see John 11:35, 43).

2 Prayers of Dependence

Whether praying for help with hostile relationships or for the healing of our country, we can be certain that God is able. When we humble ourselves before Him, pray, seek His face, and turn away from our sins, God is delighted to hear us and heal our land (see Deut. 30:2–3).

3 Sacrifice of Food

Nehemiah knew his people were in desperate need. In ancient Near Eastern countries, meals were long, leisurely social gatherings. By sacrificing his meals, Nehemiah gained several hours in his schedule for undisturbed prayer. The critical needs of the moment eclipsed his normal pleasures.

5 Covenant of Character

A *covenant* is an agreement between two people or two groups that involves promises on the part of each one to the other. A covenant can be monumental as with God and His people, or it can be small and private as with the friendship between Jonathan and David (see 1 Sam. 18:3).

7 Sobering Sovereignty

The word *sovereign* means the unlimited power of God, who has complete control over the affairs of heaven, nature, and history. In countries ruled by a monarchy, people think of the king or queen as a sovereign political ruler.

9 Recipe for Delicious Prayers

Prayer comes naturally when we are in times of distress or pain. No matter the circumstance, the apostle Paul gave us the recipe for effective prayer: start with rejoicing, add prayer and stir constantly, sprinkle liberally with thanksgiving, and be confident that your prayer will rise (see 1 Thess. 5:16–18).

8. a. Have you ever been struck down with sadness or grief?

b. Who did you immediately turn to for comfort and guidance?

c. Is it easier to turn to sympathetic people or to a righteous God?

9. a. How often did Nehemiah pray?

b. Do you pray daily and routinely, or only in times of great need?

c. When did you last pray?

10. Are you experiencing affliction? Are you about to undertake a great work? Write your thoughts and concerns about your circumstances in your journal. Pray and ask God to be attentive to your prayer. Remember, "You have not, because you ask not."

————————————

When George H. W. Bush was inaugurated as president of the United States on January 20, 1989, he inherited some of the goodwill from the Reagan administration, but he also faced his own challenges, including the following:

- Fall of the Berlin Wall (1989)
- Valdez oil spill (1989)
- *Anita Hill v. Clarence Thomas* (1991)
- Breakup of the Soviet Union (1991)
- Race riots in Los Angeles (1992)

His first act as commander in chief was to pray for the nation:

Heavenly Father, we bow our heads and thank You for Your love. Accept our thanks for the peace that yields this day and the shared faith that makes its continuance likely. Make us strong to do Your work, willing to heed and hear Your will, and write on our hearts these words: "Use power to help people."

The Lord our God be with us, as He was with our fathers; may He not leave us or forsake us, so that He may incline our hearts to Him, to walk in all His ways … that all peoples of the earth may know that the Lord is God; there is no other. Amen.[7]

Listen To …

Prayer is reaching out after the unseen; fasting is letting go of all that is seen and temporal. Fasting helps express, deepen, confirm the resolution that we are ready to sacrifice anything, even ourselves, to attain what we seek for the kingdom of God.

—*Andrew Murray*

Honest Confession and Merciful Love

We've all heard the saying "Confession is good for the soul," and surely it is. But some confessions come as a result of great hardship or the release of a burden following a lifetime of deception. During war, members of intelligence or regular soldiers are selected for torture in order to force a confession of government secrets. In other, more common situations, imminent death can prompt a final opportunity to ease a conscience or clear the air.

Naomi Shemer, a much-loved songwriter in Israel, wrote a song called "Jerusalem of Gold" that so touched the hearts of the nation it became the unofficial Israeli anthem. For years, she was accused of plagiarizing the melody from a lullaby, which she adamantly denied. Years later, as she lay dying of cancer, she admitted to a friend that she had indeed stolen the melody. Even then, she referred to it as "a regrettable work accident," although she also said she felt her guilt and deception contributed to her deadly illness.[8]

A sincere confession is the result of a repentant heart—even if it comes as a last-minute, desperate attempt to clear the air and ease a conscience. A deathbed confession often carries the burden of a life spent in fear and regret.

Nehemiah's prayerful confession was not only for the sins of the nation Israel but for his own sinful nature that was an offense before God. His confession was honest, voluntary, and sincere.

Lift Up ...

Dear Lord, thank You for Your merciful love and the promise to forgive me when I confess my sins to You. Help me to be quick to confess, quick to turn from sin, and quick to praise You for Your forgiveness. In Jesus' name. Amen.

Look At ...

Yesterday we found a window into Nehemiah's character. Although living a comfortable life removed from the realities that were plaguing Jerusalem, Nehemiah was profoundly affected by the solemn news. He reacted with emotion, but also with wisdom and patience. He wept, prayed, fasted, and sought God's guidance.

Today we find that Nehemiah was acutely aware of the legacy of sin left by the children of Israel—a legacy that continued to bring consequences for the following generations. Even though he was not directly involved, in humility, Nehemiah took his share of the responsibility that was inherent in his fallen nature. He made a heartfelt confession.

Read Nehemiah 1:6–7.

Confess the sins of the children of Israel which we have sinned against You. Both my father's house and I have sinned. We have acted very corruptly against You, and have not kept the commandments, the statutes, nor the ordinances which You commanded Your servant Moses. Nehemiah 1:6–7

1. Whose sins did Nehemiah confess?

2. What word did he use to indicate he counted himself among the sinners?

3. What led to the corrupt actions of the Jews?

4. What personal confession did Nehemiah make?

5. How had the children of Israel acted toward God?

6. What specifically had they failed to do?

4 Sin

It would have been easy for Nehemiah to point his finger at the sins of people he didn't even know, but that's not what he did. Instead, he counted himself a perpetrator of sin as well. "For all have sinned and fall short of the glory of God" (Rom. 3:23).

5 Corruption

"Nehemiah was sensitive to the fact that all sin, things blatantly or carelessly done, or things selfishly or heedlessly left undone, need to be identified, acknowledged and pardoned. He knew that all such sin can be fully, immediately, and eternally forgiven."[9]

6 Acknowledgment

Commandments, statutes, and ordinances were violated. A *statute* is a decree or law issued by a ruler or governing body or especially by God as the supreme ruler. Psalm 99:1–3 tells us that the Lord is King above all; He is supreme over all the nations.

Live Out ...

7. Name some sins we as a nation commit. Are they sins of omission (things we neglect to do) or sins of commission (outright acts of disobedience)?

8. Psalm 32:1–5 is a vivid description of the physical effects of unconfessed sin and the joy of God's forgiveness. From this psalm, identify the bad effects of unconfessed sin and the blessings of forgiveness.

> Blessed is he whose transgressions are forgiven, whose sins are covered. Blessed is the man whose sin the LORD does not count against him and in whose spirit is no deceit. When I kept silent, my bones wasted away through my groaning all day long. For day and night your hand was heavy upon me; my strength was sapped as in the heat of summer. Then I acknowledged my sin to you and did not cover up my iniquity. I said, "I will confess my transgressions to the LORD"—and you forgave the guilt of my sin. (NIV84)

Bad Effects   **Blessings**

9. Do you have unconfessed sin in your life? Write a prayer in your journal, confessing it to the Lord. Trust that He will forgive you in His merciful love.

Sin can be an elaborate, premeditated attempt to deceive others, exalt ourselves, escape responsibility, or satisfy greed. It can also be a split-second decision that alters our lives and reveals our deepest character.

In 1936 renowned Polish violinist Bronislaw Huberman performed at Carnegie Hall. He had recently acquired a Guarnerius violin, so at intermission, he left his Stradivarius in his dressing room and finished the performance with the new instrument. At the close of the concert, Huberman discovered that the Stradivarius had vanished.

Twenty-year-old nightclub musician Julian Altman stole the Stradivarius and went on to become a violinist playing with the National Symphony Orchestra in Washington, DC, where he played for presidents and dignitaries.

At first glance, it would seem that there were only the best of consequences for Altman's corrupt actions. Yet the depth of his defective character was revealed when, almost fifty years later, he was imprisoned for child molestation.

On his deathbed, he finally confessed to his wife about the stolen Stradivarius. Following his death, she not only found the stolen violin, but she also found newspaper clippings about the theft.[10] It seemed that while he cherished his sin, he was totally corrupted by it. Confession may clear the conscience, but only prayerful repentance clears the soul.

For the Jews in Jerusalem, their unconfessed sins had resulted in separation from the God who loved them dearly.

7 Effects of Omission

Sometimes we fail to confess sins because we have not yet become aware of them. Other times, we willfully choose not to confess sins, which grieves God, quenches His power, and deprives us of the blessings of answered prayer (see Eph. 4:30; 1 Thess. 5:19).

9 Unconfessed

Trying to hide our sin only makes it worse. Proverbs 28:13 tells us that when we fail to confess our sin, we will not prosper, but when we both confess and repent, we will find mercy. Unconfessed sin blocks our relationship to our Father.

Listen To ...

Prayer in the sense of petition, asking for things, is a small part of it;
confession and penitence are its threshold, adoration its sanctuary, the
presence and vision and enjoyment of God its bread and wine.

—C. S. Lewis

Reliable Promise and Faithful Redeemer

Adolf Hitler and the Nazi Party assumed power in Germany in 1933 and began plans for war. The Jews were already targeted as an "impure" race, and by the time Germany invaded Poland in 1939, they were being forced out of their homes and into ghettos.

Enter Oskar Schindler, a war profiteer and a womanizer. Schindler set up a factory that produced enamelware kitchen goods in Krakow. Captured Jews and free Polish workers manned the factory. Although money was Schindler's primary motivation, he came to care for his workers and regarded them as friends. He saw the brutal effects of German policies on the Jews.

In 1941 Hitler's "Final Solution" to exterminate Jews, Gypsies, and other "impure" ethnic groups in Europe was implemented. Jews were sent to Auschwitz, Treblinka, and other death camps, as well as to gas chambers.

In part due to his well-known compromised character, Schindler found himself in a unique position to save over a thousand Jews that worked for him. He risked his life and his wealth to redeem the lives of these people.

In comparison to the millions of Jews killed in the war, Schindler's efforts saved a relatively small number of people. However, it is estimated that over six thousand descendants have resulted from the small number saved.[11]

While Schindler primarily worked to rescue people who worked for him, Nehemiah's efforts extended to people he didn't know in a place he didn't live. His motivations were pure, and an all-knowing God orchestrated the opportunity.

Lift Up ...

Dear Lord, help me understand the meaning of redemption through the eyes of the book of Nehemiah. Help me forsake my willful ways and be consumed with dwelling with You. As I walk in the world, let Your name and reputation be glorified in my life. You have delivered me from my sin and death. In Jesus' name. Amen.

Look At ...

Yesterday we saw Nehemiah sorrowfully aware of the condition of the Jewish people and the city of Jerusalem. He knew the source of their problem: a generation of stubborn disobedience to the Word of God. The consequences of sins being repeatedly swept under the rug had erupted into a dust storm of chaos. Nehemiah recognized that he had the same nature that had overcome the previous generations of Jerusalem Jews. He prayed and confessed this to God.

Today we see how Nehemiah prayed Scripture, "reminding" God of His promise, His warning, His great power, and His love for His people. Nehemiah was contrite, strong, and confident in God's promise and the plan for the redemption of His people. He knew that sin scatters and love unites.

Read Nehemiah 1:8–10.

Remember, I pray, the word that You commanded Your servant Moses, saying, "If you are unfaithful, I will scatter you among the nations; but if you return to Me, and keep My commandments and do them, though some of you were cast out to the farthest part of the heavens, yet I will gather them from there, and bring them to the place which I have chosen as a dwelling for My name." Now these are Your servants and Your people, whom You have redeemed by Your great power, and by Your strong hand. Nehemiah 1:8–10

1. What did Nehemiah ask God to remember?

2. God was specific in His command to Moses. What action of the children of Israel would result in harsh consequences?

3. Read Deuteronomy 4:25. Specifically, how were the children of Israel unfaithful to God?

      a. Their acts were _____.

      b. They carved _____.

      c. They did _____ in the sight of the Lord.

      d. They provoked God to _____.

4. According to Nehemiah 1:8, what was the consequence of the Jews' unfaithfulness?

5. What small word did God use to let His children know they still had a choice (see v. 8)?

6. What act of obedience did God require from the children of Israel *if* they returned (see v. 9)?

7. What consequence did God promise them *if* they returned to Him (see v. 9)?

Live Out ...

8. The Jews suffered the consequences of their disobedience, yet they were still the redeemed of God.

      a. Do you tend to forget the cost of your own redemption? When was the last time you considered Christ's sacrifice?

      b. What have you learned from the Jews' rebellious stubbornness?

      c. Write a prayer of contrition to the Lord.

9. To what "farthest places" have you been scattered?

1 A Respectful Reminder

In his prayer, Nehemiah did not remind God as though He had forgotten. Instead, he made a heartfelt appeal to God based on love for the Jews and the glory of His name. Nehemiah's respect for God was evident in that he knew both God's Word and God's character.

4 A Harmful Scattering

Scatter means to cause to separate and go in various directions; disperse. Another word for this scattering is *diaspora*, referring to the historical exile and dispersion of the Jews from the kingdom of Judah. The effects are still felt today.

7 A Dwelling Place

Through His prophet Moses, God told the children of Israel that if they broke their covenant with Him, they would be exiled. They broke the covenant; they were exiled. Yet God so loved them, He brought them back to the dwelling place He had promised them, Israel.

8 A Costly Redemption

Redemption means deliverance by payment of a price. In the New Testament, redemption refers to salvation from sin, death, and the wrath of God by Christ's sacrifice. Nehemiah turned to God in prayer, confession, and dependence on God's promises that despite their failings, Israel was a redeemed community.

10 Prone to Wander

Not long after the Jews set out for the Promised Land, they began to grumble about their hardships. They complained primarily about the food, missing meat, fish, cucumbers, melons, and leeks (see Num. 11:1). Their complaints angered God, frustrated Moses, and resulted in prolonged suffering and separation.[12]

❑ Depression

❑ Alcoholism

❑ Debt

❑ Overeating

❑ Sexual Immorality

❑ Other: _____

10. Draw a map to illustrate how God has gathered you back (or is still gathering you back) into fellowship with Him. What stops have you made along the way? In your wanderings, what wrong turns have you taken? How long was your journey (or how much farther do you think you have to go)?

```
                                              X God




    X You
```

_____

Oskar Schindler was a flawed man. He cheated on his wife, drank too much, and spied for the counterintelligence of the German military. Initially, his business efforts were motivated by a desire to profit from the war. Yet God used him.

As the German obsession to exterminate the Jews escalated, so did Schindler's outrage. The Nazis needed certain factories to remain operational for the war effort. Schindler used his credibility with the authorities to convince them that his factory and his trained workers were vital to their goals.

In 1944 he moved the factory and his skilled staff of Jewish workers to a more strategic location. Now the factory was commissioned to produce armaments for the war. "Schindler's List" was the transport list of names and occupations vital to this German effort. Schindler not only included the names of his eight hundred employees, but he requested three hundred "needed" women brought out from Auschwitz.[13]

Imagine the joy of having your name placed on such a list—a list of life. As believers, we have a Redeemer, a God of divine character and pure motive. He loved you so much He paid for you with His perfect blood. If you have received Him as your Savior and Redeemer, your name is written on the list of all lists: the Lamb's Book of Life.

Listen To ...

We have come to a turning point in the road. If we turn to the right mayhap our children and our children's children will go that way; but if we turn to the left, generations yet unborn will curse our names for having been unfaithful to God and to His Word.
—*Charles Spurgeon*

Humble Servant and Royal Cupbearer

In 1776 when General George Washington asked for a volunteer for a dangerous spy mission, Captain Nathan Hale of the 19th Regiment of the Continental Army stepped forward.

His mission was fraught with peril: he was to slip behind British enemy lines and gather intelligence prior to an impending battle. This subterfuge meant that Nathan Hale was about to become one of the first spies of the Revolutionary War—an unprecedented role.

The British had seized the island of Manhattan. Walking the streets disguised as a Dutch schoolmaster, the Yale-educated Hale slipped through the ranks, surreptitiously gathering information to take back to General Washington. Over the next few weeks, he successfully gathered intelligence about British troop movements.[14]

Hale knew when he volunteered for the mission that he placed both himself and his country at risk.

Nehemiah, like Nathan Hale, stepped out of the formation of safety and placed his life and security at risk. Although he was bound by the structure of the palace and the goodwill of King Artaxerxes, Nehemiah held himself accountable to a higher authority. In taking this stand, he would count on moment-by-moment guidance from his Lord and Master.

Lift Up ...

Dear Lord, before setting out on any work, I humbly seek You in prayer. Help me resist the temptation to push ahead with my own ideas and plans without first waiting on You. Thank You for the confidence of knowing that Your provision, Your plans, and Your process are perfect. In Jesus' name. Amen.

Look At ...

We saw yesterday that Nehemiah's prayer recalled the history of God's love and His discipline of the Jews. God warned the Jews and promised to redeem them if they heeded His Word. Nehemiah acknowledged God's preeminence over His people by using the words *You* and *Your* five times in just one verse (see v. 10). Nehemiah acknowledged God as faithful and true to His Word.

Today we find Nehemiah making his requests known to God. From Jewish history, he knew that the success or failure of his prayer was dependent on God's mercy and the orchestration of divine timing. In order to turn the heart of King Artaxerxes, Nehemiah knew he had to be precisely within God's will. If not, even his best efforts would avail nothing. He recognized his need for God's great provision in the task that lay before him.

Read Nehemiah 1:11.

"O Lord, I pray, please let Your ear be attentive to the prayer of Your servant, and to the prayer of Your servants who desire to fear Your name; and let Your servant prosper this day, I pray, and grant him mercy in the sight of this man." For I was the king's cupbearer. Nehemiah 1:11

1. Whose prayer did Nehemiah ask God to hear?

2. Nehemiah also wanted God to hear the prayers of whom else?

3. Read Proverbs 1:7 and Proverbs 16:6. What two virtues do these Scriptures say the fear of the Lord is the beginning of?

    1.

    2.

1 A Servant's Request

Supplication means to ask humbly or earnestly, as by praying. Nehemiah's prayer indicated he understood his relation to God and God's prerogative to either ignore or pay attention to his prayer. Clearly, he grasped that God's will reigned.

2 A Request for Servants

Nehemiah assumed that other Jews were praying for the well-being of their country and their race. He asked God to activate other people to rise to the cause of this godly mission and the work that would be required to accomplish it.

3 A Godly Fear

Fear is not always a bad thing. Fearing the Lord and gaining knowledge of a Holy God results in both wisdom and knowledge. In fact, such knowledge brings a balanced understanding of life and purpose that can actually extend our earthly existence (see Prov. 9:10–11).

7 A Trusted Position

"Writing in the same century as Nehemiah, the Greek historian Herodotus tells us that the cupbearer's office was highly esteemed among the Persian people. The wine steward was a man of recognized dignity in court circles, entirely trustworthy, the king's confidant, and next in rank to princes."[15]

8 The Promise Seekers

We don't have to look far to find biblical examples of people who were put in the waiting room. Consider Abraham and Sarah as they waited for a child. Think of Noah as he waited and trusted God for a coming flood. And step into the sandals of the grieving sisters Mary and Martha as they waited for their friend and healer, Jesus.

10 The Promise Keeper

God's promises cannot be separated from God's character. When we look at the essence of the promise, we learn the nature of the promiser. Reading Scripture in the light of the majesty of God allows us to lay hold of the glory of our Lord.

4. What was Nehemiah's first prayer request of God?

5. What was the second petition he made for himself?

6. Who was Nehemiah referring to when he prayed about "this man"?

7. What important position did Nehemiah hold in the king's royal palace?

Live Out ...

8. Waiting on the Lord can be one of the most difficult and rewarding virtues we acquire as maturing believers. Think about a time when you trusted God enough to wait for His guidance. Write a prayer asking God to help you apply that faith in a current situation.

9. Has there ever been a time in your life when you have run ahead of the Lord? What was the task? What was the outcome? What were the consequences? Write about your experience in your journal.

10. Review the promise at the beginning of each day of this week's lesson. What did Nehemiah teach us about God?

    Day 1:

    Day 2:

    Day 3:

    Day 4:

    Day 5:

In service and love for his country, Nathan Hale stepped out of the ranks and into risk and peril. He hoped to remain incognito and successful in his mission, but he also knew he must avoid the attention and scrutiny of the British.

When the British set Manhattan on fire, a new level of vigilance for patriot sympathizers was implemented. Hale knew he had to avoid any contact that would prompt examination. As the danger grew nearer, he had to take action, and he made the decision to try to cross back to American territory by sailing across Long Island Sound. He was carrying incriminating documents that, if discovered, would confirm his allegiance to and mission for the American cause.

Like Hale, Nehemiah had to be prepared for every possible scenario. He, too, risked everything—his position, the future of his country, the well-being of his compatriots, the approval of God, and his very life.

The British eventually captured Nathan Hale, and the documents he carried sealed his fate. British General William Howe ordered his execution for spying. Standing on the gallows, the twenty-one-year-old Hale was asked if he had any last words, to which he replied, "I only regret that I have but one life to give for my country."[16]

We have only one life, yet there are things worth dying for: love for others, character, passion, faith, and determination.

What about you? You also have "but one life." Is it time to look inward? If you can't think of anything you would die for, give careful thought about what you are living for.

Listen To ...

God's mercy with a sinner is only equaled and perhaps outmatched
by His patience with the saints, with you and me.

—*Alan Redpath*

The Good Hand of God

Nehemiah 2

In 1759 William Wilberforce was born into a prosperous family of merchants. William's father died early on, and while his immediate family was not religious, his aunt and uncle were strong Christian influences. Neither his mother nor his paternal grandfather was pleased by his exposure to Christianity.

William was educated at Cambridge and discovered he was not well suited to carry on the legacy of a merchant's life. He found himself drawn to political debates and was elected to Parliament at the age of twenty. He quickly became a popular and well-known figure in English and international circles. He met such notables as King Louis XVI, Marie Antoinette, and Benjamin Franklin.

During an extended trip, he had a deep spiritual experience, thanks to a Christian friend who challenged his intellect. He returned from that trip convinced that the God of the Bible existed and that Jesus was the Messiah. Over the next several years, he cemented his Christian convictions.

John Newton, former slave ship captain and author of the hymn "Amazing Grace," encouraged him to use his political position for God's glory. Wilberforce held a significant seat in Parliament from which he fought for the most important social change of that time—the abolition of the slave trade. His fight lasted eighteen years, and ultimately the slave trade was abolished in England.[1]

God often puts men and women of godly conviction in strategic places to accomplish great things. Such was the case with Nehemiah, a man with a broken heart and a high purpose.

Day 1: Nehemiah 2:1–6   **Touching the Heart**

Day 2: Nehemiah 2:7–10   **Influencing a King**

Day 3: Nehemiah 2:11–15   **Guiding a Man**

Day 4: Nehemiah 2:16–18   **Moving the People**

Day 5: Nehemiah 2:19–20   **Ignored by Enemies**

Touching the Heart

Lift Up ...

Lord, I am mindful today of the privilege of coming into Your presence whenever my heart desires. You are a King who never wavers in mood or the consistent desire for Your best in my life both now and forever. Through Your Son, Jesus Christ, I have found favor in Your sight. Thank You. In Jesus' name. Amen.

Look At ...

Yesterday we studied Nehemiah's preparation prior to asking King Artaxerxes' permission and assistance in his return to Jerusalem to rebuild the wall. The king could be unpredictable when approached at the wrong time or with a wrong attitude. Nehemiah knew that God's will and timing made the difference between success and failure.

Today, we find Nehemiah in the king's company. Because Nehemiah was a trusted and unswerving presence in the king's life, Artaxerxes noticed that Nehemiah was downcast. Rather than being angry, the king was concerned. We find that Nehemiah was ready for this moment. He had waited on God for the precise time to bring his requests before Artaxerxes. With honesty and diplomacy, Nehemiah made his requests known. He would not need to go back to the king with additional information or favors. He had done his homework. He was ready to make his appeal.

Read Nehemiah 2:1–6.

And it came to pass in the month of Nisan, in the twentieth year of King Artaxerxes, when wine was before him, that I took the wine and gave it to the king. Now I had never been sad in

1 A Moment in Time

Israel followed a twelve-
month calendar. The
following are mentioned
in the Bible: *Nisan*, the
first month; *Sivan*, the
third month; *Elul*, the
sixth month; *Chislev*, the
ninth month; *Tebeth*, the
tenth month; *Shebat*, the
eleventh month; and *Adar*,
the twelfth month.[2]

3 A Heart in Tune

Nehemiah displayed the
mark of a mature believer:
he was grieved by the
things that grieve God.
Bob Pierce, the founder
of World Vision and
Samaritan's Purse, prayed,
"Let my heart be broken
with the things that break
the heart of God."[3]

4 A Fine Line

Though cupbearers held a
prestigious and influential
position, they walked a
fine line in the presence
of the king, who held
absolute power over his
servants. To appear sad
while serving him could
be perceived as an act
of treason, punishable
by death. No wonder
Nehemiah was afraid!

his presence before. Therefore the king said to me, "Why is your face sad, since you are not sick? This is nothing but sorrow of heart." So I became dreadfully afraid, and said to the king, "May the king live forever! Why should my face not be sad, when the city, the place of my fathers' tombs, lies waste, and its gates are burned with fire?" Then the king said to me, "What do you request?" So I prayed to the God of heaven. And I said to the king, "If it pleases the king, and if your servant has found favor in your sight, I ask that you send me to Judah, to the city of my fathers' tombs, that I may rebuild it." Then the king said to me (the queen also sitting beside him), "How long will your journey be? And when will you return?" So it pleased the king to send me; and I set him a time. Nehemiah 2:1–6

1. In what month and year did the above events take place?

2. Based on the Jewish calendar, what amount of time had passed between Nehemiah's hearing of Jerusalem's dismal state and the events described here (see Neh. 1:1)?

3. Describe Nehemiah's emotional state and the king's response.

4. What was Nehemiah's initial response to the king's question?

5. Instead of impulsively answering the king's question, what did Nehemiah do?

6. Dissect Nehemiah's response: list two reasons he offered the king for granting his request and what he specifically asked for.

7. What was the king's response?

Live Out ...

8. Nehemiah waited for months before he was given an opportunity to share his burden. In the meantime he prayed, fasted, and planned.

> a. Are you waiting for God to give you an opportunity, open a door, or answer a prayer?
>
> b. What are you doing while you wait?
>
> c. What will you start doing?

9. When emotionally distraught, it's tempting to neglect our work, whether inside or outside the home. Nehemiah faithfully worked despite his grief. How does his example compare to your response to work during emotionally challenging times?

10. Today, we found that the things that grieve God should grieve His children. The opposite is also true: a believer should find joy in the things that please God. Read Ephesians 4:30–32, and list in the columns those things that grieve God and those things that please Him.

Grieves God   **Pleases God**

8 In Good Time

We are reminded, "Always give yourselves fully to the work of the Lord, because you know that your labor in the Lord is not in vain" (1 Cor. 15:58 NIV). He is with us in the waiting and prepares us so that "through faith and patience [we may] inherit the promises" (Heb. 6:12). Our wait time should be our prep time.

9 In Good Company

The Bible is filled with examples of people who kept working despite trials. Joseph became a slave after his brothers abandoned and betrayed him. Like Nehemiah, his loyalty and hard work earned him a place of influence that God was able to use later on.

William Wilberforce's long battle to abolish the slave trade was ultimately successful. He had no doubt of his calling. In his diary, he wrote that God had set before him the great objective to suppress the slave trade. His purpose was clear, and he didn't waver in getting it done. He recognized that unless God was behind his effort, he would accomplish nothing. He also knew better than to fight in his own strength. Instead, he used the weapons of prayer and Scripture. He memorized Psalm 119 and recited it during his walk home from Parliament. He had a close group of believers who prayed with and over him on a regular basis. They were known as the Clapham Circle because most of them lived in the London suburb of Clapham. Every time Wilberforce went before Parliament on an important bill or issue, the Clapham Circle prayed God would give him strength and wisdom.[4]

Like Wilberforce, Nehemiah knew the importance of prayer, preparation, and planning. When we submit to God's purpose and timing, He is faithful to accomplish amazing things through us.

Listen To ...

No great work is ever done in a hurry. To develop a great scientific discovery, to paint a great picture, to write an immortal poem, to become a minister, or a famous general—to do anything great requires time, patience, and perseverance.

—W. J. Wilmont Buxton

Influencing a King

Benjamin Franklin said, "By failing to prepare, you are preparing to fail." While some people love to plan and make lists, check them twice, add new items, and gain great pleasure from crossing things off or checking a box as "done," for most folks preparation is a lost art. Modern conveniences and easy access to information have made planning and preparing unnecessary. If you're hungry, you can swing by a drive-through restaurant. While traveling, you can rest in a picnic area or hotel. If you are looking for information, you need go no further than your smartphone. Since our survival is not dependent on preparation, we are not forced to plan.

This was not the case during ancient times. Imagine needing to store up enough food to survive the winter or defend against enemy attacks on a regular basis. Nehemiah did not have the luxury of a safety net. He began preparations as soon as he learned Jerusalem was in disrepair. He felt a call on his life and confidently moved into action. He didn't ask when it would happen, ask how it would all come together, or demand guarantees that he would succeed. He simply made himself available and prepared a detailed plan of what he needed. God honored his preparation by blessing him with more than he could have hoped for.

Lift Up ...

Dear Lord, to honor You with my life, I don't have to accomplish great missions or build great structures. You are my plan, Lord. Help me pray and pray again when I set out on a work of any kind, knowing that You will lead me from there. In Jesus' name. Amen.

Look At ...

In yesterday's lesson, Nehemiah stood before the king and carefully explained his dilemma. He had already done his weeping and praying before the King of Kings prior to making his needs known before King Artaxerxes.

Today, we see the requests Nehemiah made. During his time before the Lord, he listened for God's leading and anticipated the specific things he would need in order to leave his specialized position in the palace and complete a successful journey. Without the proper planning, travel was dangerous and time-consuming. His own safety was not his only consideration; he also thought about the supplies necessary to accomplish the great work of rebuilding when he arrived. Although God softened the king's heart at this stage of the mission, Nehemiah would face further opposition.

Read Nehemiah 2:7–10.

Furthermore I said to the king, "If it pleases the king, let letters be given to me for the governors of the region beyond the River, that they must permit me to pass through till I come to Judah, and a letter to Asaph the keeper of the king's forest, that he must give me timber to make beams for the gates of the citadel which pertains to the temple, for the city wall, and for the house that I will occupy." And the king granted them to me according to the good hand of my God upon me. Then I went to the governors in the region beyond the River, and gave them the king's letters. Now the king had sent captains of the army and horsemen with me. When Sanballat the Horonite and Tobiah the Ammonite official heard of it, they were deeply disturbed that a man had come to seek the well-being of the children of Israel. Nehemiah 2:7–10

1. What did Nehemiah request to ensure travel safety?

2. What was the second request Nehemiah made?

3. What three things did he use the supplies for?
   1.
   2.
   3.

4. Why did the king grant Nehemiah's requests?

5. What protocol did Nehemiah follow on his journey to Jerusalem?

6. Why do you think the captains and horsemen accompanied him?

7. a. How did Sanballat the Horonite and Tobiah the Ammonite react to Nehemiah's mission?

b. What in particular disturbed them?

Live Out ...

8. Neglecting to stay under the protection of our parents or our authorities can result in personal danger or other peril. Write in your journal about a time you put yourself in such a situation.

9. Once you have experienced God's good hand in your life, you can offer a helping hand to someone else who needs it. Take a moment to contact someone who might need "safe passage" through a trying time.

10. Write about a time when you experienced opposition when carrying out God's will in your life.

_____

Marco Polo, an Italian merchant and trader like his father and uncle before him, is known for his travels to Central Asia and China. While not the first of such explorers, his detailed writings gave Europeans

3 A Prepared Plan

Nehemiah was thoroughly prepared before asking for the king's support. He had a plan. He prepared spiritually through prayer and practically by asking for safety and supplies. We, too, can go to our King who will gladly provide for us. "You do not have because you do not ask" (James 4:2).

4 A Gracious Response

It was the grace of God—the good hand of God—that moved the king to grant Nehemiah safe passage and supplies for the rebuilding project. "The king's heart is in the hand of the LORD, like the rivers of water; He turns it wherever He wishes" (Prov. 21:1).

5 A Long Journey

Nehemiah's journey was long and treacherous; highwaymen, rough terrain, and hostile officials were just a few of the dangers he faced. Due to the size of his entourage and the supplies acquired as he traveled, Nehemiah's trek would have taken at least two months.

7 A Dangerous Rift

Tobiah the Ammonite came from a nomadic race descended from Lot's son Ammon. The Ammonites were enemies of the Israelites. In Exodus, God instructed the Israelites not to associate with them. The Bible doesn't give us a reason for such hostility, but the rift between the two peoples continued over the centuries.[5]

8 A Safe Passage

The Bible instructs us to submit to our parents (see Eph. 6:1), rulers (see Heb. 13:17), and God (see James 4:7). The Father safeguards every stage of our lives, not to oppress us, but to protect us and make it possible to carry out His will rather than impede it.

9 A Lifeline of Hope

Do not underestimate the power of an encouraging word, note, or deed. With minimal effort, you may be giving someone a lifeline of hope. "Do not withhold good from those to whom it is due, when it is in the power of your hand to do so" (Prov. 3:27).

the first glimpse of an advanced and sophisticated society. Prior to his travels, his father, Niccolo, and uncle Maffeo traveled to China and met the great Chinese emperor Kublai Khan. When they left for Venice, the emperor sent them with a letter to the pope, asking for learned men to teach his people about Christianity and Western science and to bring him oil from the Holy Sepulchre in Jerusalem. In order to assure their safe travel, Kublai Khan gave them a golden tablet with the following inscription: "By the strength of the eternal Heaven, holy be the Khan's name. Let him that pays him not reverence be killed." This was a VIP passport to obtain necessities during their travels.[6] It took Niccolo and Maffeo three years to reach Venice in April 1269.

In 1271 Niccolo and Maffeo returned to China, this time with Marco in his late teens, where he subsequently served in Khan's court. Twenty-four years later, the three Polos returned to Venice.

For centuries, men have traveled under the protection of kings while undertaking important missions. We have something in common with both the Polos and Nehemiah: we operate under the protection of a mighty King who has dispatched us to accomplish a great commission with historical and eternal consequences.

Listen To ...

The one concern of the devil is to keep Christians from praying. He fears nothing from prayerless studies, prayerless work, and prayerless religion. He laughs at our toil, mocks at our wisdom, but trembles when we pray.

—*Samuel Chadwick*

Guiding a Man

On September 8, 1900, a category 4 hurricane with winds up to 145 mph descended upon Galveston, Texas. Thousands of residents perished as a storm surge of fifteen feet landed on the island, which measured only eight feet above sea level. Due to lack of warning and the disregard of evacuation warnings, it is still considered one of the deadliest natural disasters in United States history.

Close to four thousand homes were destroyed as the storm surge knocked buildings off their foundations and washed out the entire island. The city, which had been referred to as the "Wall Street of Texas," with a bustling population of thirty-six thousand people, was cut off from outside communication for two days.

The estimated number of human fatalities is counted between six thousand and eight thousand. Some were lost as the storm surge crashed over the island, others due to the lack of outside communication, which caused a delay in rescue efforts.

Within four days, relief efforts began, and within three weeks the port was once again shipping cotton. Survivors took shelter in surplus United States Army tents set up along the shore. They were down, but they were not defeated. Galveston began to rebuild.

To prevent another disaster, the Galveston Seawall was built in 1902 and the city was raised by seventeen feet above its previous elevation. Today, Galveston has a population of over fifty thousand and is home to a cruise port and two universities. The people of Galveston are resilient and met disaster with fortitude.[7]

When Nehemiah set out to rebuild Jerusalem, he was not met with enthusiasm or locals willing to help rebuild his beloved city. Instead, he had to tread carefully during his initial assessment of the destruction and formulated a plan to motivate others.

Lift Up ...

Dear Lord, in times of disaster or crisis, I pray that the first resource I turn to is You. With that link established, You will lead me and perhaps enable me to lead others through resistance and confusion. Help me remember that my strength comes from You, and there is none stronger. In Jesus' name. Amen.

Look At ...

Yesterday, we found Nehemiah packing his bags for Judah. He needed the basics: letters for safe passage and permits to acquire the needed lumber to accomplish his mission. Without these vital elements, he could not succeed. He planned for every foreseeable contingency, but he could not foresee the waiting hatred and opposition.

Today, we see Nehemiah's assessment of the situation in Jerusalem. Up to this point, he made plans based on what he had heard from others. Now he wanted to survey the scope and depth of this challenge with his own eyes. He ventured out under the cover of night, knowing there was the potential for opposition and conflict. Although he had a few men with him, he didn't tell them his mission. Once again, he waited for God's timing.

Read Nehemiah 2:11–15.

So I came to Jerusalem and was there three days. Then I arose in the night, I and a few men with me; I told no one what my God had put in my heart to do at Jerusalem; nor was there any animal with me, except the one on which I rode. And I went out by night through the Valley Gate to the Serpent Well and the Refuse Gate, and viewed the walls of Jerusalem which were broken down and its gates which were burned with fire. Then I went on to the Fountain Gate and to the King's Pool, but there was no room for the animal under me to pass. So I went up in the night by the valley, and viewed the wall; then I turned back and entered by the Valley Gate, and so returned. Nehemiah 2:11–15

1. How long did Nehemiah rest after he reached Jerusalem?

2. What was Nehemiah's next course of action?

3. To whom did Nehemiah reveal his plans?

4.   a. When did Nehemiah begin his survey of the city gates?

   b. Why do you think he chose this time of day?

5. What areas did Nehemiah first observe?

6. What was the condition of the walls and gates?

7. Following his nighttime survey of the walls, what did Nehemiah do?

Live Out ...

8. Through Nehemiah's example we learn that there is a time to keep silent and a time to speak. Write in your journal about a time you spoke when you knew you should have kept silent. What were the consequences?

9. Nehemiah needed to know the worst, so he made a survey of the ruins. While Nehemiah saw the devastation, he also saw the potential of what could be rebuilt. As believers, we too must be willing to look at our personal ruins and envision what God can do. Review previous questions about the broken walls in your life and quietly go before God and ask Him to help you see the potential He has for each area. Journal a prayer asking to see the possibilities.

10. Nehemiah encountered some rubble that hindered the continuation of his survey. This is symbolic of the secret sin that keeps us from

1 Between You and Yourself

Nehemiah showed another mark of spiritual maturity by taking time to rest following his long journey. At creation, God established the value of setting aside time for rest. Jesus said, "Come to Me, all you who labor and are heavy laden, and I will give you rest" (Matt. 11:28).

3 Between You and God

Nehemiah showed spiritual maturity by keeping God's plan private and taking time to reflect and do more research. He did not want to speak hastily or to step ahead of God. Mary did similarly following the birth of Jesus. "Mary kept all these things and pondered them in her heart" (Luke 2:19).

4 Between Dark and Light

Nehemiah was aware he was being watched both by his enemies (Tobiah and Sanballat) and the people of Jerusalem. He needed to gather facts before he formulated a plan; this was best done in secret. Nehemiah was looking not only at the damage but at the potential of what could be.

moving forward. Write a prayer confessing those things that have become an obstacle to your spiritual growth.

—————————————

7 Between Hell and Heaven

Nehemiah now knew the worst. In the dark of night, he came face-to-face with the ruins he was called to rebuild. Similarly, on a dark night in the garden of Gethsemane, Jesus came face-to-face with the ruins caused by sin. It would cost Him everything to rebuild the lives of His people.

8 Hold Your Tongue

The Bible counsels us to carefully consider our words before we speak. "He who answers a matter before he hears it, it is folly and shame to him" (Prov. 18:13). It is better to gather enough information and understand a situation before we offer an opinion.

10 Let Go of Sin

We can always go to God and ask Him to clear the path and forgive us. "If we confess our sins, He is faithful and just to forgive us our sins and to cleanse us from all unrighteousness" (1 John 1:9). "In all your ways acknowledge Him, and He shall direct your paths" (Prov. 3:6).

In 2005 the United States experienced one of the deadliest hurricanes in history when Hurricane Katrina hit the Gulf Coast. The most significant impact was on New Orleans, Louisiana, as it flooded when the levee system catastrophically failed. The majority of the city was underwater and remained so for weeks after the storm. The following months were filled with criticism and accusations about the failure to handle the devastation and protect human life. The confirmed death toll, primarily in Louisiana and Mississippi, was 1,836.

Unlike Galveston, New Orleans struggled to rebuild. Currently, about 80 percent of the levees have been rebuilt and about 80 percent of the prestorm population has returned. Slowly, retail establishments are returning, but problems with crime and schools remain.

Rebuilding a city is challenging. Throughout history, from Nehemiah's time to modern day, destroyed cities have risen from the ashes. No effort has ever been completed without a plan and the resources to execute them. When God is behind the effort, as He was in Nehemiah's case, the outcome is a testament to His great plan.

Listen To ...

For not only does sound reason direct us to refuse the guidance of those who do or teach anything wrong, but it is by all means vital for the lover of truth, regardless of the threat of death, to choose to do and say what is right even before saving his own life.

—A. W. Tozer

Moving the People

Modern film has captured some of the most inspirational speeches ever given on the eve of battle. In *Braveheart*, Mel Gibson played William Wallace, who roused the Scottish warriors to fight against their English enemies. He gave them a vision of the future and the privilege of fighting for it with these words:

> Fight and you may die. Run and you will live at least awhile. And dying in your bed many years from now, would you be willing to trade all the days from this day to that for one chance, just one chance, to come back here as young men and tell our enemies that they may take our lives but they will never take our freedom![8]

Can't you hear Gibson shouting the last few words? Inspiring!

In Shakespeare's *Henry V*, Kenneth Branagh delivered a magnificent performance of Shakespeare's most famous battle speech when Henry appealed to his soldiers' sense of unity:

> From this day to the ending of the world, but we in it shall be remembered. We few, we happy few, we band of brothers; for he today that sheds his blood with me shall be my brother.[9]

Movies can give us a glimpse of warriors fighting a daunting enemy. In the book of Nehemiah, we find a man tackling a huge task with enemies determined to thwart God's plans. He appealed to others using the most powerful motivation of all: the chance to do a mighty work under the good hand of God.

Lift Up ...

Dear Lord, sometimes I am not prepared to deal with evil because I don't recognize the Enemy. You have told us that we are not wrestling with flesh and blood but with powers, rulers of darkness, and hosts of wickedness. Guide me through those forces with Your strong hand. In Jesus' name. Amen.

Look At ...

Yesterday, we observed Nehemiah in a discovery mode. He needed to understand what he was dealing with and then determine a method to achieve a mighty goal. He wisely chose to assess the situation at night with the Lord as his only knowledgeable advisor.

In today's lesson, we see that Nehemiah revealed his plan to the people who not only would benefit the most from its accomplishment but would also have to participate in its execution. Once again, Nehemiah was prepared. He informed everyone involved at the same time. He showed them the need and led them to the solution. He appealed to their sense of national pride and assured them that they would be part of a godly work.

Read Nehemiah 2:16–18.

And the officials did not know where I had gone or what I had done; I had not yet told the Jews, the priests, the nobles, the officials, or the others who did the work. Then I said to them, "You see the distress that we are in, how Jerusalem lies waste, and its gates are burned with fire. Come and let us build the wall of Jerusalem, that we may no longer be a reproach." And I told them of the hand of my God which had been good upon me, and also of the king's words that he had spoken to me. So they said, "Let us rise up and build." Then they set their hands to this good work. Nehemiah 2:16–18

1. Who was unaware of Nehemiah's actions?

2. Why didn't Nehemiah reveal his plans before this?

3. The time had come for Nehemiah to motivate the people to work. What did he say to remind them of the reality of their situation?

4. What did Nehemiah say to motivate the people to change the reputation of God's city?

5. What was Nehemiah's personal testimony concerning God's intervention?

6. How did the people verbally and physically respond to Nehemiah's motivational speech?

7. Why do you think the work of rebuilding the walls was called "good work" (v. 18)?

Live Out ...

8. Nehemiah motivated the people by identifying with them and offering himself as part of the solution. Rather than pointing a finger of blame, he offered a hand of assistance. Describe something that caused you to say, "*They* really should do something about that."

9. Now describe some ways you could personally be a part of the solution in this situation or join with others to help out.

10. After motivating the people by asking them to reflect on their ruined walls, Nehemiah gave his personal testimony of how God's good hand led him to Jerusalem to rebuild. Now it's your turn. Write about how God's good hand led you to your own time of reconstruction (i.e., this study in Nehemiah, a small group, a mentor, a prayer partner, etc.).

———————

3 The Right Time

Nehemiah must have gathered the priests, nobles, officials, and the rest of the Jewish people in one place to deliver his message. In this way, he would have one audience hearing the same message at the same time. When casting a vision that will require the help of many people, proper timing is essential.

4 The Right Tone

Another mark of Nehemiah's spiritual maturity was personally identifying with the people. He used the words *we* and *us* instead of *you* and *them*. This foreshadows Christ's identification with us when He "made Himself of no reputation, taking the form of a bondservant, and coming in the likeness of men" (Phil. 2:7).

5 The Right Hand

The hand of God is powerful indeed. It united Judah in "singleness of heart to obey the command of the king and the leaders" (2 Chron. 30:12). Also, Solomon acknowledged, "the righteous and the wise and their works are in the hand of God" (Eccl. 9:1). He is in control.

9 Divine Priorities

God has given us clear priorities. First is our relationship with Him, then our families, and finally, our work in or outside the home (Matt. 22:36–39). In the midst of these responsibilities, He invites us to participate in "good works, which God prepared beforehand that we should walk in them" (Eph. 2:10).

10 A Divine Plan

We can be sure that God wants us to know Him better. David wrote, "The LORD will work out his plans for my life—for your faithful love, O LORD, endures forever. Don't abandon me, for you made me" (Ps. 138:8 NLT). Let Him work out His plans for you.

J. R. R. Tolkien's *The Lord of the Rings* was originally published in three volumes in 1954–55. Director Peter Jackson turned the books into a film trilogy: *The Fellowship of the Ring* in 2001, *The Two Towers* in 2002, and *The Return of the King* in 2003. In the final battle of the last installment, Aragorn, heir to the throne of Gondor, addressed his soldiers as they faced an overwhelming source of evil with very few warriors.

> I see in your eyes the same fear that would take the heart of me. A day may come when the courage of men fails, when we forsake our friends and break all bonds of fellowship, but it is not this day. An hour of wolves and shattered shields, when the age of men comes crashing down, but it is not this day! This day we fight! By all that you hold dear on this good Earth, I bid you stand, Men of the West![10]

The scene continued with Aragorn rushing into battle toward the ominous Black Gate, his people charging after him.

Just as Aragorn inspired his soldiers to fight with courage, so Nehemiah inspired the Jewish people to rebuild the ruined walls of the city. They were no strangers to hardship, and the pain of captivity was still fresh upon them. Sometimes it takes one person to lead the charge so others can be inspired to follow.

Listen To ...

We are building many splendid churches in this country, but we are not providing leaders to run them. I would rather have a wooden church with a splendid parson than a splendid church with a wooden parson.

—*Samuel Smith Drury*

Ignored by Enemies

Bullying has become a serious and prevalent concern in our society. It happens not only on the schoolyard but in the workplace and even in the home. Entire websites, organizations, and books are dedicated to addressing the problem and equipping teachers, parents, and the public at large to deal with this social problem. According to bullyingstatistics.com, it can take several different forms:

- *Verbal.* This type of bullying usually involves name-calling and/or teasing.
- *Social.* Spreading rumors, intentionally leaving others out of activities, and breaking up friendships are all examples of social bullying.
- *Physical.* This traditional form of bullying involves hitting, punching, shoving, and other acts of intentional physical harm.

Bullies use strength and power to harm or intimidate to get what they want. The damage from bullying can be traumatic and long-lasting.

In today's lesson, we see that Nehemiah faced some bullies. These men used each form of bullying mentioned above. Experts encourage victims of bullying to get authorities involved, whether school administrators, parents, or bosses. Nehemiah appealed to the absolute highest authority available—the God of heaven Himself.

Lift Up ...

Dear Lord, when I think of the bullies in my life, I consider the bully of fear, the bully of doubt, and the bully of pride. Lord, intervene for me when I am being pushed around. Help me stand strong in Your shadow and dwell peacefully in Your Word. In Jesus' name. Amen.

Look At ...

In yesterday's lesson, Nehemiah made a thoughtful appeal to those who stood to gain the most and, therefore, would need to contribute the most. He was ready. He demonstrated the need and the benefits. He was succinct and efficient. He awakened a long-neglected sense of identity and national pride in the residents of Jerusalem.

In our study today, we find Nehemiah dealt with naysayers, bullies, and outsiders. They mocked his mission and hinted at the danger of his bold initiative. Nehemiah's clear determination and confidence in the King of Kings is evident. He rose up with the shield of righteousness to fend off the darts of doubt.

Read Nehemiah 2:19–20.

But when Sanballat the Horonite, Tobiah the Ammonite official, and Geshem the Arab heard of it, they laughed at us and despised us, and said, "What is this thing that you are doing? Will you rebel against the king?" So I answered them, and said to them, "The God of heaven Himself will prosper us; therefore we His servants will arise and build, but you have no heritage or right or memorial in Jerusalem." Nehemiah 2:19–20

1. What two familiar enemies heard the Jew's plan to rebuild the walls?

2. Who was the third person to join their conspiracy?

3. What two things did the conspirators do to discourage the Israelites from building the walls?

    1.

    2.

4 Predicted Rebellion

Ezra 4 records how the Jews' efforts to rebuild the temple in Jerusalem were stopped when accusations of treason were leveled against them. The Samaritans sent a letter to King Artaxerxes, warning him that allowing the Jews to rebuild would lead to rebellion, as was the Jews' tendency.

5 Divine Backing

Nehemiah had the king's permission to rebuild the wall. In addition, he had the blessing of the King of Kings—the God of heaven. He did not try to intimidate his enemies with his strength, but he reminded them of who they were really opposing—God.

7 Divine Abode

Jerusalem means possession of peace. God commanded the Israelites to "seek the place where the LORD your God chooses, out of all your tribes, to put His name for His dwelling place" (Deut. 12:5). David established Jerusalem as the capital city of Israel and as God's dwelling place via Solomon's temple.

4. How did they imply the Jews were committing treason?

5. What did Nehemiah tell his enemies about God's ability to overcome their opposition?

6. What did Nehemiah say to show that he and the people were determined to build the wall?

7. What three things could the enemies *not* claim in Jerusalem?
1.
2.
3.

Live Out ...

8. The first tactic these enemies used against God's people was to laugh at them. Reword the following psalm into a personal prayer about those who laugh at you because of your faith.

> You have made us a strife to our neighbors, and our enemies laugh among themselves. Restore us, O God of hosts; cause Your face to shine, and we shall be saved! (Ps. 80:6–7)

9. The second tactic these enemies used was to despise the people. What is your experience? Has the criticism of others stopped you from fully obeying God, or have you pressed on in the face of contempt?

10. The third tactic the three men used was accusation. The Bible tells us that Satan, our Enemy, is the "accuser of our brethren" (Rev. 12:10). James 4:7–8 gives us the counterattack against him: "Submit

8 Delayed Weeping

People may mock you for spending time and effort doing God's work, but the Lord is not impressed by their taunts. Jesus, speaking of enemies who laughed at God's plans, said, "Woe to you who laugh now, for you shall mourn and weep" (Luke 6:25). The day will come when laughing ceases.

9 Prompt Obedience

We are to obey God regardless of how we are treated. Psalm 119:22 says, "Remove from me reproach and contempt, for I have kept Your testimonies." Being hated because we follow God is to be expected, but we can pray for God to intervene on our behalf.

to God. Resist the devil and he will flee from you. Draw near to God and He will draw near to you." Write a prayer of submission to God, placing yourself in His protective custody, in your journal.

––––––––––––––––

The pressure of opposition can be overwhelming. Add fear to the mix, and this combination can stop progress in its tracks. Nehemiah did not let bullies stop the work he was called to do. Teddy Roosevelt said, "Do what you can, with what you have, where you are." Nehemiah was a man overcome with grief by the condition of God's Holy City. So he did what he could—he prayed and waited. He used what he had—the power of prayer and a position of influence. He went to work where he was—in the throne room of a king. Then he willingly journeyed to a distant land to begin a new work there.

Because of Nehemiah's willingness to be used, God touched the heart of the most powerful man on earth to support Nehemiah's plan and provide safe passage and ample supplies for the construction project. God used Nehemiah to move the hearts of the people to restore the walls and the reputation of His Holy City and people. Nehemiah boldly stood against the enemies of God's chosen people through prayer, obedience, and submission to God.

If you are willing and sensitive to His will, God can use *you* to touch the hearts of the people around you and build His kingdom on earth. Through your prayers, your obedience, and your submission to His will, God will enable you to stand against bullies and accomplish the work He has called you to do—and you will experience the good hand of God on your life.

Listen To ...

The joy of the Lord will arm us against the assaults of our spiritual enemies and put
our thoughts out of taste for those pleasures with which the tempter baits his hooks.
—*Matthew Henry*

Lesson Three

The Helping Hands of Men

Nehemiah 3

Near the end of World War II, a great explosion destroyed much of the center of a town in Southern Europe. As patrolling soldiers began to search through the ruins of what they knew to be a church, a young soldier came across a statue lying in the rubble. Slowly, he lifted the stone statue back to standing position. It was a life-size sculpture of Jesus. His two extended hands had been blown off in the explosion, but the statue was still in relatively good condition.

The soldier called for his comrades to help him search for the hands of Jesus. They sifted through the smoldering rubble only to find bits and pieces of obliterated stone. While they searched, the young soldier found a scrap of cardboard and a piece of charcoal left from a burning timber. With the charcoal and a heavy hand, he began to write upon the cardboard. He removed a shoelace from his boot, attached it to the cardboard, and hung his newly made sign around the neck of the handless statue of Jesus. The sign read: "Now I have no hands but yours!"[1]

Nehemiah 3 records the process of rebuilding the wall around Jerusalem and the names of those who followed Nehemiah's godly leadership. Priests, families, leaders, and servants rallied together with willing hands to rebuild Jerusalem's wall. As we study this chapter, may we be inspired and encouraged to put forth effort in the areas God has called us to. May we, like the rebuilders of Nehemiah's day, serve with passionate hearts and willing hands for the glory of our great God!

Day 1: Nehemiah 3:1–2   **Priests Were Helpers**

Day 2: Nehemiah 3:3–5   **Families Were Helpers**

Day 3: Nehemiah 3:6–14   **Diverse Helpers**

Day 4: Nehemiah 3:15–25   **Leaders Were Helpers**

Day 5: Nehemiah 3:26–32   **Servants Were Helpers**

Priests Were Helpers

Lift Up ...

Dear Father, I want to be Your servant, always willing to do Your work. Help me see areas in my home and in my heart that need repair and rebuilding. Give me the strength to diligently and joyfully build up the places that have broken down around me. In Jesus' name. Amen.

Look At ...

Last week, we learned that Nehemiah inspected the walls surrounding Jerusalem and found them in ruins. He dealt with opposition at every turn, including ridicule and threats, yet he remained steadfastly confident in his Lord and his mission.

This week, we take a look at the process of rebuilding and repairing the walls that were essential to the security and protection of God's people. We will see the God-ordained division of labor and how different workers cooperated in the process. Although Nehemiah 3 is a series of names and locations, it records the rich heritage of believers who united and served God for His glory. Today, we focus on the priests who rebuilt the Sheep Gate.

Read Nehemiah 3:1–2.

Then Eliashib the high priest rose up with his brethren the priests and built the Sheep Gate; they consecrated it and hung its doors. They built as far as the Tower of the Hundred, and consecrated it, then as far as the Tower of Hananel. Next to Eliashib the men of Jericho built. And next to them Zaccur the son of Imri built. Nehemiah 3:1–2

1. Who were the first people involved in rebuilding?

2. What portion of the wall was rebuilt first?

3. Look up John 10:1–2. Who is the person Jesus described as the shepherd?

4. Now read John 10:7.
    a. Who did Jesus say is the gate?
    b. Symbolically, why do you think the Sheep Gate was the first to be rebuilt?

5. What occurred *after* the Sheep Gate had been repaired?

6. Name the next group of people mentioned in rebuilding the wall.

Live Out ...

7. Think about the actions in these verses: repairing and consecrating. Now consider your own life and the areas needing repair. There may be areas of small cracks of dissension or the rubble of broken relationships. Record these areas and dedicate them to God as you pray to rebuild.

8. The workers on the wall of Jerusalem served with passion. Are there areas of service where you have found yourself going through the motions? List them here and allow God to either rekindle your passion or lead you to a new way to serve. "Whatever your hand finds to do, do it with your might" (Eccl. 9:10).

9. Circle any additional areas in your life that need major repair and renovation:

2 Profit for Priests

It was not a coincidence that the first gate to be rebuilt was the Sheep Gate. It was through this gate that sheep were brought for sacrifice in the temple. The priests were zealous in their duties because these offerings to the Lord were their inheritance; therefore, they stood to benefit most by the repair.[2]

4 Loss of Self

Jesus said that salvation comes to those who enter through the most important gate: Himself. He is the only way, the truth, and the life. No man or woman can come to the Father except through Him (see John 10:7; 14:6).

5 Sacrifice for Sin

The priests dedicated and consecrated the Sheep Gate. The sacrifice of sheep for the Israelites' sins pointed to the ultimate sacrifice of the Lamb, Jesus Christ, who died for our sins. When John the Baptist saw Jesus at the Jordan River, he proclaimed, "Behold! The Lamb of God who takes away the sin of the world!" (John 1:29).

A broken relationship with a friend
A marriage on shaky ground
A neglected time with the Lord
Other: ____________________

7 Set Apart

The meaning behind *consecration* and *dedication* is to recognize something as special and uniquely set apart for God's glory and service. Nehemiah and the priests regarded the work on the walls and the city gates as special to God and uniquely set apart unto Him.

9 God-Glorifying

Used thirty-five times in this chapter of Nehemiah, the word *repair* means to make strong and firm. Nehemiah wasn't interested in a quick fix. He and those who gathered to serve were building to the glory of God. They did their very best.[3]

Nehemiah 3 gives us a close look at the team of workers who gathered to rebuild the walls of Jerusalem. Like these men and women, we are called and equipped to put our hands to the areas of service that God has prepared for us. The task may be difficult, but we can be assured that God will strengthen our hands to do His work.

J. Hudson Taylor, a missionary to China in the late 1800s, stated, "I have found that there are three stages in every great work of God: first, it is impossible, then it is difficult, then it is done."[4] Often the job before us seems overwhelming, even impossible, but as we take the first step of faith and commit our work to the Lord, He will establish us and give us the strength we need. May our hands and hearts be given to the work of our Savior. God be glorified as we choose to honor Him.

Listen To ...

God's work, done in God's way, will never lack God's supply.

—J. Hudson Taylor

Families Were Helpers

During the time of Nehemiah, walls around cities provided security for both physical and spiritual well-being. Strong walls provided needed protection from enemy advances. For the Jewish people, the walls also offered protection from the infiltration of worldly ways that might pollute hearts and minds. What outsiders might construe as a limitation or a form of captivity was regarded as peace and security to the residents.

In today's culture, we see the walls of the family unit breaking down. Divisive attacks of lies, selfishness, and temptation are bringing destruction to the modern home. How can we protect our hearts and families as the Enemy attempts to divide, conquer, and bring ruin? We need to build walls of truth around our hearts and homes. The foundation of truth is God's Word alone—the Scriptures. These walls of truth are designed to guard our hearts and give us and our families a safe place to retreat, grow, and rest. Within these walls, our homes become fortresses, dwellings of safety amid the raging battles.

Living in God's Word of Truth will always be a place of safety. From Nehemiah we learn that, like the Israelites, we have an obligation to build strong walls of truth around our lives.

Lift Up ...

Dear Lord, perhaps I have allowed the walls that protect my loved ones to become unstable. Maybe some of the mortar is loose and there are rocks about to fall. Help me learn about rebuilding walls that will protect and nurture but will not separate me from those who need my help. In Jesus' name. Amen.

2 A Fishermen's Gate

The Fish Gate, which was located west of the Sheep Gate, was the gate the fishermen used when they came in from fishing in the Jordan River and Sea of Galilee. The fish market was probably located nearby. Think of it: this was the same gate used by Peter, James, and John, the best-known fishers of men!

3 A Proud Legacy

Here we see the importance of the names of the sons, fathers, and even grandfathers. Today, we each bear a heritage that is passed on in our family. We might be a proud daughter of a God-fearing father or a blessed mom of believing children.

Look At ...

Last week, we considered the rebuilding and repair of walls that were essential to the Israelites' security and national identity as God's people. We learned that even when God has ordained a great work, planning and delegating responsibilities are essential to its success. The names and locations of those who participated in rebuilding Jerusalem's wall were recorded for all time.

Today we continue our tour of the beams, bolts, bars, gates, and walls that surrounded the city. We meet the participating families and learn their names. The faithful chronicling of names indicates the importance of this endeavor. To this day, they are part of a proud legacy. Similarly, those who shunned their responsibility are also remembered, to their lasting shame.

Read Nehemiah 3:3–5.

Also the sons of Hassenaah built the Fish Gate; they laid its beams and hung its doors with its bolts and bars. And next to them Meremoth the son of Urijah, the son of Koz, made repairs. Next to them Meshullam the son of Berechiah, the son of Meshezabel, made repairs. Next to them Zadok the son of Baana made repairs. Next to them the Tekoites made repairs; but their nobles did not put their shoulders to the work of their Lord. Nehemiah 3:3–5

1. What was the next section of the wall to be repaired?

2. a. Which family repaired the gate?

    b. What did their repairs entail?

3. Draw a line connecting the names of the sons who repaired the next section of the wall with their fathers and grandfathers.

Son	Father	Grandfather
Meshullam	Baana	Meshezabel
Zadok	Urijah	Koz
Meremoth	Berechiah	

4. Who were the ones who did *not* participate in the work?

5. What reasons might the nobles have given for not wanting to "put their shoulders to the work"?

6. During His earthly ministry, Jesus showed us the greatest example of servanthood. What kind of attitude should we have concerning service in our homes, workplaces, or churches?

Live Out ...

7. How do you honor God and establish strong protective gates and walls in your home? Even simple things can make a big difference. Share some practices that have made a difference in your life.

8. a. What are some ways you enjoy serving your family?
b. What are some ways your family enjoys serving God together?

9. Many served side-by-side to accomplish God's work. Some, like the nobles of Tekoa, missed out on the blessing of serving God.

4 A Prideful Legacy

The Tekoites were a group of people who had travelled approximately eleven miles from Tekoa, near Bethlehem. They built at two different places around the wall. The nobles of Tekoa did not assist in the labor, feeling too important to perform manual labor.

7 The Weak Point

Much of the rebuilding involved gates in the wall. The gates were the critical entry and exit points to the city; as such, they were most likely to see an enemy attack. The work started at each of the seven gates and moved out from there.[5]

8 The Strong Point

Christian service begins at home. A Chinese proverb says, "Better to be kind at home than to burn incense in a far place." The apostle Paul wrote, "Let them first learn to show piety at home" (1 Tim. 5:4).

Are you living out God's plan for serving in your life? If not, what is holding you back from accomplishing great things for Him?

A professional home renovation can result in an inspiring change. A house can undergo a dramatic transformation in a relatively short amount of time. Some renovations only require rearranging the furniture and applying fresh paint, but others call for a major teardown before construction even begins.

When that's the case, the work is demanding, messy, expensive, and time-consuming. In the end, however, the broken-down home is transformed into a strong, beautiful, and refreshing place to live. How satisfying to see the tangible results of such efforts.

In the same way, it's wonderful to see the results of God's work in our hearts and in our homes when He guides our transformation. When we take inventory of our lives, we often realize that some of our protective walls have crumbled. By God's grace, we are given an opportunity to rebuild.

Rebuilding is rarely quick or easy. In the process, we may feel inadequate and weak, but God has promised to be our strength in our weakness. When we live in mindful obedience, He shows us where to erect walls of truth, holiness, and love. When we stand back and see our work, we find a place of peace and security to live our lives and raise our families.

Listen To ...

The God who made us also can remake us.

—*Woodrow Kroll*

Diverse Helpers

In March of 1981, President Reagan was shot in an assassination attempt. He was hospitalized for several weeks. Although Reagan was the nation's chief executive, his absence due to his hospitalization had little impact on the nation's activity. Government continued as usual.[6]

In February 1968, seven thousand sanitation workers gathered in New York City Hall Park and voted to go on strike in order to get a decent contract. For years, they had been bound by policies that required their pay to be lower than that of firefighters or police. The strike lasted only eight days before Governor Nelson Rockefeller was compelled to send in the National Guard to pick up the garbage and stem rising health and safety concerns.[7]

Our society needs a president, but it also needs sanitation workers. We can't underestimate the less-esteemed work that contributes to the smooth functioning of our country, our cities, our homes, and our churches. Paul said, "And the eye cannot say to the hand, 'I have no need of you'; nor again the head to the feet, 'I have no need of you.' No, much rather, those members of the body which seem to be weaker are necessary" (1 Cor. 12:21–22).

In Nehemiah, God used all kinds of people—leaders, sons, daughters, servants, perfume makers, and goldsmiths. They all worked side-by-side. Each member was important, and each had a special function to perform.

Lift Up ...

Dear Lord, I am often guilty of seeing one ministry as more meaningful and appealing than others. This attitude hurts not only me, but it hurts others as well. I want to be useful, Lord. Give me eyes to see the worth in every effort for Your glory. In Jesus' name. Amen.

Look At ...

In yesterday's lesson, we took a walking tour of the various gates and the components that went into the construction and repair of the wall. We met the families whose names were memorialized in this grand effort. We also learned about the people who shirked their duties and "did not put their shoulders to the work of their Lord."

Today we see that the workers were not limited to carpenters or construction workers but were from all walks of life. In their unified efforts, this community of people drew together. They did not opt out because repairing walls and gates was not their calling or the best use of their gifts. They did their part, whether a goldsmith, perfumer, or community leader. Repairs were not limited to walls and gates but extended to the residence of the governor.

Read Nehemiah 3:6–14.

Moreover Jehoiada the son of Paseah and Meshullam the son of Besodeiah repaired the Old Gate; they laid its beams and hung its doors, with its bolts and bars. And next to them Melatiah the Gibeonite, Jadon the Meronothite, the men of Gibeon and Mizpah, repaired the residence of the governor of the region beyond the River. Next to him Uzziel the son of Harhaiah, one of the goldsmiths, made repairs. Also next to him Hananiah, one of the perfumers, made repairs; and they fortified Jerusalem as far as the Broad Wall. And next to them Rephaiah the son of Hur, leader of half the district of Jerusalem, made repairs. Next to them Jedaiah the son of Harumaph made repairs in front of his house. And next to him Hattush the son of Hashabniah made repairs. Malchijah the son of Harim and Hashub the son of Pahath-Moab repaired another section, as well as the Tower of the Ovens. And next to him was Shallum the son of Hallohesh, leader of half the district of Jerusalem; he and his daughters made repairs. Hanun and the inhabitants of Zanoah repaired the Valley Gate. They built it, hung its doors with its bolts and bars, and repaired a thousand cubits of the wall as far as the Refuse Gate. Malchijah the son of Rechab, leader of the district of Beth Haccerem, repaired the Refuse Gate; he built it and hung its doors with its bolts and bars. Nehemiah 3:6–14

1. Who laid the bars and beams?

2. Which gate were they repairing?

3. Men skilled in things other than construction or carpentry helped restore the walls.

    a. What two trades were mentioned here?

    b. What did they repair?

    c. Name the government official who worked on the wall.

4.   a. Who made repairs in front of his own house?

    b. Who was next to him?

5. This section of Scripture shows that there were some persons that you might be surprised to find working on the wall. Who were they?

6.   a. Where were the men who repaired the Valley Gate from?

    b. How thorough were they in completing their job?

    c. How far did they build?

7.   a. Who rebuilt the Refuse Gate?

    b. What else did he do?

Live Out ...

8. We saw that the daughters of Shallum labored to help rebuild the wall. In what ways do you work for the Lord?

1 Hooks and Catches

The word *beam* used here and in Nehemiah 3:6, 13–15 is thought to mean a crossbar rather than a lock, while the word *bars* denotes the hooks or catches that held the crossbar at its two ends. The residents created a secure system for protection.

2 Old and New

The Old Gate, also called the Mishneh Gate, was probably located at the northwest corner of the city. This led to the new quarter, a portion of Jerusalem built after Nehemiah's time. Commentator Warren Wiersbe says, "It is from the old that we derive the new; and if we abandon the old, there can be nothing new."[8]

5 Male and Female

Throughout Scripture, women played an important part in the ongoing work of God. In this case, it is not surprising to find that the daughters of Shallum put their hands to work on the repairing of the wall. Are you a woman who desires to work for Him?

8 A Humbling Place

For Nehemiah, the Valley Gate represented a low place because of the spiritual damage to the people and the physical damages to the city. Sometimes we come to a place where we must be humbled as well. This gate represents a believer's valley—our humbling place.

10 A Cleansing Place

The Refuse Gate, or Dung Gate, led to the Valley of Hinnom, where all the garbage was deposited. Important in its function, it represents the need for cleansing. As Warren Wiersbe wrote, "We must rid ourselves of whatever defiles us before it destroys us."[9]

❑ Praying

❑ Raising kids in a Christlike home

❑ Teaching Sunday school

❑ Supplying food for the needy

❑ Praying for missionaries

❑ Cleaning up parks and playgrounds

❑ Building homes for veterans or homeless

❑ Working on church committees

❑ Supporting missionaries financially

❑ Using your God-given gifts

❑ Tithing to your church

❑ Supporting/undergirding your spouse

❑ Delivering meals to elderly shut-ins

9. Is your labor done with a willing spirit? Look up 1 Corinthians 3:8. What does it say about our efforts for the Lord?

10. In God's kingdom, is some work more important than other work? Why or why not?

_____

A conductor was rehearsing with his great orchestra. The organ rolled a beautiful melody, the drums thundered in the background, the trumpets resounded their support, the violins wept their refrain, when suddenly, something was wrong.

The conductor threw up his arms and said, "Where's the piccolo?"

The piccolo player replied, "I'm obscure. I don't amount to much. With all of the other instruments playing, I didn't think I would be missed."

The conductor with the trained ear said, "Every one of us is necessary to create a masterpiece."[10]

The great wall surrounding Jerusalem required a symphony of workers orchestrated by Nehemiah, who saw the vision of the completed task. In the church today, we must partner with one another to complete the work that God has called us to do. When we feel obscure, we must remember that God has something significant planed for our lives. We must play our part and keep our eye on the Master Conductor.

Listen To ...

Alone we can do so little; together we can do so much.

—*Helen Keller*

Leaders Were Helpers

A story is told about Samuel, who from a young age knew he wanted to be a great man of God and a teacher of His Word. After he graduated from seminary, he traveled around the nation, preaching sermons that were received enthusiastically. He became well known as a preacher and was offered a position to pastor a large church on the East Coast.

While prayerfully considering this offer, Samuel began to sense God was leading him to temporarily serve for the Salvation Army. Because he was well known in the community, he assumed he would be quickly promoted to a position of leadership. However, on the first day, he was stunned to learn that he would not be preaching. Instead, he was assigned to clean and polish the boots of his fellow officers.

The following morning, sitting in a room surrounded by muddy shoes and a jar of polish, he was tempted to quit. This was an obvious waste of his time and talent. He had proved himself to be a brilliant preacher. How could he be given such a demeaning task? He wondered if he had made a huge mistake. Yet there, in the midst of the smelly boots, Samuel thought of Jesus, picturing Him washing the dirty feet of His disciples. Samuel realized that Jesus, the King of Kings, had set a great example by taking the form of a servant, with love and humility. He cried out, "Lord, You washed their feet; I will polish their boots."

In Nehemiah we see this same humble attitude in the leaders who worked right alongside the people to rebuild the wall.

Lift Up ...

Dear Lord, it is easier to talk about humility than to practice it. I struggle with wanting to be admired and acknowledged for my efforts. Make me mindful that You are the One who always sees and always knows. Lord, that is more than enough. In Jesus' name. Amen.

Look At ...

Yesterday, we considered the varied group of people involved in the initiative to repair the wall surrounding Jerusalem. There were men and women, laborers and leaders, all working with a common goal to restore the place of their heritage and find, once again, their sense of national and spiritual dignity. Repairs were not limited to walls and gates but extended to the residence of the governor.

Today, we learn that several leaders offered hands-on help to the effort. There was a progression to the work—one thing followed another. Certainly there was camaraderie that generated momentum from working side-by-side. If one man built a handsome gate near his home, the next would likely want his efforts to be equal to it. This was a diverse effort from men and women of various skills and talents.

Read Nehemiah 3:15–25.

Shallun the son of Col-Hozeh, leader of the district of Mizpah, repaired the Fountain Gate; he built it, covered it, hung its doors with its bolts and bars, and repaired the wall of the Pool of Shelah by the King's Garden, as far as the stairs that go down from the City of David. After him Nehemiah the son of Azbuk, leader of half the district of Beth Zur, made repairs as far as the place in front of the tombs of David, to the man-made pool, and as far as the House of the Mighty. After him the Levites, under Rehum the son of Bani, made repairs. Next to him Hashabiah, leader of half the district of Keilah, made repairs for his district. After him their brethren, under Bavai the son of Henadad, leader of the other half of the district of Keilah, made repairs. And next to him Ezer the son of Jeshua, the leader of Mizpah, repaired another section in front of the Ascent to the Armory at the buttress. After him Baruch the son of Zabbai carefully repaired the other section, from the buttress to the door of the house of Eliashib the high priest. After him Meremoth the son of Urijah, the son of Koz, repaired another section, from the door of the house of Eliashib to the end of the house of Eliashib. And after him the priests, the men of the plain, made repairs. After him Benjamin and Hasshub made repairs opposite their house. After them Azariah the son of Maaseiah, the son of Ananiah, made repairs by his house. After him Binnui the son of Henadad repaired another section, from the house of Azariah to the buttress, even as far as the corner. Palal the son of Uzai made

1 Essential Water

An underground conduit known as Hezekiah's Tunnel fed the Fountain Gate, near the Pool of Siloah. In the Bible, drinking water is a metaphor of the Holy Spirit (see John 7:37–39). Spiritually, we each must travel from a humbling place (the Valley Gate), to a recognition of our defilement (the Refuse Gate), to a place of the cleansing refreshment of the Holy Spirit.[11]

3 Humble Leaders

The leaders worked alongside the people. Jesus was the ultimate example of servant leadership. He told us the power of this kind of commitment: "But he who is greatest among you shall be your servant. And whoever exalts himself will be humbled, and he who humbles himself will be exalted" (Matt. 23:11–12).

7 Prison Rebuilt

Commentators reference the court of the prison as being close to the royal palace. It was a place where the prisoner would have constrained activity and very little liberty. Throughout the book of Jeremiah, the prophet often found himself in the court of the prison (Jer. 32:2; 33:1; 37:21; 39:14).[12]

repairs opposite the buttress, and on the tower which projects from the king's upper house that was by the court of the prison. After him Pedaiah the son of Parosh made repairs. Nehemiah 3:15–25

1. Who was the person primarily responsible for repairs to the Fountain Gate?

2. How did Shallun reflect what Jesus said in Mark 9:34–35?

3. Five men were specifically mentioned as leaders in this passage of Scripture. List their names and the work they accomplished on the repairs and the wall.

Name	Extent of Work Done
1.	
2.	
3.	
4.	
5.	

4. Who was the high priest at this time?

5. In these verses, a select group of people repaired the wall. Who were they?

6. What portions of the wall did Benjamin, Hasshub, and Azariah repair?

7. What was the name of the man who did the repairs on the court of the prison?

Live Out ...

8. The Holy Spirit is described by the Greek word *paracleo*, meaning "to come alongside." In a sense, we can act in the same manner by coming alongside another person, whether at home or in our workplace. In what ways do you come alongside others?

9. What is the emphasis in the following Scriptures?

Psalm 133:1   It is pleasant to live in unity with one another.

Mark 3:25

Ephesians 4:3

Ephesians 4:13

10. Do you believe that you inspire a sense of unity when you are serving in your home or in your workplace? Are you leading with the heart of a servant? If not, why not?

_____

As Canada snow geese head south for the winter, they fly in a distinct V-formation. In doing so, the flock can move considerably faster and maintain flight longer than if they were to fly alone. As the lead goose deals with the headwinds and debris, it takes on the greatest effort of the flock. When it becomes tired, it drops to the rear of the V, while another goose serves as the point leader. If one goose struggles, two geese fly out to support the struggling bird and bring him back into formation. They are a united flock, flying as a team and looking out for one another.

This is a good picture of the unity required to build the wall of Jerusalem. Leaders understood the importance of serving side-by-side

9 Drawing Together

Unity is defined as the state of being drawn together or joined as a whole. The term implies strength and empowerment. Division in the body of Christ or in our homes is a tactic of the Enemy. When we stand strong in unity and prayer with fellow believers, we defeat his plans.

10 Pleasing God

It pleased God to see His people working together as one. God will put us into situations where we must work together and learn how to lead, how to follow, and how to work together with one heart and mind.[13]

with other men and women to complete God's work. Nehemiah's plan for rebuilding the wall required all the people to work together—each group taking a certain section of the wall and working on it with a servant's heart. The unified effort yielded the awesome result of a repaired and restored wall surrounding the city of God.

Listen To ...

> *Sense shines with a double luster when it is set in humility. An able*
> *and yet humble man is a jewel worth a kingdom.*
>
> —*William Penn*

DAY 5

Servants Were Helpers

In the heart of our nation's capital stands a reflective memorial honoring fallen Vietnam veterans. Dedicated in 1982, the memorial stretches five hundred feet and is inscribed with the 58,286 names of all American men and women who lost their lives fighting in the Vietnam War.

People walking along the solemn walls of the Vietnam Veterans Memorial will see their reflections in the polished black stone along with the etched names of the war heroes. This was the designer's intention. She wanted people to relate to the fallen veterans, because they were women, men, mothers, fathers, daughters, and sons, just as we all are.[14]

As you study Nehemiah 3 and read the names of the valiant workers at the wall in Jerusalem, look closely. Behind those names, your reflection shines back at you. For you are just like them—a person whose heart's desire is to honor her heavenly Father and glorify His name among the nations.

As you serve the Lord today, know that He sees your heart, and He is blessed by your acts of worship and service. He knows your name. Someday when you humbly kneel before our Father in heaven, you will hear Him lovingly speak your name and say, "Well done, good and faithful servant. Enter into the joy of the Lord!"

Lift Up ...

Dear Lord, it humbles me to realize my name is etched on Your heart. I pray that my life may be a beautiful reflection of You. In Jesus' name. Amen.

2 A Place Fortified

Not only was Ophel
located on a hill; it was
also located near the
all-important Water Gate
that led from the old City
of David to the Gihon
Spring, just adjacent to
the Kidron Valley. Ophel
was a strategic place of
fortification and proximity
to water.[15]

6 A Gate of Prominence

Traditionally, it is said that
the East Gate was the
gate through which
Jesus entered Jerusalem
on Palm Sunday. It was
the gate nearest to the
temple. Today, it is called
the Golden Gate and was
sealed during the time
of Sulayman, a Turkish
sultan.

Look At ...

Yesterday we looked at the various workers on the wall and the part
each one played in the reconstruction and new construction. It was a
unified effort that demonstrated the power of believers when called to
a God-glorifying task. Personal status and egos were noticeably absent
while leaders worked alongside the citizenry.

Today, we see the final group of helping hands who restored the
wall. While the efforts that begin an endeavor can be filled with enthusiasm, the work that brings the project to completion is a glorious thing.

Read Nehemiah 3:26–32.

*Moreover the Nethinim who dwelt in Ophel made repairs as far as
the place in front of the Water Gate toward the east, and on the projecting
tower. After them the Tekoites repaired another section, next to the great
projecting tower, and as far as the wall of Ophel. Beyond the Horse Gate the
priests made repairs, each in front of his own house. After them Zadok the
son of Immer made repairs in front of his own house. After him Shemaiah
the son of Shechaniah, the keeper of the East Gate, made repairs. After
him Hananiah the son of Shelemiah, and Hanun, the sixth son of Zalaph,
repaired another section. After him Meshullam the son of Berechiah made
repairs in front of his dwelling. After him Malchijah, one of the goldsmiths,
made repairs as far as the house of the Nethinim and of the merchants, in
front of the Miphkad Gate, and as far as the upper room at the corner. And
between the upper room at the corner, as far as the Sheep Gate, the goldsmiths and the merchants made repairs.* Nehemiah 3:26–32

1. What is the first name listed?

2. Where was the projecting tower located?

3. In this passage, we see that unlike the nobles in Nehemiah 3:5, this group of Tekoites put their shoulders to the work and accomplished something. What did the Tekoites repair?

4. What part of the Horse Gate was repaired?

5. Another group of people were mentioned as working in front of their homes.

    a. Who were they?

    b. Why do you think it was important to repair in front of their homes?

6.   a. There are five persons named doing repairs; list their names.

    b. What was the name of the East Gate keeper who made repairs?

7.   a. In the above passage two groups of people did repairs. Who were they?

    b. What was the name of the goldsmith, and what was the extent of his repairs?

Live Out ...

8. The builders of the wall knew they must fortify the gates because they expected to encounter warfare. Read Ephesians 6:11. What should we put on daily to ensure victory in the battle?

7 A Corner of Inspection

The Miphkad Gate or Inspection Gate was at the northeast corner of Jerusalem, where the army was registered and reviewed. One day we, too, will come before God for His inspection. Let Him find that you are a soldier in His army who is not ashamed of the work you have done to His glory.

8 Locked Shields

When battles were fought in ancient times, the shields the warriors carried could lock together to form a larger shield that would give greater protection from the enemy's flaming arrows. Likewise, today we are to partner in prayer and faith with other believers to fight the battles that come our way.

9 A Ready Response

Thirty-eight workers are named in this chapter, and forty-two different groups are identified. Whether their names were recorded or not, each servant responded to the call to rebuild.

9. Read Isaiah 6:8. God had a message to share; he asked, "Whom shall I send?"

    a. Who heard God's voice, and how did that person respond?

    b. How did this response show that this person was God's servant?

10. Why is it essential to seek God's will for your life if you are truly His servant?

Write a prayer in your journal, asking the Lord to show you how to become the servant He wants you to be.

———————————

Nehemiah 3 demonstrates the power of servanthood within the body of Christ and encourages us to build and maintain the walls and gates of our lives. There is a particular beauty that results from the unified efforts of lives yielded to God's will and His work.

Through our tour of the wall, the Sheep Gate is both the beginning and the ending place of the work on the walls surrounding the Holy City. Jesus is the ultimate Alpha and Omega in God's plan for our salvation. He is the ultimate sacrifice, the ultimate gate through which we must enter to be blessed with salvation. Are you one of the sheep who hears the Shepherd's voice and follows Him?

As we continue our exploration of the book of Nehemiah, remember to put on the whole armor of God, fortify the walls around your heart and soul, and take shelter in prayer and in God's Word.

Listen To ...

In the morning, prayer is the key that opens to us the treasures of God's mercies and blessings;
in the evening, it is the key that shuts us up under His protection and safeguard.

—*Jacques Ellul*

Armed for Victory

Nehemiah 4

C. S. Lewis wrote the hugely popular *The Screwtape Letters* in 1940 after being mesmerized by a radio speech from Adolf Hitler. Lewis realized that the power of charisma could sway people even if they knew what they heard was wrong.

Published as a series of weekly episodes in a church publication called the *Guardian*, these thirty-one "letters" between Screwtape, a senior demon, and his nephew, Wormwood, a less-experienced demon, discussed a "Patient" they were trying to sway away from the "Enemy" (God) and toward "Our Father Below" (Satan). While Wormwood's novice attempts failed, Screwtape took a subtle approach: "The safest road to Hell is the gradual one—the gentle slope, soft underfoot, without sudden turnings, without milestones, without signposts."[1] Eventually, the demons' attempts failed and the "Patient" died and went to heaven.

While *The Screwtape Letters* is fiction, the premise is fact. Satan wants our utter destruction by whatever means necessary. Lewis said writing the book was not fun because of the seriousness of the issue.[2] Lewis would never write another "letter" of this kind.

Just as Satan goes into battle armed for victory, so must we. With the sword of God's Word, we can victoriously overcome evil. And just as the "Patient" faltered but never failed, we too can prevail over our enemies: "For whatever is born of God overcomes the world. And this is the victory that has overcome the world—our faith" (1 John 5:4).

As a believer, you have the power to overcome sin and darkness, but like Nehemiah, you must be ready for the battle. Are you armed for victory?

Sticks and Stones

Lift Up ...

Dear Lord, when others seek to ridicule and belittle me, help me remember Your example of meekness. Words can be hurtful, but I do not have to defend myself, because You are my Defender. May the words of my enemies never gain a foothold in my thoughts and actions. In Jesus' name. Amen.

Look At ...

Last week, we saw the Israelites come together to begin rebuilding the wall. People from every trade banded together and divided the work. Each family was given their section to complete. Not only were they building a wall, but they were also rebuilding their homes. In spite of their enemies, the Israelites knew their safety depended on the wall standing strong.

In today's lesson, we see that while facing scorn from the enemies, Nehemiah kept calm under pressure. While those against the Israelites intensified their opposition with mockery and intimidation tactics, he kept his focus on God. Rather than striking out at them himself, he brought his concerns to the One who could do something about them. When you have struggles with people in your life, where do you take your concerns—to heart or to God?

Read Nehemiah 4:1–5.

But it so happened, when Sanballat heard that we were rebuilding the wall, that he was furious and very indignant, and mocked the Jews. And he spoke before his brethren and the army of Samaria, and said, "What are these feeble Jews doing? Will they fortify themselves? Will they offer sacrifices? Will they complete it in a day? Will they revive the stones from the heaps of rubbish—stones that

1 A Thorn

Sanballat means thorn in secret, and that's what he was to Nehemiah—a pain! Paul also had a thorn (see 2 Cor. 12:7), which Jon Courson said was "sent Paul's way to keep him from being puffed up in pride, to keep him in a place of humility and brokenness."³ It may have served the same purpose for Nehemiah.

are burned?" Now Tobiah the Ammonite was beside him, and he said, "Whatever they build, if even a fox goes up on it, he will break down their stone wall." Hear, O our God, for we are despised; turn their reproach on their own heads, and give them as plunder to a land of captivity! Do not cover their iniquity, and do not let their sin be blotted out from before You; for they have provoked You to anger before the builders. Nehemiah 4:1–5

1. Who came into opposition against Nehemiah and the Israelites?

2. What was Sanballat's response to the Israelites' productivity?

3. Who did he rally to intimidate the Jews?

4. Sanballat ridiculed every aspect of the Israelites' efforts—the workers, the work, and the materials—in an attempt to prevent the reconstruction of the walls. He presented five questions that served five purposes. Match the question with the purpose behind it.

a. What are these feeble Jews doing?

b. Will they fortify themselves?

c. Will they offer sacrifices?

d. Will they complete it in a day?

e. Will they revive the stones from the heaps of rubbish—stones that are burned?

___ To magnify their problems of recovering materials from the rubble.

___ To undermine their confidence by calling attention to the immensity of the project.

___ To blaspheme Jehovah God, denying God would help His people.

___ To mock their ambitions of rebuilding the wall for protection.

___ To belittle the Jews.

5. a. Who joined Sanballat?

   b. In what way did he demean the Israelites?

6. How did Nehemiah first respond to the taunts of Sanballat and Tobiah?

7. How did Nehemiah describe the way Sanballat and Tobiah felt about the Israelites?

8. a. What did Nehemiah ask God to turn against them?

   b. What did he ask God *not* to do?

9. Against whom had the enemy sinned, and why?

4 A Test

Sanballat showed nothing but contempt for the Israelites. Consider how Jesus was ridiculed, mocked, and beaten as He was led to the cross. Insulted, scorned, and taunted, He responded to their mistreatment with prayer and forgiveness: "Father, forgive them, for they do not know what they do" (Luke 23:34).

5 A Taunt

Tobiah joined Sanballat by joking about the Israelites' building skills, perhaps hoping they would be embarrassed and quit. Laughter is a good thing, but not at the expense of others. "A merry heart does good, like medicine, but a broken spirit dries the bones" (Prov. 17:22).

10 A Tussle

In the Bible, we see glimpses
of the spiritual world,
so we know a battle
rages between good and
evil. "But the prince of
the kingdom of Persia
withstood me twenty-one
days; and behold, Michael,
one of the chief princes,
came to help me, for I had
been left alone there with
the kings of Persia" (Dan.
10:13).

Live Out ...

10. Words can wound, but not if we don't let them infiltrate our minds. Read Ephesians 6:12, and answer the questions below.

a. What do we wrestle against?

b. Where does this battle take place?

11. Sanballat hurled angry words at the Jews when he learned they were making progress on the wall. Nehemiah returned with prayer to God.

a. How do you respond when you are angry?

❑ Scream/yell   ❑ Silence   ❑ Sarcasm

❑ Prayer   ❑ Patience   ❑ Other: _____

b. Now read Galatians 5:19–26. What sins of the flesh does the Lord ask us to put off? If we live in the Spirit of Christ, what righteousness are we to put on? List your answers below.

Put Off	Put On

c. Write a prayer in your journal asking God to help you put off the things that are not pleasing to Him and put on those things that delight Him.

12. Satan will stop at nothing to get a foothold in your mind and keep you from doing what God has called you to do.

a. What lies does the Enemy want you to believe about your work for the Lord?

b. What important truth should you keep in mind?

c. What should you keep before your eyes?

12 A Truth

Satan wants us to believe our kingdom work means nothing to God. "For God is not unjust to forget your work and labor of love which you have shown toward His name, in that you have ministered to the saints, and do minister" (Heb. 6:10). God knows what we do in His name.

Most of us are familiar with the rhyme "Sticks and stones will break my bones, but words will never hurt me." It first appeared in the *Christian Recorder* in March 1862.[4] While words cannot physically harm us, in today's world of cyberspace and cell phones, online bullying is on the rise, with devastating effects.

Here are some staggering statistics from nobullying.com:

- Twenty-five percent of teenagers report that they have experienced repeated bullying via their cell phones or the Internet.

- Often, bullies and cyberbullies turn to hate speech to victimize their targets. One-tenth of all middle school and high school students have been on the receiving end of "hate terms" hurled against them.

- More than 80 percent of teens regularly use cell phones, making them the most popular form of technology and therefore a common medium for cyberbullying.

- The most common types of cyberbullying tactics reported are mean, hurtful comments and the spreading of rumors.

- Victims of cyberbullying are more likely to suffer from low self-esteem and to consider suicide as a result.[5]

Nehemiah was face-to-face with his bullies and subject to direct, repeated harassment. He could have responded by returning insults or even giving up and running away. Instead, he prayed. He didn't give any more thought to Sanballat and Tobiah because, as Warren Wiersbe wrote, "If we spend time pondering the Enemy's words, we will give Satan a foothold from which he can launch another attack closer to home…. Anything that keeps you from doing what God has called you to do will only help the Enemy."[6] Nehemiah would not be swayed from his task, and neither should we.

Listen To …

The tests of life are to make, not break us. Trouble may demolish a man's business but build up his character. The blow at the outward man may be the greatest blessing to the inner man. If God, then, puts or permits anything hard in our lives, be sure that the real peril, the real trouble, is that we shall lose if we flinch or rebel.

—Maltbie Davenport Babcock

Partners in Prayer

Partners in crime are collaborators or accessories to crimes. Oftentimes, when a crime looks more complicated than one person could pull off, the police look for an accomplice and almost always find one. Partners in crime can be as close as married couples or coworkers or as random as two people looking for a leg up.

Most of us became familiar with the phrase *insider trading* in 2004 when Martha Stewart, America's homemaking queen, was sent to prison. Insider trading is when individuals with access to nonpublic information trade stock or other securities based on that knowledge. It is illegal because it is unfair to other investors who don't have access to the same information.

Recently, two partners in crime, Rajat Gupta and Raj Rajaratnam, shared sensitive information about Goldman Sachs and wound up in the same prison in Ayer, Massachusetts. Gupta was convicted of insider trading for leaking information while on the board of Goldman Sachs to Rajaratnam, a hedge fund manager.[7]

Rest assured, when you partner with God, you are partnering with the One who never falters. "God is not a man, that He should lie, nor a son of man, that He should repent. Has He said, and will He not do? Or has He spoken, and will He not make it good?" (Num. 23:19). Partners in crime can't be trusted; they always look out for themselves. God is the opposite; He is the one partner who will never leave you or forsake you.

Lift Up ...

Dear Lord, thank You that when I feel taunted, I know You are with me. No matter what comes into my life, whether good or bad, I know I can make my prayers known to You and You hear me. You work on my behalf for my good. Thank You for Your presence. In Jesus' name. Amen.

2 Hard Workers

Nehemiah's confident prayer rallied the emotionally fragile workers. He trusted God to provide abundant resources for every need during a crucial time in the construction process. Because God was faithful, morale was high and the walls were built.

Look At ...

In yesterday's lesson, we saw Nehemiah encounter mockery and insults, but he called upon God to defend the Israelites from their adversaries. While the Israelites may have been feeble in the eyes of their enemies, they served a strong God to whom they cried out to stand in their defense. Nehemiah's response was one of prayer. The Israelites prayed and then protected. They relied on God to do His part, but they also knew they had the responsibility to guard.

Today we see the Israelites' hard work and progress even in the midst of adversaries on every side. As bricks were laid higher and higher, their foes also increased and became angrier as the walls rose to half their original height. Facing conspiring opponents, the Israelites prayerfully continued to build.

In the middle of resistance, do you allow hostility to slow you down? Instead, lift your eyes. God is there.

Read Nehemiah 4:6–9.

So we built the wall, and the entire wall was joined together up to half its height, for the people had a mind to work. Now it happened, when Sanballat, Tobiah, the Arabs, the Ammonites, and the Ashdodites heard that the walls of Jerusalem were being restored and the gaps were beginning to be closed, that they became very angry, and all of them conspired together to come and attack Jerusalem and create confusion. Nevertheless we made our prayer to our God, and because of them we set a watch against them day and night. Nehemiah 4:6–9

1. In spite of enemy opposition, what were the Israelites able to accomplish?

2. What attitude did the people have? Why do you think they had it?

3. Who else joined Sanballat against the Israelites?

4. What news did this group hear about the Israelites' progress?

5. What reaction did they have to the news?

6. a. What attack did they formulate?

   b. What was their goal?

7. a. What was the Israelites' response as the warfare intensified?

   b. How did Nehemiah impact them in this area?

8. a. With what precaution did they balance their prayers?

   b. How often did they do this?

Live Out ...

9. What walls have you begun to rebuild in your life? Are they the walls of your marriage, family, business relationships, friendships, or relationship to God? Draw your walls to the height they have been constructed and give them names. Include the gaps that still need to be filled. (Example: If the wall you are rebuilding is your marriage, draw a wall structure, label it "marriage," and include the specific areas in your marriage that you

3 Angry Foes

Jerusalem was now surrounded on all four sides—the Samaritans to the north, the Arabs to the south, the Ammonites to the east, and the Ashdodites to the west. Ashdod was a major city of the Philistines, and its inhabitants had been an ever-present enemy of Israel, from the time of the judges through the reign of King David.

6 Secret Plans

First, the enemy ridiculed and fired contempt at the builders. Nehemiah's defense was a cry of prayer. Angered by defeat, the enemy determined to attack with confusion. Satan doesn't give up easily when we are walking in God's will. "For God is not the author of confusion but of peace" (1 Cor. 14:33).

still need to work on—the "gaps"—such as being grateful, being faithful, being kind, slowing down, working harder.)

Completed Wall

10 Blatant Lies

Satan has opposed God's plan of salvation from the very beginning. He wants to make us believe that God is against us and will eventually give up on us. Hold fast, "for I am persuaded that neither death nor life, nor angels nor principalities nor pow- ers, nor things present nor things to come, nor height nor depth, nor any other created thing, shall be able to separate us from the love of God which is in Christ Jesus our Lord" (Rom. 8:38–39).

11 Powerful Prayers

R. A. Torrey said, "Anticipate your battles; fight them on your knees before temptation comes, and you will always have victory." In the garden of Gethsemane, Jesus said, "Watch and pray so that you will not fall into temptation. The spirit is willing, but the flesh is weak" (Mark 14:38 NIV). Be alert—watch and pray.

Ground Level

10. The Devil gets angry when we close the gaps in our walls. Where are you experiencing opposition against the closing gaps in your rebuilding project? What weapons is the Devil using to attack you?

❑ Hate   ❑ Jealousy   ❑ Anger
❑ Resentment   ❑ Worry   ❑ Discouragement
❑ Fear   ❑ Anxiety   ❑ Lies
❑ Pride   ❑ Laziness   ❑ Other: _____

11. In the midst of enemy attacks, the Israelites partnered together in prayer and developed a plan. Our battle is not against flesh and blood but against Satan and his opposing forces. To fight the invisible enemy, we need God's resources and supportive partners.

    a. In your journal, write a specific prayer to your great God about the opposition you face.

b. Think of someone you can partner with in prayer, or if you already have a prayer partner, write the name of that individual here.

c. Reach out to that person this week to share your prayer requests. Don't forget to ask how you can pray for her.

––––––––––––––

With the wall progressing to half its height, the Israelites were surrounded: Sanballat to the north, the Arabs to the south, the Ammonites to the east, and the Ashdodites to the west. Nehemiah's enemies partnered together in hopes of stopping the progression of the wall. Matthew Henry said, "Those who disagree in almost every thing, will unite in persecution."[8] They didn't have to be the best of friends to come against a common enemy: the Israelites.

Partners in crime aren't limited to the stock market. Even the animal kingdom shows examples of banding together for a common good. Pack hunters such as wolves and lions work together in groups; they rely on strategy, communication, and well-planned ambushes to capture their next meal.

While Sanballat and his band of thugs were hunting for Nehemiah and the Israelites, they didn't realize Nehemiah had already partnered with an entity stronger than the four of them combined—the living God.

Does it feel like your enemies are banding together to try to take you down? Like Nehemiah, partner with the God of heaven in prayer against your enemies. "Let us then approach God's throne of grace with confidence, so that we may receive mercy and find grace to help us in our time of need" (Heb. 4:16 NIV).

Listen To ...

Suffering overcomes the mind's inertia, develops the thinking powers,
opens up a new world, and drives the soul to action.
—*Anthony Harrison Evans*

DAY 3

Faith or Fear?

Phobias are extreme or irrational fears or aversions, such as xanthophobia, the fear of the color yellow, or one of the most common, coulrophobia, the fear of clowns. A phobia can develop after a frightening event, but it is often an inexplicable and illogical fear of a particular object, class of objects, or situation. Fear then causes a fight-or-flight response to kick in, causing us to react to threatening situations.

Phobias develop when people are not able to adjust adequately to the situation. One method of dealing with phobias is to expose the person to the very thing he or she fears most: "Exposure therapy, a form of cognitive-behavior therapy, is widely accepted as the most effective treatment for anxieties and phobias, and the vast majority of patients complete treatment within ten sessions. During exposure therapy, a person engages with the particular fear to help diminish and ultimately overcome it over time. An individual might, for example, look at a photograph of the dreaded object or become immersed in the situation he or she loathes."[9]

Nehemiah went through a kind of exposure therapy as he repeatedly faced his enemies. Either the Israelites could allow fear to cause them to give in to their enemies or they could rise up in faith, knowing that "the eyes of the LORD run to and fro throughout the whole earth, to show Himself strong on behalf of those whose heart is loyal to Him" (2 Chron. 16:9). When facing phobias, God will make Himself strong on your behalf if you stand in faith rather than fear.

Lift Up ...

Dear Lord, thank You for hearing my prayers and forgiving me when I fall into fear. When I focus on the circumstances in front of me, I get overwhelmed and afraid. I know I can trust You. Thank You for standing in my defense and fighting my enemies. In Jesus' name. Amen.

Look At ...

Yesterday, we saw that Nehemiah and the Israelites had a mind to work. They built the wall back up to half its height, which was no small feat, considering it is estimated to have been up to twelve feet! When his attackers banded together, Nehemiah knew he faced foes on every side, but he also knew that his one chance at survival was turning to God.

Today, we see weary Israelites. When confronted with massive piles of rubble, their task seemed daunting and hopeless. Through bold proclamation, Nehemiah reminded the Israelites to combat their adversaries with faith and courage. We can learn the same lesson today: when faced with rubble and enemies, turn to the Lord!

Read Nehemiah 4:10–14.

Then Judah said, "The strength of the laborers is failing, and there is so much rubbish that we are not able to build the wall." And our adversaries said, "They will neither know nor see anything, till we come into their midst and kill them and cause the work to cease." So it was, when the Jews who dwelt near them came, that they told us ten times, "From whatever place you turn, they will be upon us." Therefore I positioned men behind the lower parts of the wall, at the openings; and I set the people according to their families, with their swords, their spears, and their bows. And I looked, and arose and said to the nobles, to the leaders, and to the rest of the people, "Do not be afraid of them. Remember the Lord, great and awesome, and fight for your brethren, your sons, your daughters, your wives, and your houses." Nehemiah 4:10–14

1. Who came to speak to Nehemiah?

2. What did he say about how the Israelites were feeling?

3. What was hindering them?

4. What were their enemies plotting?

5 Rumors!

Rumors of the enemies' plot circulated among the Israelites. The enemies hoped fear would cause the workers to abort their project. If that failed, they would try to kill them. Jesus said, "The thief does not come except to steal, and to kill, and to destroy. I have come that they may have life" (John 10:10).

6 Revolt!

Jews from the surrounding communities of Jericho, Tekoa, Gibeon, Mizpah, and many others were helping rebuild Jerusalem. With enemies on all four sides, the workers were bound to live near some of them. Not only were the workers threatened, but so were their families.

8 Remember!

Nehemiah knew what it was like to be overcome by terror. "So I became dreadfully afraid" (Neh. 2:2). He conquered his fear by faith in the great and awesome God: "So I prayed to the God of heaven" (Neh. 2:4). Faith and fear cannot coexist.

5. How do we know their adversaries planned it as a stealth attack?

6. What fearful reports from home did the Jews bring to Nehemiah?

7.   a. According to verse 12, how many times did the Jews repeat the warning?

b. Considering what you have learned so far about Nehemiah's spiritual maturity, why do you think he did not respond immediately?

8.   a. According to verse 14, what public assembly did Nehemiah address?

b. What did he admonish them not to do?

c. What two things did he tell them to do?

Live Out ...

9. Answer the following questions about the countermeasures Nehemiah took to arm the people and the wall against the impending crisis.

a. Where did Nehemiah position some of the men as guards?

b. Why do you think he posted them there?

c. How did he position the rest of the people? Why do you think he grouped them like this?

d. With what weaponry were they equipped?

e. Put yourself in their shoes. In your own words, describe how you would feel about their physical condition, the depressing working conditions, and their ability to continue.

10. Just like the laborers in today's lesson, we can become discouraged and afraid when we take our eyes off God and focus on our own troubles. Look up the following verses to find out what God's Word says about discouragement and fear. Record God's commands and His promises for you when you obey Him.

Scripture	God's Command	God's Promise
Joshua 1:9		
1 Chronicles 28:20–21		
John 14:27		
Revelation 1:17		

11. Today, we learned that faith and fear cannot coexist in the same heart.

    a. What paralyzes you with fear and keeps you from effective service? (Be specific.)

    b. What will help you overcome your fears?

    c. What mind-set do you have to exhibit?

    d. Review today's lesson. What is the most important thing you learned about combating discouragement and fear?

Some fears are irrational, like turophobia, the fear of cheese, or omphalophobia, the fear of the navel (yes, the belly button). In 2005 Oprah Winfrey admitted in an interview that she had a fear of chewing gum. Her grandmother used to chew it and then stick it in the cabinet. Rows upon rows of gum caused a fear in Oprah to the point where even now, she doesn't allow chewing gum in the building where she works.[11]

9 Reluctant!

Discouragement kept the Israelites from the Promised Land. Warren Wiersbe said, "'We are not able!' is the rallying cry of all who take their eyes off the Lord and start looking at themselves and their problems."[10] God wants us to look up instead of looking around.

10 Rally!

Satan knows exactly which tool to use at the exact moment it's most impactful. He knows that if he can discourage us, we will defeat ourselves and he doesn't have to lift a finger. After weeks of hard labor, the Israelites were physically, mentally, and emotionally exhausted. Nehemiah knew they needed to rally.

While phobias are illogical, the physical and spiritual fears that Nehemiah and the Israelites faced were understandable. Satan uses any tactic he can to hinder us from the work God has for us. He is a very real Enemy: "The thief does not come except to steal, and to kill, and to destroy" (John 10:10). Satan has been trying to destroy the Jewish nation from the beginning of time, and he doesn't intend to stop.

But along with a very real Enemy, we have the living God who stands on our behalf. When you are fearful, know that God is on your side: "Be strong, do not fear! Behold, your God will come with vengeance, with the recompense of God; He will come and save you" (Isa. 35:4). Don't look around and don't look down; look up, because the God who has orchestrated the battle has a plan for victory.

Listen To ...

Self-pity is our worst enemy and if we yield to it, we can never do anything wise in this world.

—*Helen Keller*

Builder Be Aware

Caveat emptor, Latin for "Let the buyer beware," is a warning that notifies buyers that the goods they are purchasing are "as is" or subject to defects. The buyer understands and assumes the risk that the item could be defective or unsuitable. It is up to the buyer to examine, judge, and test a product for purchase.[12]

Nehemiah and the Israelites were in the thick of a raging war of wills. As they continued building the wall, they had no idea what opposition they would encounter, but Nehemiah remained faithful. Building the wall would not be a simple task, but he assumed the risk and pushed forward, having faith that God would be on his side.

Nehemiah knew that victory was certain if the people trusted the Lord. He continually boosted the morale of the Israelites by reminding them that God would fight for them. As they built with one hand holding a brick and the other holding a sword, they were aware of the dangers of their endeavor. Through trials, attacks, rumors, and threats, they persevered.

What risk have you assumed in a task God has asked you to take on? You can go in knowing that while it might be difficult, God has assumed the responsibility for the outcome.

Lift Up ...

Dear Lord, thank You that no matter what godly risk I am facing, You assume all responsibility for the conclusion. I know I can arm myself daily with Your promises and that I fight *from* victory, not *for* it. I praise You for Your faithfulness. In Jesus' name. Amen.

Look At ...

Yesterday, we saw how Nehemiah countered enemy aggression with faith and courage. The Israelites were weary and discouraged. Clearing away rubble was a daunting task in itself,

3 Stand Guard

God used the courage of the builders to thwart the plot of their enemies. The Israelites stood united, with God as their guard, and the enemy retreated. "For the eyes of the Lord run to and fro ... to show Himself strong on behalf of those whose heart is loyal to Him" (2 Chron. 16:9).

but then came the hard labor of rebuilding. Even though the people were losing heart, Nehemiah reminded them that God would fight for them. He knew that by rallying them as families, the Israelites would defend their own.

Today, we see how Nehemiah armed the Israelites with confidence and weapons as they persevered to battle and build. Some built with bricks and others defended with weapons, and this is how God's work continues today. Some of us build and some battle, but we work together as one body to accomplish God's work.

Read Nehemiah 4:15–20.

And it happened, when our enemies heard that it was known to us, and that God had brought their plot to nothing, that all of us returned to the wall, everyone to his work. So it was, from that time on, that half of my servants worked at construction, while the other half held the spears, the shields, the bows, and wore armor; and the leaders were behind all the house of Judah. Those who built on the wall, and those who carried burdens, loaded themselves so that with one hand they worked at construction, and with the other held a weapon. Every one of the builders had his sword girded at his side as he built. And the one who sounded the trumpet was beside me. Then I said to the nobles, the rulers, and the rest of the people, "The work is great and extensive, and we are separated far from one another on the wall. Wherever you hear the sound of the trumpet, rally to us there. Our God will fight for us." Nehemiah 4:15–20

1. What had been revealed to the Israelites' enemies?

2. How had their plans been obstructed?

3. How did this confirm Nehemiah's admonition in verse 14 and reward the Jews' obedience to his commands?

4. According to verse 15, what did the community do next?

5. How did Nehemiah set up a defense plan to protect everyone and keep the work from being interrupted?

6. a. How were the soldiers armed?

    b. Who supported Nehemiah's strategy?

7. How were the laborers prepared to build and battle at the same time?

8. a. What weapon did each builder gird at his side?

    b. According to Ephesians 6:17, what does the sword represent?

9. According to verse 18, who did Nehemiah keep beside him?

Live Out ...

10. Answer the questions below concerning Nehemiah's additional defense plan.

    a. Who did Nehemiah inform about his warning system?

    b. Why did he believe a warning system was needed?

    c. What action were the people to take when they heard the trumpet sound?

    d. Who did he say would ultimately come to their defense?

7 Stand Ready

Whatever work we do, we are to work at it with all our heart, as working for the Lord (see Col. 3:23). The Bible confirms that we will experience spiritual attack in our work, but it also assures us of God's defense. We are to stand battle-ready in the spiritual armor of God (see Eph. 6:13–17).

8 Stand Firm

Christian warriors must gird themselves with the Word of God in their hearts and minds. We must use it to protect ourselves and those God has placed around us. "How can a [woman] stay on the path of purity? By living according to your word.... I have hidden your word in my heart that I might not sin against you" (Ps. 119:9, 11 NIV).

10 Stand Confident

God promises us that in Him, we can be confident. "'No weapon formed against you shall prosper, and every tongue which rises against you in judgment you shall condemn. This is the heritage of the servants of the LORD, and their righteousness is from Me,' says the LORD" (Isa. 54:17).

12 Stand Delivered

Deliver means to save, rescue, or set free. "The LORD is my rock and my fortress and my deliverer; the God of my strength, in whom I will trust; my shield and the horn of my salvation, my stronghold and my refuge; my Savior, You save me from violence" (2 Sam. 22:2–3).

e. How can you apply this same theory of defense to your life?

11. Today, we saw that though the people were armed for battle, they recognized it was God who fought for them. He alone could ensure their victory. Write in your journal about how God has delivered you from the hand of the enemy—from depression, fear, physical illness, or a bad habit, for example. How have you tasted victory?

12. Just as the builders were girded with their swords as they worked, we also must gird ourselves with the sword of the Spirit, the Word of God, in our daily lives.

a. Look up Scriptures that talk about deliverance. (Use keywords like *deliver, Deliverer, delivered.*)

b. Choose a few verses to write down and commit to memory.

———————————

When looking for a home, most people hope not to hear "Buyer beware." Unfortunately, it can become a reality, as it did for one Missouri woman who rented a home for a steal and later learned why. She loved the house she found in St. Louis and signed the lease without question. Then she watched a cold case documentary about serial killers and discovered her home had been the scene of torture and murder at the hands of serial killer Maury Travis. According to a real estate expert, murder, suicides, and violent crimes don't require disclosure. With the help of the St. Louis Housing Authority, the woman was able to break her lease and move.[13]

Nehemiah also found himself in the middle of an unexpected situation, one that left the Israelites threatened, vulnerable, and exposed to enemy forces. But Nehemiah knew where his defense lay. Even when we find ourselves in menacing situations, God has our best interest at heart. We must do our portion by being ready to defend, and He will do His by fighting for us.

Listen To ...

When a man has no strength, if he leans on God, he becomes powerful.

—D. L. Moody

DAY 5

Sacrifice of Service

Louis Zamperini was born in Olean, New York, in 1917. His Italian-immigrant parents moved their family to Torrence, California, when he was two. His older brother introduced him to track and field, which led him to the 1936 Olympics in Berlin, Germany. He finished eighth in the five-thousand-meter race, but with a final lap of fifty-six seconds, he impressed the dignitaries enough to earn him a meeting with Adolf Hitler.

In 1941 he enlisted in the United States Army Air Forces and was deployed to the Pacific as a bombardier on a B-24 Liberator bomber. While on a search for a lost aircraft and crew, his plane had mechanical difficulties and crashed in the ocean, killing eight of the eleven crew members.

Zamperini and the two other survivors drifted for forty-seven days, surviving on rainwater, fish, and birds they caught with their hands and ate raw. One of the two other survivors, Francis McNamara, died at sea. Upon arriving in the Marshall Islands, Zamperini and the other survivor were captured by the Japanese Navy and held as prisoners of war for more than two years.[14] Through bravery and a strong will to live, he survived.

Louis Zamperini was a valiant illustration of sacrifice and service, as was Nehemiah, who sacrificed to serve those he was in charge of. Nehemiah labored alongside the Israelites he had rallied to build the wall. He battled shoulder to shoulder with those he commanded and didn't take any luxury that the people he led couldn't take.[15] He was a true servant leader, like Jesus.

Lift Up ...

Dear Lord, thank You for Your example of sacrificial service. Help me to emulate Your model of a servant spirit with those You have put in my life. I want to be obedient to Your command, "Do as I have done to you." In Jesus' name. Amen.

Look At ...

In yesterday's lesson, we saw God's victory through the practical faith of Nehemiah and the builders. While they put their faith in God and His promise to fight on their behalf, they also took practical steps to protect each other. God used Nehemiah and the Israelites for His purpose. Jon Courson said, "The man with a brick in one hand, the Word of God in the other, and a mind to work is the man God uses."[16]

Today, we see what they sacrificed to serve God. The people worked from the moment the sun came up until the stars appeared in the night sky. They guarded while they constructed. As the final portion of the wall started coming together, no one gave up. They laid brick upon brick on the promises of God.

3 To Defend

Each builder worked to clear rubble and labored at heavy construction with the added burden of a weapon. The soldiers continuously stood guard dressed in full armor, holding shields, spears, and bows. The whole community sacrificed in hard labor under strenuous conditions for twelve to fourteen hours a day.

Read Nehemiah 4:21–23.

So we labored in the work, and half of the men held the spears from daybreak until the stars appeared. At the same time I also said to the people, "Let each man and his servant stay at night in Jerusalem, that they may be our guard by night and a working party by day." So neither I, my brethren, my servants, nor the men of the guard who followed me took off our clothes, except that everyone took them off for washing. Nehemiah 4:21–23

1. Despite being heavily armed, the community continued to pursue what goal?

2. How do you know Nehemiah rolled up his sleeves and worked?

3.   a. What job did half of the men perform?
     b. How long did they do this?

5 To Guard

Nehemiah asked the workers to continue working despite their exhaustion. Sometimes God requires that we go above and beyond our normal daily duties to serve Him. "Then He said to them all, 'If anyone desires to come after Me, let him deny himself, and take up his cross daily, and follow Me'" (Luke 9:23).

7 To Persevere

When Nehemiah asked the builders to work hard all day, stand vigilant guard all night, and stay in a constant state of battle preparedness, he was right beside them. Nehemiah was a godly leader who had faith to stand, eyes to see, ears to hear, and willing hands to work for the Lord.

8 To Serve

Jesus doesn't want lords who order people around; He wants servants who humble themselves. "Yet it shall not be so among you; but whoever desires to become great among you, let him be your servant. And whoever desires to be first among you, let him be your slave" (Matt. 20:26–27).

4. Instead of going home after a long, hard day of work, what additional sacrifice did Nehemiah ask the people to make?

5.   a. What duty would they pull at night?

b. What would they continue doing during the day?

6.   a. What other sacrifice did Nehemiah, his brethren, servants, and men of the guard make?

b. Why do you think they did this?

7. When was the only time they took off their clothes?

Live Out ...

8. Just as Nehemiah asked the people of Judah to make sacrifices for the rebuilding of the wall and the safety of the people, our Lord asks us to make sacrifices in our lives to serve Him and the kingdom of God.

In your journal, write about some ways Jesus has asked you to sacrifice and to take up your cross and follow Him.

9. God desires spiritual sacrifices. Fill in the following table to discover what spiritual sacrifices you can offer to God.

Scripture	Spiritual Sacrifice
Psalm 51:17	
Psalm 51:19	
Psalm 107:22	
Psalm 141:2	

10. Choose one of the spiritual sacrifices listed above, and then write in your journal about how you will offer that particular sacrifice.

———————————

On the fateful day that Louis Zamperini washed ashore into the hands of enemy captors, he remembered thinking to himself, *Six weeks ago, I was a world-class athlete.* Then, for the first time in his life, he cried. After being released at the end of the war in 1945, he struggled with post-traumatic stress, rage, depression, and alcoholism.[17]

9 To Sacrifice

God calls each of us to sacrifice. For all He has done for us, it is the least we can give in return. "For whoever desires to save his life will lose it, but whoever loses his life for My sake will save it" (Luke 9:24).

In 1949 at the urging of his wife, Cynthia, Louis attended a Billy Graham crusade and gave his life to Jesus. Graham later helped him begin a career as a Christian speaker. He spoke often about forgiveness and even wrote a letter to one of his Japanese guards, nicknamed "The Bird," and forgave him. He went on to visit many of the guards who had imprisoned him, extending forgiveness and grace. He died at the age of 97 in July of 2014, leaving a beautiful legacy of forgiveness and grace.[18]

Knowing the God who died on the cross for our sins can make all the difference in the world. It allowed Zamperini to be freed from the pain of imprisonment, and it brought the Israelites to finish the task before them. Neither situation was easy, but because of the living God, both were successful. James Montgomery Boice said, "What a pattern for us when we are faced with opposition: prayer and persistence, faith and good works."[19]

Listen To ...

No character is ultimately tested until it has suffered.
—*Harry Emerson Fosdick*

Greed and Generosity in the Gates

Nehemiah 5

Aida Skripnikova was nineteen years old and stunningly beautiful. She stood on the street corner handing out small cards containing her original poetry. Each poem declared the love and joy she possessed from knowing Jesus as her Lord and Savior. Many passersby, compelled by her beauty and the deep love expressed in her smile, accepted the cards. For this activity, she was arrested and sentenced to one year in a Russian jail.

Aida was as bold in her faith as she was beautiful. When she was released from prison, she went right back to sharing the love of Jesus Christ. Although repeatedly arrested, she never wavered in her faith or dedication. By the age of thirty, after four prison terms, Aida was a changed woman. Her physical beauty was depleted, and she looked older than her years. Those who saw her face would never have recognized her were it not for one thing: her radiant smile that still reflected the love and beauty of the Jesus she longed to share.[1]

Aida worked hard to share Jesus, yet the spiritually deceived Russian authorities worked hard against her. We see a similar scenario in our lesson this week. Nehemiah tirelessly worked to do right by his people while the Jewish leaders and merchants simultaneously took advantage of them. Years of moral decline manifested in the physical deterioration in Jerusalem. Nehemiah could rebuild the walls, but the attitudes and selfishness within the walls required a more subtle kind of repair.

Greedy Merchants

Lift Up ...

Dear Lord, stay close to me. As I study Your Word, remind me that there are relevant lessons and guidance that apply to me all these generations later. Help me see the interior rooms of my heart and mind as I study this week. In Jesus' name. Amen.

Look At ...

Last week, we saw the Israelites' enemies outside the gates, plotting against them. In response, Nehemiah and the laborers set a guard around the walls and continued their work. We found that regardless of the weaponry—be it fear, ridicule, disappointment, or physical attack—the counterattack begins with turning to the Lord. The enemy looms large in our minds until we set our eyes on God.

This week, we see that the Jews faced economic and social problems inside the gates and walls of Jerusalem. We witness a sharp sense of insult and betrayal when brother turns against brother. In this case, wealthy Jews were exploiting poor Jews. Neither a new wall nor a polished gate could conceal the corruption that resided within.

Read Nehemiah 5:1–3.

And there was a great outcry of the people and their wives against their Jewish brethren. For there were those who said, "We, our sons, and our daughters are many; therefore let us get grain, that we may eat and live." There were also some who said, "We have mortgaged our lands and vineyards and houses, that we might buy grain because of the famine." Nehemiah 5:1–3

2 Close Ties

The Hebrew word *ach* refers to a brother or near relation. It also implies a friend or fellow countryman. The term expresses relationship, whether by blood or by choice.[2] The Israelites who worked on the wall were mistreated by their fellow Jews, their kin, and their families.

4 Needy Families

The family breadwinners left their occupations for two months to rebuild Jerusalem. As a result of their sacrificial efforts, they struggled to feed their families but believed that God would honor their efforts. "I beseech you therefore, brethren, by the mercies of God, that you present your bodies a living sacrifice, holy, acceptable to God, which is your reasonable service" (Rom. 12:1).

5 Greedy Merchants

The wealthy merchants in Israel took advantage of their poorer brethren by forcing them to borrow money for grain and then requiring them to mortgage their property in order to secure the loans. These leaders sacrificed the workers' well-being to achieve their own prosperity.

1. What type of emotional appeal did the people employ?

2.   a. Who cried out for help?

b. Who did they cry out against?

3. What physical need did the Israelites experience?

4. What did they ask of Nehemiah?

5. What did some of the people do in order to obtain grain?

6. Exodus 22:25–27 spells out specific guidelines for financial dealings between God's people. Read the passage, and record the instruction given there.

7. Why was there a shortage of grain in the land?

Live Out ...

8. Famine is a recurring hardship for God's people in Scripture. Several reasons and purposes for famine are mentioned. Read the following verses, and match the famine to its cause or purpose.

2 Chronicles 20:9	Misplaced priorities
Haggai 1:9–11	Punishment
Luke 21:10–11	Realization that God is near
Ezekiel 5:16	Future signs
2 Samuel 21:1	Judgment

9. Just as the Israelites experienced a famine in their land, believers today can experience spiritual famine. Read and meditate on the

Scriptures below, then note the various aspects of spiritual famine they address.

Scripture	Spiritual Famine
Amos 8:11–12	
Psalm 33:18–20	
Romans 8:35–38	

8 A Call for Famine

As we see in Scripture, God often used a famine to achieve His will and complete His plan. God does nothing without cause (see Ezek. 14:23). He used famine for His work and His glory. "Moreover He called for a famine in the land; He destroyed all the provision of bread" (Ps. 105:16).

10. The people initially did the wrong thing in response to the famine—they turned to greedy people instead of seeking spiritual direction. If you are experiencing a spiritual famine, go to your spiritual leader—God—for famine relief. Reword the following psalm into a personal prayer, asking God to rescue you in times of spiritual famine.

> The blameless spend their days under the LORD's care, and their inheritance will endure forever. In times of disaster they will not wither; in days of famine they will enjoy plenty. (Ps. 37:18–19 NIV)

_____

10 Reliance on God

God's Word clearly tells us to rely on God—and God alone—for anything and everything we need. In all circumstances, God is the perfect and final authority; He desires our complete and constant reliance on and trust in Him (see Ps. 62:7–8).

Scripture is filled with examples of righteous people like Nehemiah who remained obedient to God's directive while being bombarded by the sin of this world. Job was a blameless man, yet in one night, Satan, the "father of sin," destroyed Job's children, his servants, and his livelihood (see Job 1). For 120 years, Noah diligently labored, building the ark to the exact specifications given to him by God. Throughout those years, Noah was subjected to taunts and ridicule. Not one individual outside of his family respected his dedication or believed his message (see Gen. 6–7).

But the preeminent example of dedication and obedience is Jesus Christ, who came to save the lost. While surrounded by sin, He remained sinless and blameless. The authorities put Jesus to death for His words, His mission, and His love. Jesus did right but was confronted at every turn by wrong.

We must strive to respond like Jesus—whether we are met with obstacles and resistance like Nehemiah, attacked by evil like Job, ridiculed like Noah, or hated like Jesus. In the midst of wrong, strive to do right. When surrounded by sin, pray to be sinless. When prompted to quit, persist in good works. Follow your Leader.

Listen To ...

Few things are impossible to diligence and skill. Great works
are performed, not by strength, but perseverance.

—*Samuel Johnson*

Grasping Moneylenders

When is enough, enough? This question has plagued the human race since the beginning of time. One young man was once asked by an older gentleman, "When is a covetous man rich enough?" The boy thought and answered, "When he has a thousand pounds." The gentleman said, "No." "When he has two thousand pounds?" The gentleman shook his head and said, "No." Then the boy gave an answer he was convinced would settle the question: "A hundred thousand!" Once again, the gentleman said no. Frustrated, the boy confessed that he could not say, and the gentleman gravely said, "A man is rich enough when he has a little more than he currently possesses. And that is never!"[3]

The desire to acquire more and more is called greed. The *Macmillan Dictionary* defines *greed* as a strong desire to have more money, things, or power than you need. Greed is always about more and never about enough. This was the case with the wealthy moneylenders who exploited the men and women helping to build the wall.

Throughout the Word of God, greed is always sin. Jesus addressed it many times during His earthly ministry. He summed up its danger when He said, "Watch out! Be on your guard against all kinds of greed; life does not consist in an abundance of possessions" (Luke 12:15 NIV).

Lift Up ...

Lord, check my heart and my motives. Mesh my outward actions with the desire of my heart to become more like You. Caution me when greedy desires threaten to influence my decisions and actions. In Jesus' name. Amen.

1 Taxing Issues

Nehemiah knew taxes were necessary to maintain the government. Jesus did not dispute the need for taxes but rather said, "Render therefore to Caesar the things that are Caesar's, and to God the things that are God's" (Luke 20:25). The issue was the treatment of those who were unable to pay.

Look At ...

Yesterday, we saw that greedy merchants caused economic trouble for the Israelites and their families. Grasping moneylenders were willing to hold their own people captive, causing not only economic trouble but social heartbreak as well. Their struggles were real: hunger, loss of property, and conflict. Several factors converged to create a time of extreme unrest.

Today, we see the people still in great distress. They were mortgaged to the hilt, taxed beyond reason, and helpless to stop the defilement. Left without dignity and power, their appeal reached Nehemiah. His reaction was neither gentle nor mild, but it was entirely appropriate.

Read Nehemiah 5:4–6.

There were also those who said, "We have borrowed money for the king's tax on our lands and vineyards. Yet now our flesh is as the flesh of our brethren, our children as their children; and indeed we are forcing our sons and our daughters to be slaves, and some of our daughters have been brought into slavery. It is not in our power to redeem them, for other men have our lands and vineyards." And I became very angry when I heard their outcry and these words. Nehemiah 5:4–6

1. Another group came to Nehemiah for help. Why had they borrowed money?

2. Because they could not repay the moneylenders, what did the indebted Israelites do to meet their financial obligations?

3. Read Nehemiah 5:5 in two different Bible translations. In your own words, record the concerns and frustrations the people experienced.

4. Read Exodus 21:2. What provision did God make for those forced to sell family members into slavery?

5. According to Nehemiah 5:5, what were these people unable to do, and why?

6. How did Nehemiah respond to the people's concerns?

7. Nehemiah's anger should be evaluated with a biblical perspective. Read and record what the following verses say about anger. Explain why Nehemiah's response was or was not justified.

Scripture	Anger
Psalm 4:3–4	
Proverbs 16:32	
Ephesians 4:26–27	
James 1:19–20	

Live Out ...

8. The rulers and moneylenders chose personal gain over the care of their Jewish brethren. We all need to evaluate our motives and responses when it comes to helping others. Read Philippians 2:3–4, then complete the following chart.

4 Debts Canceled

The practice of selling family members into slavery was not uncommon in Old Testament times. However, the Mosaic law provided for the Jewish slaves to be set free and their debt canceled every seventh year or in the fiftieth year of Jubilee (see Lev. 25). The wealthy Israelites disregarded these laws and took advantage of their compatriots.

5 Unredeemed

Redemption means to deliver by payment of a price. In the Old Testament, redemption was applied to freedom from financial obligation or slavery by payment of a sum of money. In the New Testament, redemption refers to salvation from sin and death by the payment of Christ's sacrificial death.

Do This …   **Don't Do This …**

9 Freed from Sin

Not only does God want to free us from sin, but He also wants to adopt us into His family and make us heirs to His kingdom. Being held captive by this world can bring us down; redemption through Christ lifts us higher than we can imagine.

10 Guided in Anger

God knows that as sinful humans, we deal with unrighteous anger. He gave us clear and helpful instructions on how to deal with that anger: be slow to anger (see James 1:19), don't hold on to anger (see Eph. 4:31), overlook the offense (see Prov. 17:9), and think before you respond (see Prov. 15:1).

Search your heart and evaluate your response to those around you. Think of an individual or relationship that requires the application of these principles. Ask God to guide you in this process.

9. The Israelites did not have the power to redeem (buy back) their children from slavery. Likewise, we don't have the power to buy our freedom from the slavery of sin. Read Galatians 4:4–7, and answer the following questions:

    a. Who did God send to redeem humanity (see v. 4)?

    b. Where did God send the Spirit of His Son (see v. 6)?

    c. Fill in the blanks. Because of the Son's redemption, we are no longer _____, but God's _____ and _____ (see v. 7).

10. Nehemiah became righteously angry when he heard the Israelites were being oppressed by their own people. His actions showed he was angry at the sin, but he dealt with the sinners in love. Write a prayer in your journal, pouring out to God your righteous anger at an injustice or oppression. Now ask Him to help you hate the sin while loving the sinner.

"When is enough, enough? When is more just more?" The greed of the rich leaders and moneylenders had far-reaching and devastating consequences in the lives of their fellow Jews. Greed yielded not happiness and security but sorrow and hardship.

Once upon a time, a man found a magic cup and discovered that if he wept into the cup, his tears turned into pearls. The man had always been poor, but he had always been extremely happy. So he rarely shed tears.

In order to become rich, he had to find ways to make himself sad so his tears could become pearls. As the pearls multiplied, his greed and sorrow also multiplied. The story ends with the man sitting on a mountain of pearls, alone, and weeping helplessly into the cup.[4]

As we learned today, our greed or the greed of others can also have far-reaching effects. Either way, the lesson is the same: continually striving for more of anything can become an addiction that eventually brings pain to others and ourselves.

Charles Haddon Spurgeon said it well: "You say, 'If I had a little more I should be very well satisfied.' You make a mistake: if you are not content with what you have, you would not be satisfied if it were doubled."[5]

Listen To ...

You have succeeded in life when all you really want is only what you really need.
—Vernon Howard

Great Assembly

One day, Hugh Latimer was preaching in the presence of King Henry VIII and said to himself, "Latimer! Remember that the king is here. Be careful what you say." Then he reminded himself, "Latimer! Remember that the King of Kings is here. Be careful what you do *not* say." Latimer was eventually burned at the stake because of his faithful obedience to the King of Kings, but he died fearing God more than he feared man.[6]

The fear of the Lord is foundational in Christian life. Believers embrace a holy, healthy fear of the Lord above and beyond fear of anyone or anything else. When we fear the Lord, we seek Him and are obedient, regardless of what it costs us or what others think.

In today's lesson, we find that Nehemiah acted in the fear of God as he boldly and obediently confronted people's sin. Fear of man could have kept him silent, but Nehemiah publicly rebuked the wealthy noblemen out of love and respect for the Law of God. He did what was right, not what was comfortable or politically correct.

As we study today, search your heart. Do you possess a healthy fear of God? If you fear man more than God, three steps can help you put yourself in a right perspective: (1) confess your fear of man and repent, (2) question your fear of man and determine what you are truly afraid of, and (3) confront your fear of man with courage. Just as Nehemiah knew that trusting God was the right choice, so can we, no matter what enemy awaits.[7]

Lift Up ...

Lord, as I go about this day, let me strive for obedience to Your leading and instruction. Help me desire Your will, approval, and honor above any other. In Jesus' name. Amen.

Look At ...

Yesterday, we considered the situation of oppressed and abused people. In their desperation to stay alive and keep their families together, the Israelites risked their precious land, were in trouble with taxes, and were betrayed by wealthy brethren. They were a broken people.

Today, we find an angry Nehemiah. Although angry, he was fully in control of himself and the message he had to deliver. Because the sin was public and national, Nehemiah called everyone together to address it at one time. He was uncompromising in his message while being an exemplary leader. He confronted the sin of his people in order to restore them as a people and a nation under God.

Read Nehemiah 5:7–11.

2 Unfair Interest

Usury is unreasonable interest charged on borrowed money, and the Old Testament forbade the Jews to practice it (Lev. 25:35–37). The needs of the people were not to be used as an opportunity to make a profit. However, foreign traders and merchants could be assessed interest (see Deut. 23:20).

After serious thought, I rebuked the nobles and rulers, and said to them, "Each of you is exacting usury from his brother." So I called a great assembly against them. And I said to them, "According to our ability we have redeemed our Jewish brethren who were sold to the nations. Now indeed, will you even sell your brethren? Or should they be sold to us?" Then they were silenced and found nothing to say. Then I said, "What you are doing is not good. Should you not walk in the fear of our God because of the reproach of the nations, our enemies? I also, with my brethren and my servants, am lending them money and grain. Please, let us stop this usury! Restore now to them, even this day, their lands, their vineyards, their olive groves, and their houses, also a hundredth of the money and the grain, the new wine and the oil, that you have charged them." Nehemiah 5:7–11

1. What phrase lets you know Nehemiah didn't immediately react in his anger?

6 Obvious Oppression

Nehemiah pointed out that the people were not walking in the fear of the Lord; they were disobeying His command to provide for the poor and needy. "He who oppresses the poor reproaches his Maker, but he who honors Him has mercy on the needy" (Prov. 14:31).

7 Appropriate Restoration

Nehemiah instructed the Israelites to follow the Jubilee year pattern of forgiving debts by releasing the property they had taken as security against loans and returning the interest they had charged. "A hundredth of the money" would be about 12 percent annual interest.[8]

2. What did he accuse the aristocracy of doing?

3. What situation compelled Nehemiah to publicly bring up the matter of usury?

4. Nehemiah began to reason with the people by pointing out an obvious inconsistency in their past and present actions toward those who were enslaved. Explain the difference between how the Jews had dealt with their enslaved compatriots in the past and what they were doing in the present.

5. How did the people respond to Nehemiah's reasoning?

6. Next, Nehemiah appealed to their sense of morality by reminding them that what they were doing was not _____. Rather than continuing in the behavior that would bring reproach in the eyes of their enemies, Nehemiah urged them to walk in _____ _____ _____ _____.

7.   a. What did Nehemiah urge the people to restore?
     b. What amount of interest did he urge them to repay?

Live Out ...

8. Nehemiah offered a simple template of how to deal with anger: *think before you act.* Compare Nehemiah 5:7 in several Bible translations, and record the words used to explain Nehemiah's thought process.

NKJV—"After serious thought ..."

_____ — _____

_____ — _____

_____ — _____

Write a prayer in your journal asking God to help you apply these methods when you are angry.

9. Nehemiah pointed out that the way the wealthy Israelites treated their struggling compatriots was tarnishing God's character in the eyes of their adversaries. Their enemies would be skeptical to embrace a religion where the people treated each other harshly.

> a. Ask God to search your heart and reveal any area where you are misrepresenting God or His Word in your treatment of others. Are there people you treat as though they are less worthy than yourself?
>
> b. Read Psalm 5:8, and write a prayer in your journal asking God to teach you to be a worthy ambassador of Christ to unbelievers.

10. Nehemiah encouraged the people to walk in the fear of God. Read Psalm 112:1–9, and record the blessings awarded to those who fear the Lord.

Our reverent fear of God should bring us to our knees in submission and honor to Him. We should be completely awestruck in the presence of our perfect, powerful, and Holy God. He calls us to Himself (see Matt. 11:28–29), He calls us His friends (see John 15:14–15), and He calls us little children (see 1 John 3:2). But we must never forget that He is the almighty, sovereign, and creator God.

One author gave a beautiful example of this when she said, "My father never lost his temper with us, never beat us, but we had for him that feeling often described as fear, which is something quite different and far deeper than alarm.... One does not fear God because He is

8 Put It Away
God's Word offers directions on how and how not to deal with anger. Instruction in anger management is found in Ephesians 4:31–32: "Let all bitterness, wrath, anger, clamor, and evil speaking be put away from you, with all malice. And be kind to one another, tenderhearted, forgiving one another, even as God in Christ forgave you."

10 Bring It Out
"'The fear of our God' is not the servile dread of a slave toward a master but the loving respect of a child toward a parent. To fear the Lord means to seek to glorify God in everything we do. It means listening to His Word, honoring it, and obeying it."[9]

terrible, but because He is literally the soul of goodness and truth. To do Him wrong is to do wrong to some mysterious part of oneself."[10]

What does the Lord your God require of you but to fear Him, walk in His ways, and to love and serve Him with all your heart and soul?

Listen To ...

It is only the fear of God that can deliver us from the fear of man.

—*John Witherspoon*

Grave Promise

It was late and the man's young sons had been in bed for at least an hour when he and his wife returned home from their Bible study group. A good father, he crept into the boys' bedroom to kiss them goodnight. To his surprise, the younger boy, Peter, was awake and asked if he could have some ice cream. Dad said, "No, it is way too late."

"But Dad, you promised!" He was right. Peter had asked for ice cream earlier in the day, but there had been none in the freezer. His father had said, "I'll get some for you later, I promise." Peter had not forgotten. So, at ten o'clock that night, Dad hopped in the car and drove to the convenience store for ice cream. He and Peter enjoyed a late-night snack of chocolate-vanilla swirl. This father had a promise to keep.[11]

God, our heavenly Father, is a promise keeper, and He expects nothing less of us. A man's word, given and kept, is more valuable than all of the riches of this world. "Better is the poor who walks in his integrity than one who is perverse in his lips, and is a fool" (Prov. 19:1).

Lift Up ...

Dear Lord, thank You that Your instructions are perfect and require me to be honorable. I want to be a promise keeper; therefore, help me speak nothing that is untrue or unattainable. In Jesus' name. Amen.

Look At ...

Yesterday, we read about a different side of Nehemiah's character and personality. He was capable of righteous anger, but he also dealt with his anger in a productive, rather than damaging, way. He focused on his mission, and he was in control of himself. He determined the most

2 A Solemn Promise

An *oath* is a solemn statement by which a person
promises or guarantees
that a vow will be kept
or that a statement is, in
fact, true. Oaths were
often accompanied and
evidenced by the raising
of hands toward heaven
or by placing the hand
under the thigh (see Gen.
24:2–3; Dan. 12:7).

effective way of dealing with the many individuals who needed to be confronted and compelled to proceed as God's people.

Nehemiah brought the people together to expose their social and moral sins. In short, the greed of usury had inflicted suffering on some of the people. He made it clear that these actions evoked the judgment of the Lord. The people responded to the conviction and were willing to right the wrongs.

Read Nehemiah 5:12–13.

So they said, "We will restore it, and will require nothing from them; we will do as you say." Then I called the priests, and required an oath from them that they would do according to this promise. Then I shook out the fold of my garment and said, "So may God shake out each man from his house, and from his property, who does not perform this promise. Even thus may he be shaken out and emptied." And all the assembly said, "Amen!" and praised the LORD. Then the people did according to this promise. Nehemiah 5:12–13

1. What three things did the people promise as a result of Nehemiah's assembly?

　　1.

　　2.

　　3.

2. What did Nehemiah require from the people?

3. Who did Nehemiah ask to serve as witnesses to the solemn oath?

4. What symbolic action did Nehemiah take to show the Israelites a visual picture of what God would do to those who failed to keep their oath?

5. How did the people audibly agree to the oath?

6. How did the people spiritually respond to the Lord?

7. How did they follow up on their oath?

Live Out ...

8. The people of the assembly took an oath to confirm that they would keep their promise. The priests witnessed their oath, which implies that God was a witness to it. Making a promise to God is a serious matter. Read Ecclesiastes 5:4–5, then complete the following:

> a. In your own words, explain the seriousness of a vow made before God.
> b. Are there vows (promises, oaths) you have made in the presence of God that are left unfulfilled? Get right with God.
> c. Write a prayer in your journal asking God to help you keep your promises.

9. The importance we place on keeping our word is a reflection of our integrity. Look up the following Scriptures, and note what each says about the role of integrity in our lives. Ask God to show you where you are not walking in integrity.

4 A Shaken Robe

Nehemiah shook a garment to show that God would "shake out" or punish anyone who promised to do the right thing but went back on his word. Paul used a similar demonstration in Acts 18:6, and Jesus spoke of shaking the dust from your feet in Matthew 10:14.[12]

5 A Unified "Amen"

Amen is the translation of the Hebrew word signifying something as certain, sure, valid, truthful, and faithful. It is translated "so it." The people agreed to God's terms for restoration. In Revelation 3:14, Jesus is called the Amen, because He is the reliable and true witness of God.

8 A Thoughtful Word

New Testament believers are held to a high standard. We must say what we mean and mean what we say. "But above all, my brethren, do not swear, either by heaven or by earth or with any other oath. But let your 'Yes' be 'Yes,' and your 'No,' 'No,' lest you fall into judgment" (James 5:12).

9 A Bowed Heart

One day, God will require an oath of every person. Those who walk in righteousness and integrity desire to declare their allegiance to His name. "Every knee will bend to me, and every tongue will declare allegiance to me" (Isa. 45:23 NLT).

Scripture

Psalm 7:8

Psalm 25:20–21

Proverbs 11:3

Proverbs 12:22

Role of Integrity

10. God requires our treatment of one another to meet His high standards. His instructions on how to meet those standards are simple and straightforward. Read the following verse, and rewrite it, asking the Lord to solidify these principles in your heart.

"He has shown you, O man, what is good; and what does the LORD require of you but to do justly, to love mercy, and to walk humbly with your God?" (Mic. 6:8).

———————————

Captain Robert Campbell had been held captive for two years in a German World War I prison camp when he received news that his mother was close to death. He wrote to Kaiser Wilhelm II, begging to be allowed to see his mother one last time before she died. Incredibly, the German leader granted the young officer leave on the sole condition that he give his word, as an officer, to return. After visiting his cancer-stricken mother in 1916, Campbell kept his promise and returned to the German prison camp. He remained there until the end of the war in 1918.[13]

Captain Campbell made a promise on his honor, and he kept it. It took sacrifice, courage, and integrity, because he knew he would have to return to the consequences and constraints of being a prisoner.

But we can find no better example of integrity than Jesus. He gave His promise to save us, and He followed through by sacrificing

His life. "For all the promises of God in Him are Yes, and in Him Amen, to the glory of God through us" (2 Cor. 1:20).

Listen To ...

Promises may get friends, but it is performance that must nurse and keep them.

—*Owen Feltham*

Generous Governor

An old fable tells of an elderly man who was traveling with a boy and a donkey. As they walked through a village, the man was leading the donkey and the boy was walking behind. The townspeople said the old man was a fool for not riding, so to please them, he climbed up on the animal's back. When they came to the next village, the people said the old man was cruel to let the child walk while he enjoyed the ride. So, to please them, he got off and set the boy on the animal's back and continued on his way. In the third village, people accused the child of being lazy for making the old man walk, and they suggested that the two should both ride. So the man climbed on, and they set off again. In the fourth village, the townspeople were indignant at the cruelty to the donkey because he was made to carry two people. The frustrated man was last seen carrying the donkey down the road.[14]

In our world, many voices clamor to influence our decisions: the voice of tradition, the voice of culture, the voice of pride, and the voice of doubt. We need to listen and follow only one voice—the voice of our Lord. Nehemiah chose to listen to God's voice. He did things God's way and, as a result, was respected and admired. Whose voice do you follow?

Lift Up ...

Dear Lord, help me walk in the love and fear of You. You alone are worthy of honor, praise, and worship. I want to do what is right and well pleasing to You. In Jesus' name. Amen.

Look At ...

Yesterday, we saw that Nehemiah acted as the spiritual conscience for the nation. The Jews had fallen away, as was their tendency, and in the process, betrayed their own people and their God.

When confronted as a group, there was no escaping the truth—no justification could release them from responsibility. Convicted, they agreed to make humble restoration.

Nehemiah brought social justice to the people of Israel. In today's lesson, we find that he was able to bring justice because he was a generous man who feared the Lord. His generosity was an extension of his personal relationship with his generous God. Part of his selfless service manifested by not making his needs a burden to anyone else while simultaneously helping others in need.

Read Nehemiah 5:14–19.

Moreover, from the time that I was appointed to be their governor in the land of Judah, from the twentieth year until the thirty-second year of King Artaxerxes, twelve years, neither I nor my brothers ate the governor's provisions. But the former governors who were before me laid burdens on the people, and took from them bread and wine, besides forty shekels of silver. Yes, even their servants bore rule over the people, but I did not do so, because of the fear of God. Indeed, I also continued the work on this wall, and we did not buy any land. All my servants were gathered there for the work. And at my table were one hundred and fifty Jews and rulers, besides those who came to us from the nations around us. Now that which was prepared daily was one ox and six choice sheep. Also fowl were prepared for me, and once every ten days an abundance of all kinds of wine. Yet in spite of this I did not demand the governor's provisions, because the bondage was heavy on this people. Remember me, my God, for good, according to all that I have done for this people. Nehemiah 5:14–19

1. Contrast Nehemiah's actions as governor with the actions of the former governors.

Nehemiah	**Former Governors**

2. What reason did Nehemiah give for acting righteously toward the people?

2 God-Pleasing

Nehemiah's goal in life was not to make a personal profit but to please God. He did not ask, "Will this help me?" Instead, he asked, "Will this make God happy?" When faced with financial decisions, make sure you ask the right questions.

3 God's Domain

Nehemiah could have followed the example of the worldly leaders and loaned the people money, requiring their land as collateral. He was in a position to use his knowledge as an insider to buy land at a steal. However, Nehemiah's goal was not to build his own domain but to build God's domain.

6 God's Solution

Nehemiah came to Jerusalem to help the people, not exploit them. As governor, he could have imposed a tax to pay for his expenses, but instead he chose to be generous. Nehemiah refused to become part of the people's problem when it was in his power to be part of the solution.

3. What did Nehemiah say to reveal that he and his servants did not seek personal profit through real estate transactions?

4. Nehemiah used his position to extend a helping hand to those in need.

a. How many people did Nehemiah feed on a daily basis?

b. Looking at what he provided, estimate about how much his grocery bill would be today.

5. What phrase reveals that Nehemiah didn't charge these provisions to his "expense account"?

6. Why did Nehemiah pay for these provisions from his own pocket?

7. What one thing did Nehemiah ask of God in return for his goodness to the people?

Live Out ...

8. We have learned that Nehemiah was concerned not with personal profit but with pleasing God. Fill in the chart below to discover some ways *you* can please God.

Scripture	Pleases God
Psalm 69:30–31	
Proverbs 16:7	
Romans 8:8–9	
Hebrews 11:6	

9. Based on what you wrote in the table above, do you live a life that is pleasing to God? Write in your journal about an area of your life that could be more pleasing to God. What needs to change?

10. Nehemiah was a wise and godly man; he exhibited many strong leadership qualities. Thinking about today's text, consider the traits listed below and check those you believe could be improved in your own life.

_____ Consider others' needs above your own

_____ Seek the Lord in your decision making

_____ Work alongside other people

_____ Treat everyone equally

_____ Serve other people, not yourself

_____ Work to please the Lord

Cultivating these practices will manifest in stronger, godlier leadership in your life.

———————————

Four young college men rented a house together. One Saturday morning, a bedraggled-looking old man came to their door. He was unkempt, his eyes were foggy, and his clothes were ragged. His shoes were mismatched—in fact, both shoes were for the left foot. He carried a wicker basket full of unappealing vegetables that he wanted to sell. The boys wanted to help him out, so they bought the vegetables.

From that week on, every Saturday, the man came to their door selling his produce. The roommates got to know him and learned that he lived in a shack at the end of the road. His eyes were foggy due to cataracts, he played the harmonica, and he loved God. They began to look forward to his visits and devised a plan to help him. The next

9 The Work of Our Hands

Pleasing God is never to be a burden, but a privilege and a gift. We are able to please God only because He enables us to do so because our good works come from Him. "And let the beauty of the LORD our God be upon us, and establish the work of our hands for us; yes, establish the work of our hands" (Ps. 90:17).

10 Servant Leadership

Nehemiah was a servant leader. "Jesus knew that the idea of leader as 'loving servant' would not appeal to most people. Securing our own creature comforts is the more common mission. But becoming a servant is His requirement for those who want to lead in His Kingdom"[15] (see Mark 10:43–44).

Saturday when he came by, the old man proclaimed, "God is good!" He explained that outside his door that morning he found boxes full of clothes, shoes, and food. The boys traded coy smiles as the man continued, "God is good because I know a very needy family, and I was able to give all the gifts to them."[16]

When we care more for others than ourselves, we become truly generous. Generosity is all about listening to the voice of the Lord as He personally prompts us to share and care for others more than ourselves (see Phil. 2:3–4).

Listen To ...

> *That's what I consider true generosity. You give your all and*
> *yet you always feel as if it costs you nothing.*
>
> —*Simone de Beauvoir*

Overcoming Opposition with Integrity

Nehemiah 6

A well-known tale first published in the *New York Tribune* in 1906 is attributed to a sermon by a Brooklyn preacher whose church had finally paid off their mortgage. This was how he illustrated the long process.

A little railroad engine, used for light jobs, was waiting for its next call when a long train of freight cars asked for help getting over a steep hill. "I can't; that is too much of a pull for me," said other, stronger engines in the rail yard, but the smallest locomotive agreed to assist. As it pulled, the little engine kept bravely puffing faster and faster, saying, "I think I can, I think I can." Struggling higher, it went slower and slower but kept going by repeating, "I—think—I—can, I—think—I—can." It reached the top and coasted down the other side, crying, "I thought I could, I thought I could."[1] Perseverance and determination, undergirded by God's grace, helped this Brooklyn congregation to pay off their mortgage.

They also enabled Nehemiah to continue his work. Along the way, he encountered opposition, plotting, bullying, and lies, but he refused to be daunted. He held fast to an I-think-I-can mentality in the certainty that he would eventually triumph in his mission. When our service for God feels like an uphill climb, we benefit by remembering Nehemiah's steady example.

Day 1: Nehemiah 6:1–4 **Foiling Opposition with Patience**

Day 2: Nehemiah 6:5–9 **Foiling Opposition with Perseverance**

Day 3: Nehemiah 6:10–14 **Foiling Opposition with Insight**

Day 4: Nehemiah 6:15–16 **Completing the Job**

Day 5: Nehemiah 6:17–19 **A Man of Questionable Influence**

Foiling Opposition with Patience

Lift Up ...

Dear Lord, help me understand the stories from the Bible so I can learn the wise lessons they contain. When the story of my life is told one day, I want it to be said that I was a woman who lived for You, followed Your will, obeyed You in the face of opposition, and prevailed despite the Enemy's best efforts. In Jesus' name. Amen.

Look At ...

Last week, we learned more about three of the powerful forces of opposition that threatened to defeat God's plan for Nehemiah to rebuild the wall surrounding Jerusalem. The pagans were behind the first two: ridicule of the Jews and threats of violence. Wealthy Israelites were the third, as their greed led them to oppress the poor. Nehemiah handled these challenges with grace and ongoing prayer.

Today, we see the Israelites' enemies at work in manipulations to sidetrack Nehemiah from his mission. They came at him with lies, distractions, ploys, and repeated efforts to lure him away from his God-given work. Nehemiah stayed on task. His discernment was heightened by his constant dependence on God. Nehemiah was not contentious, but neither was he gullible to methods employed against him.

Read Nehemiah 6:1–4.

Now it happened when Sanballat, Tobiah, Geshem the Arab, and the rest of our enemies heard that I had rebuilt the wall, and that there were no breaks left in it (though at that time I had not hung the doors in the gates), that Sanballat and Geshem sent to me, saying, "Come, let us meet

1 Enemies of the Wall

Geshem, the Arabian ruler of Kedar; Sanballat, the governor of Samaria; and Tobiah, an Ammonite who had political authority in the territory, continued to join together to oppose the rebuilding of the wall.[2] A protected Jerusalem would diminish their power and control.

3 The Noble Truth

Nehemiah showed his truthfulness when he stated that although enemies had heard there were no breaks left in the wall, the doors still needed to be hung in the gates. As Alexander Pope stated, "An honest man's the noblest work of God."[3]

4 Grief on the Horizon

The plain of Ono is part of a wadi (a dry creek bed that fills during the rainy season) located about twenty miles northwest of Jerusalem. It was home to the fortified town of Ono, which means grief.[4] Nehemiah realized grief awaited him there.

together among the villages in the plain of Ono." But they thought to do me harm. So I sent messengers to them, saying, "I am doing a great work, so that I cannot come down. Why should the work cease while I leave it and go down to you?" But they sent me this message four times, and I answered them in the same manner. Nehemiah 6:1–4

1. Which three of Nehemiah's enemies are specifically named?

2. At this point, what had Nehemiah accomplished on the wall?

3. What did Nehemiah admit had not yet been accomplished?

4. Who messaged Nehemiah, and what was the request?

5. Nehemiah could see the truth in Sanballat and Geshem. What were their true intentions?

6. In response, Nehemiah sent messengers of his own. What message did they carry?

7. Ongoing communication commenced between Nehemiah and his enemies. How many times were the same messages sent and returned?

Live Out ...

8. His enemies changed their tactics and tried to convince Nehemiah that they wanted to meet and work something out. Nehemiah discerned that their manipulations were an attempt to slow him down in his service to the Lord.

a. What is your primary area of service for the Lord?

b. How were you inspired to serve?

c. Have you ever felt manipulated by someone who wanted to end your service out of jealousy or insecurity? How did you respond?

9. When we are determined to complete an assignment God has given to us, we are likely to encounter resistance from the Devil. Think back and record a time when you started a specific project based on your understanding of God's plan for you.

a. My project was to:

b. Circle the methods below that Satan employed in an attempt to divert you from your purpose.

- Increased responsibilities at work or in the home
- Increased opportunities for pleasurable activities like sports, entertainment, travel, shopping, watching television, surfing the Internet
- Illness of family members, pets
- Needed repairs in your home or car
- Other: _____

c. At the time, did you recognize that you were being sidetracked? How did you respond?

8 Seeing Clearly

To *discern* is to recognize something that is separate or different from what it appears to be. Things are not always what they seem. Cyril Barber said Nehemiah's "ability to see all the issues clearly and stand firm under pressure safeguarded him from succumbing to the wiles of his adversaries."[5]

10 Unwavering Values

Integrity is defined as the quality of being of sound moral principle, faithfully supporting a standard of values. Being a person of integrity requires an unwavering uprightness, honesty, sincerity, blamelessness, and righteousness.

10. Nehemiah responded to his enemies with integrity. He was impeccable with his words, clearly and consistently stating that he could not benefit his cause by interrupting his work. When words are spoken in love and truth, threats can be diminished or even dismantled. Fill out the following table to learn about other people of the Bible who behaved with integrity.

Scripture	Other Biblical People of Integrity
Genesis 6:9	
Genesis 17:1	
Judges 4:4–5	
1 Samuel 25:32–35	
1 Kings 9:4	
Job 1:1	
Titus 2:7	

Winston Churchill is known for is famous words about perseverance when he addressed the Harrow School on October 29, 1941. He said, "Never give in, never give in, never, never, never, never—in nothing, great or small, large or petty—never give in except to convictions of honor and good sense. Never give in." Then he sat down.

Throughout his life, he met failure and defeat, yet Churchill did not give in to it. As a child, he failed sixth grade. In his political career, he was defeated in every election for public office until he became prime minister of England at the age of sixty-six.[6]

Nehemiah's life is also defined by perseverance. He never wavered to do what he thought was right and consistent with God's plan. He did not allow himself to get frazzled by circumstances as he maintained his resolve to continue with the work at hand. He did not give up. Nor should we.

Listen To ...

Never cut what you can untie.

—*Joseph Joubert*

Foiling Opposition with Perseverance

Most of us are familiar with the story of Cinderella, the sweet daughter of a wealthy widower who took a proud and haughty woman to be his second wife. Cinderella suffered unmercifully, bullied by her stepmother and two stepsisters. She dared not tell her father because he was under the control of his new wife. The stepfamily forced Cinderella to work all day doing chores and then sent her to a cold room where she slept near a fireplace to stay warm.

One day the prince invited all the girls in the kingdom to his ball, but Cinderella's stepmother lied, saying that Cinderella was a servant, and told her she could not go. Ultimately, Cinderella triumphed over the bullying stepfamily thanks to her fairy godmother, who transformed her into the most beautiful girl at the ball and helped her win the heart of the prince.

Just as Cinderella knew her stepfamily lied about her being merely a servant girl, Nehemiah knew his enemies were spreading lies about him. They came together to create a means to publically humiliate Nehemiah, using propaganda in the form of an open letter that would damage his relationship with the king. Cinderella turned to her fairy godmother, who transformed her; Nehemiah turned to his heavenly God-Father, who strengthened him so he could finish His work. Turning to our source of strength allows us to continue on in the face of opposition.

Lift Up ...

Dear Lord, I ask You to strengthen my resolve so that I can handle the threats of this life. I realize that You told us, "Vengeance is Mine, I will repay" (Rom. 12:19). Help me remember You are always aware and always available to hear my prayers. In Jesus' name. Amen.

1 Open Letter

This was playing dirty. Letters between leaders were treated respectfully, sealed and bagged, so only the recipient would be able to read them. Everyone who handled it during its journey would read an open letter. By the time Nehemiah received the letter, insinuations would have already begun.

Look At ...

Yesterday, we saw Nehemiah having to deal with his enemies' attempts to slow down the building of the wall. Nehemiah was not an easy mark. He was aware of anything that competed with achieving his God-ordained mission. His distracters were loud, persistent, and annoying, but this servant-soldier of God did not leave his post.

Today, we find Nehemiah in escalating circumstances. Unable to lure him away from his work on the wall, the enemies resorted to "leaking" their accusations by way of an unsealed letter. This seeming mistake was overt disrespect and a way of causing others to question Nehemiah's true motives through his work on the wall of Jerusalem. Their lies were an attempt to use fear and intimidation to quell the efforts to strengthen Jerusalem.

Read Nehemiah 6:5–9.

Then Sanballat sent his servant to me as before, the fifth time, with an open letter in his hand. In it was written: It is reported among the nations, and Geshem says, that you and the Jews plan to rebel; therefore, according to these rumors, you are rebuilding the wall, that you may be their king. And you have also appointed prophets to proclaim concerning you at Jerusalem, saying, "There is a king in Judah!" Now these matters will be reported to the king. So come, therefore, and let us consult together. Then I sent to him, saying, "No such things as you say are being done, but you invent them in your own heart." For they all were trying to make us afraid, saying, "Their hands will be weakened in the work, and it will not be done." Now therefore, O God, strengthen my hands. Nehemiah 6:5–9

1. Who used a servant to deliver a fifth letter, a shamefully open one, to Nehemiah?

2. Who reported that Nehemiah and the Jews planned to rebel against the king?

3. Based on circulating rumors, Sanballat jumped to what two conclusions?

4. a. What else was Nehemiah accused of doing?

b. How were the prophets expected to respond?

5. Who would hear these reports?

6. Sanballat once again asked to take counsel with Nehemiah. How did Nehemiah respond?

7. To whom did Nehemiah turn for support?

Live Out ...

8. Nehemiah's enemies attempted to destroy his reputation by circulating a letter that contained lies about his character. His response was to deny their accusations, saying that they were invented in the enemy's heart. Look up the verses below to learn what the Bible says about the heart.

Verse	What Comes from the Heart
Proverbs 27:19	
Jeremiah 17:9	
Matthew 15:18–19	
Luke 6:45	

4 Prophetic Call

An essential mark of a prophet is a call from God. The prophet's job is to call God's people to obedience, relaying His message by both deed and word.

6 Smoke and Mirrors

Nehemiah discounted all the accusations contained in this letter. He discerned that his enemies were inventing slanderous statements to stall or derail construction. The goal was to instill in the builders the notion that their leader was out to serve only himself, not God.

8 Slander

Slander is saying something false and damaging about someone. Clearly, this tactic was used in this attack on Nehemiah's character. Perhaps Nehemiah was drawn to pray Psalm 27:12: "Do not deliver me to the will of my adversaries; for false witnesses have risen against me."

9 Our Defender

Let God come to your defense. Hebrews 13:6 tells us, "The Lord is my helper; I will not fear. What can man do to me?" Warren Wiersbe said, "If we take care of our character, we can trust God to take care of our reputation."[7]

9. In the past year, was there a time when you felt you were under attack? Describe that time.

I felt under attack when:

I defended myself by:

What people say about you is a representation of them, not you. If you ignore their actions and opinions, you can free yourself from the suffering they are trying to impose.

10. For God to defend you and give you strength, you must be in a relationship with Him that was established by accepting His Son as your Lord and Savior. Maintaining our relationship with God requires both an ongoing study of His Word and a time commitment. List below any "busy work" you could give up in order to solidify your connection to God.

Example: I will stop staying up so late and not getting enough rest.

I will:

———————————

Born on April 4, 1928, and going home to be with the Lord on May 28, 2014, Maya Angelou, a Pulitzer Prize nominee and recipient of the Presidential Medal of Freedom, lived through many changes in the world. Her childhood was spent in Arkansas, where prejudice against blacks was a powerful force. When she was around eight years old, her mother's boyfriend raped her and was subsequently murdered, supposedly by her uncles. For the next five years, she refused to talk. Although she had been thoroughly bullied, over time Maya managed to recover and become a celebrated civil rights leader, teacher, and writer, creating poems and memoirs about her experiences of living all around the world. Her life was marked by grace and dignity.[8]

A section of her poem "Still I Rise" is reminiscent of Nehemiah's patient perseverance in response to the attacks of his adversaries.

> You may shoot me with your words,
> You may cut me with your eyes,
> You may kill me with your hatefulness,
> But still, like air, I'll rise.[9]

Listen To ...

I found that I knew not only that there was God but that I was a child of God, when I understood that, when I comprehended that, more than that, when I internalized that, ingested that, I became courageous.

—Maya Angelou

Foiling Opposition with Insight

The classic fairy tale *Little Red Riding Hood* comes in many variations, all of which teach that we must be cautious when we listen to strangers. Most of us know the story of the little girl who went through the woods to visit her ailing grandmother. When Little Red Riding Hood arrived, she did not find her grandmother at home. Instead, she encountered a wolf wearing her grandmother's clothes and lying in her grandmother's bed. Depending on which version of the story you read, the wolf either consumed both the girl and the grandmother or was killed by a passing woodsman, thereby freeing them both.[10]

Life is full of circumstances in which we encounter "wolves in sheep's clothing." The Bible warns us, "Beware of false prophets, who come to you in sheep's clothing, but inwardly they are ravenous wolves" (Matt. 7:15). Similarly, Matthew 10:16 tells us, "I send you out as sheep in the midst of wolves. Therefore be wise as serpents and harmless as doves." We must be alert and use our keen insight to discern whether we are dealing with a harmless, innocent sheep or a harmful, disguised wolf.

That is what Nehemiah did when dealing with his enemies.

Lift Up ...

Dear Lord, I trust that You have gifted me with the ability to discern the truth in any situation. Please sharpen my capability to sense when I am dealing with falsehood rather than truth. In Jesus' name. Amen.

Look At ...

Yesterday, we found that Nehemiah was under subtle, and not-so-subtle, attacks. His enemies were spreading rumors about him in an open letter that should have been private. But their attempts to distract him from his work failed. Nehemiah listened only to the voice of his Lord. When public opinion and scrutiny of his motives swirled around him, his fundamental integrity and resolve to follow God stood the test.

Today, we learn about a different kind of deceit: lies cloaked as a warning. The false prophet Shemaiah was aware that fear for one's life had the power to override calm discernment in many cases. So he used that tactic on Nehemiah. Fear can cause even good men to forget they are God's men and act in haste and foolishness.

1 Dark Prophet

Shemaiah was regarded as a prophet but had gone to the dark side, becoming a paid secret informer for Tobiah and Sanballat. He pretended to fear that assassins were coming for him and Nehemiah and suggested they both hide in the temple.

Read Nehemiah 6:10–14.

2 Temple of Doom

In ancient times, killers could ask for sanctuary in cities of refuge, but there was no safety available inside the Jewish temple. Only the Levites could enter the inner portions of the temple. "The outsider who comes near shall be put to death" (Num. 18:7).

Afterward I came to the house of Shemaiah the son of Delaiah, the son of Mehetabel, who was a secret informer; and he said, "Let us meet together in the house of God, within the temple, and let us close the doors of the temple, for they are coming to kill you; indeed, at night they will come to kill you." And I said, "Should such a man as I flee? And who is there such as I who would go into the temple to save his life? I will not go in!" Then I perceived that God had not sent him at all, but that he pronounced this prophecy against me because Tobiah and Sanballat had hired him. For this reason he was hired, that I should be afraid and act that way and sin, so that they might have cause for an evil report, that they might reproach me. My God, remember Tobiah and Sanballat, according to these their works, and the prophetess Noadiah and the rest of the prophets who would have made me afraid. Nehemiah 6:10–14

1. a. After praying, Nehemiah arrived at whose house?

    b. What was that person's secret?

2. What did Shemaiah suggest to Nehemiah?

4 Insight into Sin

Nehemiah's insight allowed him to understand that entering the temple was a sin and that Shemaiah was a false prophet whose message contradicted God's Word (see Deut. 18:20–22). Nehemiah knew God could protect him while continuing his work on the wall. He did not need to hide.

7 False Prophetess

Noadiah means God has met. As you remember, the essential mark of a prophet is a call from God. Noadiah was a false prophetess whose goal was to discourage and frighten Nehemiah." A true prophet would offer enlightenment or encouragement.

8 Finding Your Way

God is in control of everything, but we still must do our part, being wise and prudent and avoiding assumptions. Using biblical principles, we can courageously consider circumstances, asking questions that clarify the situation.

3. Nehemiah objected to meeting in the temple. What was his reason for refusing?

4. What two truths did Nehemiah perceive?

5. Shemaiah was hired for what three reasons?

1.

2.

3.

6. Nehemiah asked God to remember those who wished to make him afraid. What do you think he meant by that request?

7. What familiar names do you see? Whose name is new to you?

Live Out ...

8. Describe a time when you were confronted with a situation that seemed to be in the Lord's will but turned out poorly.

a. What happened that made you realize you were on the wrong path?

b. How did you change course?

When in doubt, stand strong in integrity and character, and prayerfully confirm that your actions are consistent with God's Word.

9. a. When do you feel fearless?

b. How do you avoid feeling fearful when someone is pushing you to be afraid?

c. Look up the following Scriptures, and find some help for dealing with fear.

Scripture	How the Lord Helps You Deal with Fear
Psalm 27:1	
Psalm 51:10	
Isaiah 41:10	
Luke 12:6–7	
Romans 8:31	
Ephesians 6:10–18	

10 Steeped in Prayer

Pray before undertaking a course of action, then pray again after acting to confirm you are in the right place. "Lead me in Your truth and teach me, for You are the God of my salvation; on You I wait all the day" (Ps. 25:5).

10. Nehemiah found himself in a crisis situation (see Neh. 6:14) and followed his pattern of response by shooting up an "arrow" prayer to the Lord. His lifelong commitment to prayer added strength and accuracy to his crisis prayers.

a. How can Nehemiah's example of a life lived in prayer help you when you are tempted to stop your work for the Lord?

b. What can you change so you are able to commit more of your time to prayer?

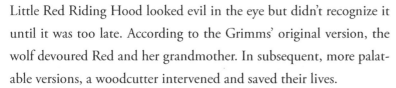

Little Red Riding Hood looked evil in the eye but didn't recognize it until it was too late. According to the Grimms' original version, the wolf devoured Red and her grandmother. In subsequent, more palatable versions, a woodcutter intervened and saved their lives.

Are you deluded into expecting to be saved at the last minute of your life? In reality, your salvation comes only from receiving Jesus Christ as your Lord and Savior. If you do not yet know Him, won't you pray right now to be saved? Tell Him you know you are a sinner and ask for His forgiveness. Tell Him you believe He died for your sins and rose from the dead and that you trust Him and will follow Him as your Lord and Savior. Ask Him to guide your life and help you to do His will.

Did you pray that prayer either in the past or right now? Amen! You are a child of God!

Listen To ...

Do the thing you fear and the death of fear is certain.

—*Ralph Waldo Emerson*

Completing the Job

The writer Aesop lived during the sixth century BC in Athens, Greece. Very little is known about him, but people surmise he was an intelligent and resourceful slave. He wrote fables that often represented him as the character who was smarter than his master and wiser than the wisest.[12]

One of his familiar fables is the story of the tortoise and the hare. In that story, a speedy hare challenged a slow but steady tortoise to a race. The hare was so confident that he stopped during the race to nap, eat, and nap again, while the tortoise kept on walking. In the end, the tortoise beat the hare by a whisker. The moral was "slow and steady wins the race."[13]

The wall around Jerusalem was finished quickly, but the daily pace was most likely a slow and steady one as the laborers worked in the hot summer climate. Nehemiah focused on doing everything he could to keep his workers from becoming distracted by various opposing forces. He wanted them to steadily continue their efforts. In the end, with God's approval, the job was completed in only fifty-two days. Nehemiah and his people were able to win the race.

Lift Up ...

Dear Lord, please help me remember that You are watching over me. Too often, I have not acknowledged the way You have preserved me from harm and enabled me to accomplish Your work. Forgive me for the times I failed to rightly give You the glory. In Jesus' name. Amen.

Look At ...

Yesterday, we saw how Shemaiah attempted to instill fear in Nehemiah. In doing so, he hoped to coax him into hiding in the temple—an action that would lead to his death. In response to

1 A Radical Accomplishment

Elul is the sixth month of the Hebrew year and includes parts of August and September.[14] Nehemiah started the work on August 1, 444 BC, and completed it fifty-two days later, on September 21. About two miles of stone walls were erected, and Jerusalem was again protected from attack.

2 A Unified Effort

Seven weeks plus three days seems like a short time in which to finish a city wall, but keep in mind that Nehemiah was leading several thousand men in at least thirty groups that were all laboring simultaneously, without distraction, and with God's help.

5 A Strengthening Result

Disheartened means being deprived of courage or enthusiasm. The quick finish of the rebuilding of the wall fortified Jerusalem. Now her enemies no longer saw the inhabitants of the city as fearful and vulnerable.

this strategy, Nehemiah stood firm—he stood on his faith in God and his determination to see his mission through.

Today, we find that mission accomplished. In the span of a mere fifty-two days, the wall was completed—a feat that could only be orchestrated by God. In the wake of accomplishment, the enemies of Nehemiah were jealous, threatened, and annoyed.

Read Nehemiah 6:15–16.

So the wall was finished on the twenty-fifth day of Elul, in fifty-two days. And it happened, when all our enemies heard of it, and all the nations around us saw these things, that they were very disheartened in their own eyes; for they perceived that this work was done by our God. Nehemiah 6:15–16

1. On what date was the wall finished?

2. How much time did it take to reconstruct the wall?

3. What group of people was dismayed to hear that the wall was finished?

4. Who observed the completion of the restoration?

5. How did the surrounding nations react to this accomplishment?

6. In whose eyes were they disheartened?

7. What did the nations around them perceive?

Live Out ...

8. We all have jobs to do, both for ourselves and for our Lord. Let's first look at the work we generally do for ourselves. Number the following chores in order of their importance to you.

____ Earn money

____ Clean house

____ Take care of dependents, family, pets

____ Pray

____ Maintain health

____ Other: _____

8 In Constant Prayer

Note that prayer is a requirement for the completion of all work. First Thessalonians 5:17–18 tells us to "pray without ceasing, in everything give thanks; for this is the will of God in Christ Jesus for you."

What work do you feel has been assigned to you by God? Number these as well.

____ Help the unfortunate: the homeless, sick, elderly, lonely

____ Contribute in Bible study and church

____ Volunteer in other ways to serve others

____ Pray

____ Other: _____

What guidelines do you use to choose which job is most important to you as well as how you make yourself persevere in your work until you complete the job?

9. Nehemiah did his best to minimize distractions and stick to the business at hand of rebuilding a serviceable wall for the city and his people.

a. What distractions hinder you from the work at hand?

10 Let Go(d)

In studying Nehemiah, we've seen the demonstrated truth, "If God is for us, who can be against us?" (Rom. 8:31). Do your best with the knowledge you've been given. Then watch God do the rest. Avoid feelings of self-condemnation and regret. You couldn't do any of it without God. Give Him the glory.

b. How do you combat these distractions to stay focused?

c. What are some other ways you can help yourself to stay on track and continue in the work God has called you to do?

10. The enemies within and the nations outside Jerusalem realized that finishing the work on the wall was possible only by God's blessing and support. Sometimes we believe that we have accomplished things apart from Him, but we are only His servants, and He is the one to whom glory is due. Fill out the table below, answering the "How Related?" part after completing the three main thoughts.

Scripture	Main Thought	Related How?
Leviticus 10:3		
Isaiah 49:3		
2 Corinthians 4:15		

Like the tortoise, Nehemiah would not be swayed from completing his race. We don't know what the tortoise was thinking as he steadily crawled along, nor what contributed to his ability to persevere, but we have learned something about Nehemiah.

James Montgomery Boice enumerated five leadership characteristics of Nehemiah that helped him complete this work. First, he stayed close to God through prayer. Second, he felt that he was specifically called by God to lead the rebuilding of the wall. Third, he recognized that his ability to successfully undertake this project was a gift from God. Fourth, he could discern the truth, thanks to his innate spiritual understanding. Fifth, he was courageous—Nehemiah was able to do what God wanted even when he was afraid, disturbed, and hurt.[15] He gave his fears to the Lord and persevered in his task. Lord, may we adopt his characteristics as our own.

Listen To ...

> *Let us be as watchful after the victory as before the battle.*
>
> —Andrew Bonar

A Man of Questionable Influence

Another story involving a wolf concerns the three little pigs. First published in 1886, this tale now appears in the form of various books and cartoons. The fable begins with three brother pigs being sent out of the family home in order to seek their fortune. The first and second pigs built houses out of straw and sticks, and a big, bad, hungry wolf blew the structures down. The two little pigs ran to the third little pig's house, which was built of brick. This house withstood the wolf's best efforts to blow it down. In the end, Mr. Wolf decided to attack the pigs from inside the house, headed up to the roof, fell down the chimney, and ended up as a meal of soup for the pigs.[16]

Nehemiah had just completed the rebuilding of his own brick walls and was ready for a rest, but there was still a "wolf" attacking him. Sometimes despite our efforts, we remain under attack. The Devil comes after all who serve the Lord. He will try to stop you by ridicule, assault, and discouragement. The battle was not yet over for Nehemiah, or for the Lord.

Lift Up ...

Dear Lord, help me to be a godly woman of influence in my home and my workplace. Allow me to influence others for good and not evil. Guard my tongue and my attitude in all circumstances. In Jesus' name. Amen.

Look At ...

Yesterday, we celebrated with the Jews and their leader when the wall around Jerusalem was completed. Nehemiah considered his project carefully, made a plan, prayed for God's guidance, motivated the people, and resisted his enemies efforts to dissuade him.

Today, we meet up with Tobiah, another enemy of Nehemiah. Tobiah was a crafty man, probably Jewish by marriage, who sought to influence people in authority. He was not to be trusted, for behind his manipulations were evil intentions against Nehemiah.

Read Nehemiah 6:17–19.

Also in those days the nobles of Judah sent many letters to Tobiah, and the letters of Tobiah came to them. For many in Judah were pledged to him, because he was the son-in-law of Shechaniah the son of Arah, and his son Jehohanan had married the daughter of Meshullam the son of Berechiah. Also they reported his good deeds before me, and reported my words to him. Tobiah sent letters to frighten me.
Nehemiah 6:17–19

1. Who began sending letters back and forth?

2. People from what tribe were pledged to Tobiah?

3. Why were these Judeans supportive of Tobiah?

4. What was the name of Arah's son, and how is he connected to Tobiah?

5. Who had Tobiah's son, Jehohanan, married?

6. What two things did the nobles report?

7. What was the purpose of Tobiah's letters to Nehemiah?

1 Letters of Dissent

The nobles of Judah sent informative letters to Tobiah, and in return, Tobiah sent them letters of persuasion. These people believed his lies and cooperated with Jerusalem's enemy even though God had promised that a King and Savior would come from their tribe (see Gen. 49:10; 2 Sam. 7). They turned their backs on their God.

3 Interconnected

Tobiah's father-in-law was Shechaniah, son of Arah, and his daughter-in-law was the daughter of Meshullam, son of Berechiah, who worked on rebuilding the wall. Many Jews were therefore loyal to and supportive of Tobiah, with whom they probably had trading contracts.[17]

6 Telling Tales

When the nobles reported to Tobiah about Nehemiah's words, they were gossiping. Proverbs 11:13 describes a gossip as a talebearer who "reveals secrets, but he who is of a faithful spirit conceals a matter." Do not be a talebearer.

8 Family Ties

Love of family can feel like the only thing that nails us to this earth, but strong family ties cannot be allowed to outweigh our ties to God. "And he who loves son or daughter more than Me is not worthy of Me" (Matt. 10:37). The Lord makes it clear that He comes first.

10 Fear Less

Sometimes it is hard to know whom to believe, but following God's Word can keep you from giving in to deception and fear. "Those who forsake the law praise the wicked, but such as keep the law contend with them" (Prov. 28:4). Err on the side of obedience.

Live Out ...

8. Examine your life right now. Are you permitting a human relationship to muddle your thinking to the extent that you find yourself disobeying the Word of the Lord? If so, write out the name of the person below.

I am placing my relationship with _____
ahead of my relationship with the Lord.
In what way does this relationship cause you to sin?

9. We see in Nehemiah 6, verses 9 and 19, that foes used rumors, lies, and threats in order to cause Nehemiah and his people to feel afraid. Read Philippians 4:6–7, and discover a way God will protect us from feeling fear.

a. What does this passage tell you not to do?

b. What are you reminded to do?

c. What will God then do for you?

10. The nobles actively corresponded with Tobiah, absorbing his opinions and sharing information gleaned about Nehemiah. They also sent letters to Nehemiah, praising Tobiah. These letters were most likely full of flattery and lies.

a. Can you recall a time when you were blinded by flattery and lies?

b. How did you discover you were being deceived?

c. How did you respond?

_____

In the following story, see Nehemiah as the optimistic soul, and ask yourself, *Which one am I?*

Two frogs fell into a deep cream bowl,

One was an optimistic soul;

But the other took the gloomy view,

"We shall drown," he cried, without more ado.

So with a last despairing cry,

He flung up his legs and said, "Good-bye."

Quoth the other frog with a merry grin,

"I can't get out, but I won't give in.

I'll just swim round till my strength is spent,

Then will I die the more content."

Bravely he swam till it would seem

His struggles began to churn the cream.

On the top of the butter at last he stopped,

And out of the bowl he gaily hopped.

What of the moral? 'Tis easily found:

If you can't hop out, keep swimming around.[18]

We know the good work God has given us to do will be ongoing until the day of Christ Jesus. In the meantime, He depends on us to do our part by building protective walls around our faith, our relationship with Him, and our relationships. Can you become a wall-builder in your home and workplace? Will you replace stones that have been dislodged by rumors, lies, and threats? Won't you begin this process today, remembering that if you think you can, you can, and if you think you can't, you won't? Each of us has a job to do. Discover yours, and get busy!

Listen To ...

Am I an earnest laborer together with God, or am I, after all, only a laborious trifler, an industrious doer of nothing, working hard to accomplish no purpose of the sort for which I ought to work, since I ought to live unto my Lord alone?
—*Charles H. Spurgeon*

Stand and Be Counted

Nehemiah 7

As the eldest surviving son of twelve children, Paul Revere had a strong instinct to protect those he loved. Born in 1734 to immigrant parents, he learned the art of silversmithing. At nineteen, his father died, and Revere became the main source of income for his family.

As a young man, he volunteered to fight the French. Later, he gathered intelligence and observed the movements of British soldiers. With his eyes open and his wits about him, Revere served as a courier, riding express to the Continental Congress in Philadelphia.

Then on the night of April 18, 1775, as the Revolutionary War was erupting, he received orders to ride to Lexington to warn John Hancock and Samuel Adams of the British approach.[1] His actions were forever memorialized by Longfellow's poem "Paul Revere's Ride":

> Listen, my children, and you shall hear of the midnight ride of Paul Revere, on the eighteenth of April, in Seventy-five; hardly a man is now alive who remembers that famous day and year.
>
> He said to his friend, "If the British march by land or sea from the town to-night, hang a lantern aloft in the belfry arch of the North Church tower as a signal light, one, if by land, and two, if by sea; and I on the opposite shore will be, ready to ride and spread the alarm through every Middlesex village and farm, for the country folk to be up and to arm."
>
> Wherever freedom hopes to flourish, men and women must diligently and prayerfully take part and keep watch.

Day 1: Nehemiah 7:1–3   **Be Counted Individually**

Day 2: Nehemiah 7:4–6   **Be Counted in the Community**

Day 3: Nehemiah 7:7–38   **Be Counted at Home**

Day 4: Nehemiah 7:39–60   **Be Counted in Ministry**

Day 5: Nehemiah 7:61–73   **Be Counted for Christ**

Be Counted Individually

Lift Up ...

Dear Lord, I sometimes forget to diligently protect my heart. I guard my home and care for my family, but I forget that most precious, bought-at-a-price territory of my mind and heart. Help me remember Your love and Your sacrifice. I want to be a faithful steward of my heart. In Jesus' name. Amen.

Look At ...

At the conclusion of lesson six, we reviewed the Jews' delight and celebration at the completion of the wall surrounding Jerusalem. Nehemiah's leadership and godly planning were evident to all. In this atmosphere of joy, Nehemiah's enemy Tobiah seethed with jealousy and evil intentions. Just as he did with Nehemiah's godly efforts, Satan seeks to interrupt our progress for the kingdom of God.

Today, we see Nehemiah consolidate the progress and long-term stability and safety for Jerusalem. The reconstruction efforts had been wonderfully successful, but hostilities still ran high. At this point of completion, there might have been a tendency to let down their guard. It took more than a wall to guard the city; it took leaders, residents, and watchers.

Read Nehemiah 7:1–3.

Then it was, when the wall was built and I had hung the doors, when the gatekeepers, the singers, and the Levites had been appointed, that I gave the charge of Jerusalem to my brother Hanani, and Hananiah the leader of the citadel, for he was a faithful man and feared God more than many.

And I said to them, *"Do not let the gates of Jerusalem be opened until the sun is hot; and while they stand guard, let them shut and bar the doors; and appoint guards from among the inhabitants of Jerusalem, one at his watch station and another in front of his own house."* Nehemiah 7:1–3

1 Extended Leadership

At this point, Nehemiah may have been thinking about his return to his position as the cupbearer for King Artaxerxes. Yet finishing the wall didn't finish his task. He needed to appoint good men to be trained to maintain and protect the city on a long-term basis.

2 Trusted Character

Many skills can be taught to people in management, but a good character is not one of them. Character is often revealed in challenging situations. Billy Graham once said, "When wealth is lost, nothing is lost; when health is lost, something is lost; when character is lost, all is lost."[2]

4 Specific Guidance

In the East, it was customary for the gates of a city to be opened at sunrise and closed at sunset.[3] Nehemiah knew that the enemy was lurking at the gates. In the early morning, the citizens were more likely to be sleepy and unprepared. When the sun was hot, people would be active and alert.

1. After he finished hanging the doors in the completed wall, what did Nehemiah do?

2. a. What two men did Nehemiah appoint as future leaders in Jerusalem?

   1.

   2.

   b. One of the men, Hanani, was Nehemiah's brother, so he knew him well. What two characteristics did the second man, Hananiah, possess that made him a good choice for a trusted position (see v. 2)?

   1.

   2.

3. There is more to a city than high walls and secure gates. By putting good men in leadership, what do you think Nehemiah was trying to achieve?

4. a. When were the gates of the city to be opened?

   b. What was the purpose of this timing?

5. a. Who else did Nehemiah want to stand guard?

   b. What specific areas were they to watch (see v. 3)?

6. a. Why were these areas important to the well-being of individuals and the population at large?

b. What effect would this strategy have on the relationships between neighbors?

Live Out ...

7. Nehemiah determined to do more than what was expected of him.
He knew that physical protection of the community was vital, but he also
made it a priority to create a sense of responsibility among the citizens.

Has there ever been a time when someone unexpected watched out
for your best interest? Write in your journal about that incident and
how you might prepare to watch out for someone else.

8. The men appointed to be in charge of Jerusalem were known by
their fear of God and their faithful actions. Put an X by the characteristics you believe best represent your attitudes and actions.

___ Consistent   ___ Prayerful

___ Forgiving   ___ Loving toward others

___ Reverent toward God   ___ Hopeful

___ Courageous   ___ Determined

Now put an O by the characteristics that could use
more development. Pray that God would strengthen
your weaknesses.

9. Nehemiah recognized leadership qualities in others and inspired
them to use their gifts for the common good. Think about a time when
God asked you to step out and use your gifts for the good of other people.
Write in your journal about how you responded to His urging.

Now look at the following list, and ask God if He is urging you
to step out once again:

     Provide intercessory prayer

     Give to an individual or a God-centered group

7 Vested Interest

Protecting one's property
and family is fundamental
to human nature.
Nehemiah wanted people
to begin watching out for
their neighbors as well
as for themselves. In the
United States, neighbor-
hood watch programs are
a cost-effective method
of crime prevention and
a stepping-stone to com-
munity revitalization.[4]

8 Blessed Interest

We are known by our words
and works. The apostle
Paul knew that a good
leader must be above
reproach, exhibit faithfulness, behave with dignity,
practice hospitality and
generosity, and be in
loving control of his own
household (see 1 Tim.
3:2–7). Nehemiah was
looking for men with
similar characteristics.

Use my time to volunteer

Use my talents for the good of others

Spend more time quietly focused on the Word

Remember: where God guides, He provides.

—————————

Historians believe that Paul Revere never actually uttered the famous phrase "The British are coming!" On his ride to Lexington, however, he stopped house by house to sound an alarm to the residents. He was so loud that a sentry standing guard at the house where Hancock and Adams were staying told Revere to stop making so much noise. Revere retorted: "Noise! You'll have noise enough before long. The regulars are coming out!"[5]

There are some situations that merit "noise." Jesus told us that we are expected to warn others of impending disaster and give them the opportunity to ensure they are safe and saved for eternity.

We are not involved in a military operation as was Paul Revere, but vocal believers will always be on the receiving end of hatred, conflict, and persecution. Our Leader and Master implored us to loudly proclaim the message of salvation. "Whatever I tell you in the dark, speak in the light; and what you hear in the ear, preach on the housetops" (Matt. 10:27).

Godly works evoke evil opposition. Nehemiah was prepared not only to do his work but also to make sure the people's efforts were well guarded and defended.

Listen To ...

The church that is not jealously protected by mighty intercession and sacrificial labors will before long become the abode of every evil bird and the hiding place for unsuspected corruption. The creeping wilderness will soon take over that church that trusts in its own strength and forgets to watch and pray.

—A. W. Tozer

Be Counted in the Community

Paul Revere was not only a respected defender and protector of our country; he was a devoted, hardworking family man. His American roots on his paternal side date back to 1716, when his father emigrated from France to the New World. His maternal American roots are much deeper, as his mother's English ancestors arrived in Boston in 1641.

Revere and his first wife, Sarah, were married in 1757 and had eight children. Sarah died shortly after the birth of their eighth child. Paul then married Rachel Walker in 1773, and they had eight more children.

From Revere's sixteen children, the new country of America was blessed with carpenters, silversmiths, a teacher, a diplomat, and six married daughters. His sixteenth child, John Revere, attended Harvard and became a physician.[6]

It would be a study in itself to find out the total number of people in Revere's lineage. His midnight ride captured our national attention, but his legacy is much more than that.

Lift Up …

Dear Lord, I want to see others and myself the way You see us. You are not concerned with grand cities and awesome monuments; You are interested in Your children and the legacy of faith they leave. Someday, I will stand before You. I want to be counted as one who loved and honored You. In Jesus' name. Amen.

Look At …

Yesterday, we saw a man of God who was aware of the wiles of Satan. In the aftermath of the victorious reconstruction of the wall and gates surrounding Jerusalem, Nehemiah's enemies were plotting ways to enter the city. Although Nehemiah was a wonderful leader, the city's best

2 A Word to the Wise

In Nehemiah 1:4–5, we found Nehemiah on his knees before God, pouring out his heartbreak and grief about the terrible report of Jerusalem. Rather than reacting impulsively, he sat, wept, fasted, and prayed to his good and wise God.

3 A Wall of Faith

It must have been an act of pure faith to build a wall around a deteriorated city. Nehemiah believed God's presence would return to dwell in the midst of Jerusalem. What was in tatters would one day be known as the "City of Truth" and the "Mountain of the Lord of hosts" (see Zech. 8:3).

defense was its citizenry who had worked hard and wanted to protect their homes and families.

Today, we find the city in a foundational phase of its growth. Nehemiah was tuned into the will of God, and he embarked on a mission to find and bring back the original residents of the city. What might have been humanly impossible was made possible when Nehemiah found an invaluable document that would allow the Jews to repopulate the city as God had intended.

Read Nehemiah 7:4–6.

Now the city was large and spacious, but the people in it were few, and the houses were not rebuilt. Then my God put it into my heart to gather the nobles, the rulers, and the people, that they might be registered by genealogy. And I found a register of the genealogy of those who had come up in the first return, and found written in it: These are the people of the province who came back from the captivity, of those who had been carried away, whom Nebuchadnezzar the king of Babylon had carried away, and who returned to Jerusalem and Judah, everyone to his city. Nehemiah 7:4–6

1. a. What two adjectives are used to describe the city?

    b. Based on this description, does Jerusalem sound like an appealing place to live? Why or why not?

2. Nehemiah must have considered the current habitation and condition of the community to be a problem. Who do you believe he first consulted on the matter?

3. Nehemiah arrived to find Jerusalem surrounded by broken walls and burned gates. Walls are generally built to protect what they

enclose. What did Nehemiah find when he surveyed the interior space of the city?

4. How did Nehemiah come up with the idea to find the registry of the genealogy (see v. 5)?

5. Why do you think the people who were part of the first return might have been interested in coming back to the city they had left?

6. The Jews had been taken captive and carried away to Babylon. The capturing king, Nebuchadnezzar, did not care about who they were as individuals. In view of that, why do you think it was important to list the names of all those who returned?

Live Out …

7. Do you have a hard time remembering names? Most people struggle to some degree. Our names are important to us. Describe how you feel when someone you've met several times still can't remember your name.

8. Now describe your feelings when someone you've recently met greets you by name.

9. a. Sometimes, a name is withheld—or spoken—for manipulative purposes. Circle the ways your name has been used to hurt you.

Blame   Jealousy

Sarcasm   Gossip

4 A Finder of the Lost

It is not recorded whether Nehemiah knew where the document was kept or if he simply found it. God is the Master of finding and saving—especially lost people. We are instructed to ask, seek, and knock when we are looking for both general and specific help (see Luke 11:9).

6 What's in a Name?

The name *Jesus* means "the Lord saves." The Bible consistently shows the importance of our individual names to the Savior. As an act of hatred and depersonalization during World War II, the Nazis tattooed numbers on the captured Jews. God, in His love, has inscribed your name on His hands (see Isa. 49:16).

9 The Name Game

Here are five simple suggestions to strengthen your memory: (1) meet and repeat—repeat the name immediately; (2) spell it out—in your mind, or ask the proper spelling; (3) associate—for instance, Sandy from Santa Fe; (4) make connections—Julie reminds you of a friend of the same name; (5) choose to care—it's important.[7]

b. Write in your journal about one of those times and how it affected you.

c. Now remember a time when your name was used in the context of praise, gratitude, acknowledgement, sincerity, or love.

It's a blessing to be remembered kindly, lovingly, and by name.

———————————

Paul Revere is not known for his performance in battles, although he participated in small expeditions to Rhode Island and Massachusetts. In fact, his last recorded military action, the Penobscot expedition, failed. As with most wars, some battles are won and some are lost. To look at Revere's success strictly on a military level could well consign him to a mere footnote in history. However, his passion for his country and his willingness to spread the word earned him an important place in the story of our country's beginnings.

Jerusalem was in a fragile state when Nehemiah came on the scene. He was a man of vision, determination, and obvious leadership skills. His recognition in the reestablishment of Jerusalem was well-earned. God used his skills and passion to accomplish a monumental task; however, one man does not make a nation. The strength of Jerusalem depended on the commitment and vigilance of its citizens.

Listen To ...

There is no king who has not had a slave among his ancestors,
and no slave who has not had a king among his.
—*Helen Keller*

Be Counted at Home

There is a certain status that comes from being "the first." It could be the prestige of being the first in your graduating class, the first to scale a mountain, or the first to finish a race. In America, it is a great honor and privilege to trace your family's genealogy back to the "first comers" who arrived in America on the *Mayflower*.

Those who arrived in Plymouth on the *Mayflower* in 1620 numbered a mere 102 people. It is believed that the descendants of those early arrivers now number between 20 and 30 million.

But adding your name to the list of *Mayflower* descendants demands patience and proof to verify your claim. The process of joining the General Society of Mayflower Descendants starts with a preliminary application that includes a synopsis of how many other people in your line have previously been filed and documented. Then, it gets complicated. After filling out a detailed family tree, you must provide documentation in the form of birth, marriage, and death certificates and Bibles, wills, deeds, census forms, and so on. Eventually, your materials go before the state historian for review and verification. If confirmed, you will be *considered* for election. Then, the historian general, who may contact you with more questions or other needed proofs, will review your application again.[8]

Just as the Mayflower Society seeks to identify descendants of our country's first comers, so Nehemiah was in pursuit of finding the first comers to the city of Jerusalem following their captivity.

Lift Up ...

Dear Lord, I sometimes feel invisible in the world. I'm not the smartest, the wittiest, or the prettiest. But Lord, I am visible to You. You know my name, You know my thoughts, and You know I am Your child. You love me. Thank You, Lord Jesus! Amen.

Look At ...

Yesterday, we looked at the growth and repopulation of Jerusalem. Even though the work on the wall was complete, Nehemiah was still tuned into God's guidance and will: "Then my God put it into my heart" (Neh. 7:5). He might have been under the impression that he had accomplished his mission, but then he embarked on a new challenge: to gather the people listed in the genealogy of Jerusalem.

Today, we learn the names of those individuals who could prove their Jewish ancestry. In the aftermath of many Jewish failures, this time and place marked a new beginning, a new national pride, and a new commitment to the God who had been faithful to them throughout the generations. It mattered to God that the inhabitants of the restored city were His people. Determining the purity of the Jewish line would prove of utmost importance in the lineage of Jesus Christ.

Read Nehemiah 7:7–38.

Those who came with Zerubbabel were Jeshua, Nehemiah, Azariah, Raamiah, Nahamani, Mordecai, Bilshan, Mispereth, Bigvai, Nehum, and Baanah. The number of the men of the people of Israel: the sons of Parosh, two thousand one hundred and seventy-two; the sons of Shephatiah, three hundred and seventy-two; the sons of Arah, six hundred and fifty-two; the sons of Pahath-Moab, of the sons of Jeshua and Joab, two thousand eight hundred and eighteen; the sons of Elam, one thousand two hundred and fifty-four; the sons of Zattu, eight hundred and forty-five; the sons of Zaccai, seven hundred and sixty; the sons of Binnui, six hundred and forty-eight; the sons of Bebai, six hundred and twenty-eight; the sons of Azgad, two thousand three hundred and twenty-two; the sons of Adonikam, six hundred and sixty-seven; the sons of Bigvai, two thousand and sixty-seven; the sons of Adin, six hundred and fifty-five; the sons of Ater of Hezekiah, ninety-eight; the sons of Hashum, three hundred and twenty-eight; the sons of Bezai, three hundred and twenty-four; the sons of Hariph, one hundred and twelve; the sons of Gibeon, ninety-five; the men of Bethlehem and Netophah, one hundred and eighty-eight; the men of Anathoth, one hundred and twenty-eight; the men of Beth Azmaveth, forty-two; the men of Kirjath Jearim, Chephirah, and Beeroth, seven hundred and forty-three; the men of Ramah and Geba, six hundred and twenty-one; the men of Michmas, one hundred and twenty-two; the men of Bethel and Ai, one hundred and twenty-three; the men of the other Nebo, fifty-two; the sons of the other Elam, one thousand two hundred and fifty-four; the sons of Harim, three hundred and twenty; the sons of Jericho, three hundred and forty-five; the sons of Lod, Hadid, and Ono, seven hundred and twenty-one; the sons of Senaah, three thousand nine hundred and thirty. Nehemiah 7:7–38

1. The first group listed came with what leader?

2. Compare the list of men who came with Zerubbabel in Nehemiah 7:7 with the list given in Ezra 2:2. What do you observe about these two lists?

3. What is the name of the second group of people?

4. Briefly scan Ezra 2, making a general note of the repetitions found in the lists in Nehemiah. Why do you think the individual names merited being recorded twice in the Bible?

5. The number of Jews returning to Jerusalem was relatively small to repopulate a city. Why do you think it was important to count them?

6. The books of Ezra and Nehemiah were originally combined. Scan Ezra 2 and Nehemiah 7, and list two outstanding similarities.
   1.
   2.

1 The Tribal Head

Zerubbabel had a distinguished history as the head of the tribe of Judah during the first return of the Jews to Jerusalem under Cyrus. He was recognized and referred to as the prince of the captivity. When the decree was issued to return to Jerusalem to rebuild the house of the Lord, he stood up.[9]

2 Alike but Different

Although Ezra's list of names of the men who came with Zerubbabel differs slightly from the list in Nehemiah, commentators agree that some of the discrepancies may have resulted from copy errors such as *Rehum* in Ezra transcribed as *Nehum* in Nehemiah. Other differences may be due to men who didn't survive the journey.

4 God's Very Own

In this list of names, it seems that God knows and values His own, His children. The repetition of their names indicates that God delights in His children and knows them by name. He has promised that "the righteous will be in everlasting remembrance" (Ps. 112:6).

7 The Power of One

Of all the pervasive messages of the Bible, the Trinity stands at the top. Jesus commissioned us to tell the nations not only about Himself but also about His Father and the Holy Spirit. It is by their names and their power that we are told to go and make disciples (see Matt. 28:19).

9 Who Are You?

You are a child of God. You can point to the promises of Scripture and prove that you are qualified to be listed in the Lamb's Book of Life because you have met the requirements of being rightly related to God through the blood of Jesus Christ. There! It's settled. No more genealogies needed!

Live Out ...

7. At the close of today's lesson, do you find yourself wondering what all the fuss is about with numbers? Read the following Scriptures, and draw a line connecting the verse to what we learn about numbers and our heavenly Father.

Scripture	What We Learn
Genesis 13:16	God knows every detail about us.
Psalm 90:12	God sees every tear that falls.
Matthew 10:30	God warns His children about danger.
Psalm 56:8	God keeps His promises.
Revelation 13:18	God wants us to be aware and wise.

8. a. Knowing that God's love for us extends to the point of numbering the hairs on our heads and keeping our tears in a bottle, do you believe that your Father cherishes and delights in you? Write a prayer in your journal asking your Father in heaven to heal any wounds that may have come from your earthly parents.

b. Read and meditate on Psalm 27:10.

9. There is a huge interest in searching for ancestral roots through the likes of Ancestry.com and RootsWeb.com. What do you know about your own family history? Whether you are of royal stock or common stock, you have the opportunity to leave a legacy of faith. Circle the ways you can make a lasting impact on your family history:

- Voice my faith
- Be seen reading my Bible
- Be compassionate, and give to the needy

- Be a godly woman and wife
- Pray for myself, my family, and my country
- Be joyful, hopeful, helpful, and thankful

The Society of Mayflower Descendants is determined to accurately qualify individuals who seek to join. They are equally determined to disqualify those who don't meet the standards. Even when a grandchild or a close relative applies on the strength of a previously registered member, that person may be turned down because the older application process was less stringent than it is today. As times and generations pass, documents and proof become harder to locate. Lineage, relationships, and documented proof are everything.[10]

As children of God, we needn't worry about whether we will qualify to enter the gates of heaven. Our names will be found written on the Father's hand in the blood of His Son, Jesus Christ.

Listen To ...

My dear Jesus, my Savior, is so deeply written in my heart, that I feel confident that if my heart were to be cut open and chopped to pieces, the name of Jesus would be found written on every piece.
—*Ignatius of Antioch*

Be Counted in Ministry

It's human nature to undervalue things that come easily to us. We've all heard about lottery winners who blow through their winnings so fast that they ultimately find themselves right back to where they were prior to winning. Or we learn of a privileged young person inheriting a strong family business only to run it into the ground.

As a population of Americans who have become complacent toward the comfort and security of citizenship, we can find ourselves in a similar position, feeling entitled to that which was hard-won by others and then handed to us.

For individuals who arrive in our country and become naturalized citizens, there is often a deep appreciation and understanding of their new status.

Miriam, for instance, had to flee Honduras in fear for her life because of her involvement in a union organization. She was granted political asylum in the United States and began to avidly pursue citizenship. Lack of time and money and the fear of a mistake that might lead to her deportation eventually took her to a Washington-based clinic designed to help by offering classes and free legal counsel. She practiced English and studied civics until she earned her citizenship in 2011. She was excited that she could vote in the 2012 election and immediately began helping other immigrants by volunteering for a citizenship hotline.[11]

It's only proper to help those who are seeking a safe destination. Be mindful to help others who may need guidance finding their way to the Savior and to heaven.

Lift Up ...

Dear Lord, my earthly lineage may not be noble, royal, famous, or heroic, but I am Your child—a child of the King. Lift my head so that I may walk worthy of my Father's name. In Jesus' name. Amen.

Look At ...

Yesterday, we pondered the names of the people who were to repopulate the new city of Jerusalem. It was important to God to make sure only His chosen people came to dwell in this land. We can imagine the sense of national and individual pride of those who could prove their Jewish ancestry.

Today's lesson lists more groups, including priests, Levites, temple singers, gatekeepers, and various temple servants. Priests and servants were listed in the same way and with equal emphasis. They were Jews, and that was all that mattered. They shared a sense of belonging and the knowledge that their ancestors qualified them to return to Jerusalem.

Read Nehemiah 7:39–60.

The priests: the sons of Jedaiah, of the house of Jeshua, nine hundred and seventy-three; the sons of Immer, one thousand and fifty-two; the sons of Pashhur, one thousand two hundred and forty-seven; the sons of Harim, one thousand and seventeen. The Levites: the sons of Jeshua, of Kadmiel, and of the sons of Hodevah, seventy-four. The singers: the sons of Asaph, one hundred and forty-eight. The gatekeepers: the sons of Shallum, the sons of Ater, the sons of Talmon, the sons of Akkub, the sons of Hatita, the sons of Shobai, one hundred and thirty-eight. The Nethinim: the sons of Ziha, the sons of Hasupha, the sons of Tabbaoth, the sons of Keros, the sons of Sia, the sons of Padon, the sons of Lebana, the sons of Hagaba, the sons of Salmai, the sons of Hanan, the sons of Giddel, the sons of Gahar, the sons of Reaiah, the sons of Rezin, the sons of Nekoda, the sons of Gazzam, the sons of Uzza, the sons of Paseah, the sons of Besai, the sons of Meunim, the sons of Nephishesim, the sons of Bakbuk, the sons of Hakupha, the sons of Harhur, the sons of Bazlith, the sons of Mehida, the sons of Harsha, the sons of Barkos, the sons of Sisera, the sons of Tamah, the sons of Neziah, and the sons of Hatipha. The sons of Solomon's servants: the sons of Sotai, the sons of Sophereth, the sons of Perida, the sons of Jaala, the sons of Darkon, the sons of Giddel, the sons of Shephatiah, the sons of Hattil, the sons of Pochereth of Zebaim, and the sons of Amon. All the Nethinim, and the sons of Solomon's servants, were three hundred and ninety-two. Nehemiah 7:39–60

2 Temple Leaders

The priests and the Levites were brought back to Jerusalem for the purpose of working in the temple. What good is a temple without its priests? Their services were used in Babylon and would be needed now in the efforts to revitalize Jerusalem.

3 Temple Staff

When you observe the workings of a church, it is clear that a competent staff is required. These two groups provided practical functions. Various Bible translations help clarify their roles. Gatekeepers were also called porters, temple guards, doorkeepers, and security guards. Singers were called music makers, musicians, and temple singers.

4 Temple Servants

Depending on the version of the Bible you are reading, you may find either the word *Nethinim* or the words *temple servants*. *Nethinim* is the ancient Hebrew word for temple servant. There is no clear definition of their duties, but they may have been ushers who helped manage the crowds.[12]

1. Underline and number the groups listed in this passage. How many groups are listed?

2. What are the names of the first two groups?

    1.

    2.

3. What were the names of the third and fourth groups?

    3.

    4.

4. A total of six groups are listed in this passage. What is the name of the fifth group?

    5.

5.   a. What is the name of the last group of individuals?

    b. What was the total number of servants given in the last verse?

6. What can we gather from the inclusion of servants in this list, who may or may not have been of Jewish descent?

Live Out ...

7. Jesus showed us the dignity and selfless love that characterized His servanthood. Read Isaiah 49:5.

    a. What do you learn about the Lord's view of coming to the world as a servant?

    b. Who did He come to serve above all others?

    c. How does this change your view about your activities that may quietly go without recognition?

8. Read John 15:20, and copy it in your journal.

a. What does Jesus want you to remember?

b. If Jesus was persecuted, what should you expect?

c. What impact does keeping God's Word have on your life today?

9. Look at the categories of groups found in today's verses.

- Respected leaders
- High-level assistants
- Strong, capable individuals
- Gifted and talented people
- Lower-rung helpers to others

a. Circle the categories to which you belong.

b. Check the category to which you would like to belong.

10. a. What is the common thread that unites all the groups listed above?

b. Read Galatians 3:28, and write your thoughts below.

_____

Americans are acutely tuned in to their rights. We know that we are entitled to freedom of speech, freedom to worship as we wish, the right to a prompt and fair trial by jury, the right to vote in elections for public officials, the right to run for elected office, and the right to life, liberty, and the pursuit of happiness.

We treasure and guard our rights, but there's a flip side to rights—*responsibilities*. Citizens are called to support and defend the

7 Servant Sons

Jesus was God and humbled Himself to serve others. He commands us to serve in the same way. "So when He had washed their feet, taken His garments, and sat down again, He said to them ..., 'If I then, your Lord and Teacher, have washed your feet, you also ought to wash one another's feet. For I have given you an example, that you should do as I have done to you'" (John 13:12, 14–15).

10 The Equalizer

Jesus is the great equalizer. He sees us with unprejudiced eyes. God has given us eternal life based purely on our relationship with His Son. If we have the Son of God in our hearts, we can be certain we stand tall in God's eyes. If we haven't received the Son, we do not have eternal life (see 1 John 5:11).

Constitution, participate in the democratic process, respect and obey federal, state, and local laws, respect the rights and beliefs of others, and pay income taxes honestly and on time to the federal, state, and local authorities.[13]

We are a nation bound by the common thread of freedom and equality. History has proven that when those rights are threatened, we will rise up to defend them.

In Nehemiah's time, there was more to rebuilding the city than shoring up the walls and building new gates. Jerusalem was nothing without its citizens. The call to return to their homeland was a privilege accompanied by a responsibility. No matter how strong the military or how dedicated the citizens, without the shared goals of pursuing their faith, protecting their families, and dwelling in their city, their efforts would fail.

Listen To ...

We should always look upon ourselves as God's servants, placed in God's world, to do His work; and accordingly labor faithfully for Him; not with a design to grow rich and great, but to glorify God, and do all the good we possibly can.

—David Brainerd

Be Counted for Christ

We started this week's study with the story of Paul Revere and the midnight ride that warned that the Revolutionary War was at the doorstep. At that same time in Philadelphia, another man was taking on both military and political roles: George Washington. His first political stand was against the acts of the British Parliament, but after the Lexington and Concord Battles, Washington was appointed commander-in-chief of the Continental Army.

At this point in history, there was no thought of citizenship, because in 1775, America was not yet a country. What *was* important was leadership. After the Battles of Lexington and Concord, Washington appeared before the Second Continental Congress in full military uniform, which indicated that he was prepared for war.

His prior military experience had already earned him a reputation as tough and courageous. Coupled with his commanding presence, he was a natural leader. Not only were the colonies under British attack, but the colonies themselves were not yet cohesive.[14]

Like Nehemiah, Washington was called to organize, train, discipline, and inspire his men. At the same time, he was considering logistics and military strategies and requesting support for resources to feed, clothe, and equip the troops. Washington fought side-by-side with his men.

George Washington's leadership was a godsend at a crucial time in establishing the independence of the country. Nehemiah's leadership, organization, and humility were critical to God's plan to rebuild, repopulate, reestablish, and reenergize God's people in Jerusalem.

Lift Up ...

Dear Lord, while I am waiting for Your return, help me be a servant who will be found by her Master walking worthy, honoring Your Word, guarding her heart, and standing in Your strength. I pray to be counted as faithful in Your sight. In Jesus' name. Amen.

Look At ...

Yesterday, we looked at the various groups of people whose Jewish genealogies verified their qualifications to return to Jerusalem. People from various classes and stratums were regarded with the same respect. National pride and a desire to restore the nation went hand in hand.

Today we find the account of those who came to Jerusalem but were unable to prove their genealogies. For the priests, not being found on the lists greatly compromised their ability to maintain their standing; the absence of their names meant they were essentially defiled and unable to perform their duties. These names give us a glimpse into our future. The day will come when our name must be found in the genealogy of our Savior so that we might enter into the eternal city of heaven.

Read Nehemiah 7:61–73.

And these were the ones who came up from Tel Melah, Tel Harsha, Cherub, Addon, and Immer, but they could not identify their father's house nor their lineage, whether they were of Israel: the sons of Delaiah, the sons of Tobiah, the sons of Nekoda, six hundred and forty-two; and of the priests: the sons of Habaiah, the sons of Koz, the sons of Barzillai, who took a wife of the daughters of Barzillai the Gileadite, and was called by their name. These sought their listing among those who were registered by genealogy, but it was not found; therefore they were excluded from the priesthood as defiled. And the governor said to them that they should not eat of the most holy things till a priest could consult with the Urim and Thummim. Altogether the whole assembly was forty-two thousand three hundred and sixty, besides their male and female servants, of whom there were seven thousand three hundred and thirty-seven; and they had two hundred and forty-five men and women singers. Their horses were seven hundred and thirty-six, their mules two hundred and forty-five, their camels four hundred and thirty-five, and donkeys six thousand seven hundred and twenty. And some of the heads of the fathers' houses gave to the work. The governor gave to the treasury one thousand gold drachmas, fifty basins, and five hundred and thirty priestly garments. Some of the heads of the fathers' houses gave to the treasury of the work twenty thousand gold drachmas, and two thousand two hundred silver minas. And that which the rest of the people gave was twenty thousand gold drachmas, two thousand silver minas, and

sixty-seven priestly garments. So the priests, the Levites, the gatekeepers, the singers, some of the people, the Nethinim, and all Israel dwelt in their cities. When the seventh month came, the children of Israel were in their cities. Nehemiah 7:61–73

1. In verse 61, we learn about a group of people who had the same problem. What was that problem?

2. Not being able to identify their father's house or lineage was certainly a disappointment to many of these people, but to one group, the consequences were more serious. What was the name of that group?

3. What interim restrictions were put on those priests whose lineage was uncertain?

4. In cases where the priests' names were not listed in the Jewish record of names, what final action was taken to determine their individual fitness to continue as a priest in the temple at Jerusalem?

5. The most significant part of the census was numbering people. The priests were isolated as an important group.

   a. What was the total number of Jews determined by this extensive census (see v. 66)?

   b. What three general groups are listed in verses 67–69?

   1.

   2.

   3.

6. Important resources for the future needs of running the temple are listed in the next three verses.

2 Priests without Proof

Without the certainty of pure Jewish roots originating in Aaron, priests were unable to carry out their duties, which included overseeing sacrifices, discerning God's will as expressed in the Torah, and deciding legal matters. Purity of their lineage was essential.[15]

4 Decisive Measures

The Urim and Thummin was a method of using a black stone and a white stone to determine an outcome when obvious evidence was lacking. Conducted by a priest, it was considered to be a humanly impartial way for God to make His will known.

6 Proportionate Portions

Those individuals who are identified as heads of the fathers' houses were most likely the individuals with the greatest financial resources. Throughout Scripture, we are encouraged and compelled to give generously and freely, honoring God's blessings by "offering in proportion to the blessings the LORD your God has given you" (Deut. 16:10 NIV).

8 Prospering Generations

God promises to bless all generations that abide in His commandments. "Therefore know that the LORD your God, He is God, the faithful God who keeps covenant and mercy for a thousand generations with those who love Him and keep His commandments" (Deut. 7:9).

a. What were they?

b. Which groups made the largest financial contributions to the upkeep of the temple?

Live Out ...

7. Looking back on your study of Nehemiah 7, how would you sum up the overall message? Circle the central points of this chapter.

- Character counts
- Pray about everything
- Don't give up in the face of obstacles
- Recognize leadership in others
- Trust God for His provision
- God knows you by name
- Know your spiritual genealogy
- Live with the goal to leave a godly legacy

8. Think about your own family. Can you trace your spiritual roots?

a. Check the individuals who influenced you toward your Christian belief.
   - ❑ Mother
   - ❑ Father
   - ❑ Grandmother or grandfather
   - ❑ Friend

b. When you consider the accomplishments of past generations in your family, what brings you the greatest sense of pride?
   - ❑ Evidences of active faith
   - ❑ Prestigious professions
   - ❑ Outstanding accomplishments

❏ Military or personal heroism

❏ Accrual of wealth

❏ Humanitarian works

At the end of your life, which of these accomplishments would you like noted by your name in the family tree?

9. Some people who were adopted know little or nothing about their biological roots or ancestral accomplishments. If you are one of those individuals, do you feel there is

a. a missing piece of your past you would like to know?

b. a sense of being slighted because of your adoptive status?

c. a special or chosen status as a result of your adoption?

———————————

9 Divine Adoption

Believers have the most enviable family legacy imaginable. Before the world was formed, we were chosen and blessed with heavenly blessings. We who believe in Christ enjoy an adoption with all the rights and privileges of a firstborn son, simply because it pleases and delights God. We are treasured, loved, and of a royal line—the line of Jesus Christ (see Eph. 1:5–7).

On day one of this week's study, we considered the tumultuous beginnings of our country during the Revolutionary War. Paul Revere's name is remembered because he added his voice to watch, warn, and protect the fledgling nation.

On the other side of the war, the colonial army's siege of Yorktown was the decisive battle that led to victory. But it's important to remember that even under the strong leadership of Commander-in-Chief George Washington, the number of battles lost was almost as many as those won.

In the aftermath of this final victory, the Congress was stunned when Washington humbly stepped out of his public service to return to his beloved Mount Vernon. For six years, he farmed and enjoyed his life until once again his country called him to service. Although reluctant, Washington was elected as the first president of the United States on February 4, 1789.[16]

There are visionaries, and there are leaders. Nehemiah was both. Under the guidance of God, Nehemiah was able to accomplish and oversee the repair of the wall surrounding Jerusalem as well as organize and register the returning Jews based on records from the first return.

This chapter could easily be viewed as a tedious counting of long-dead people with difficult names and doubtful contemporary importance. However, what we learned is not so much that the people were counted but that *people count* to our Lord and Savior.

Listen To ...

There are two great truths, which for this platform I have proclaimed for many years. The first is that salvation is free to every man who will have it; the second is that God gives salvation to a people whom He has chosen; and these truths are not in conflict with each other in the least degree.

—*Charles Spurgeon*

Reading Brings Restoration

Nehemiah 8

In 1963 the hundred-year anniversary of the signing of the Emancipation Proclamation by Abraham Lincoln was celebrated. In the summer of that same year, the March on Washington for Jobs and Freedom became one of the largest political rallies in United States history.

The organizers worked closely with the Kennedy administration and labor, religious, and civic leaders to coordinate the gathering. The most widely remembered orator was Martin Luther King Jr., who delivered his famous "I Have a Dream" speech, regarded as one of the finest examples of public speaking. That day, the crowd heard one of the most inspirational and influential addresses in recent history.

King called for an end to racism as he cited the Declaration of Independence, the Emancipation Proclamation, and the United States Constitution—powerful documents that helped shape the United States of America. The speech is now memorialized on the exact location King stood at the foot of the Lincoln Memorial.[1]

In today's study, we see how the Israelites gathered in a similar fashion, not to rally for personal rights, but to hear from the most important document of their time: the Law of Moses. After tending to their physical security needs by building the wall, they focused on their spiritual needs and were inspired by God's very own words.

Day 1: Nehemiah 8:1–3   **Reading the Word**

Day 2: Nehemiah 8:4–6   **Responding to the Word**

Day 3: Nehemiah 8:7–9   **Restoration by the Word**

Day 4: Nehemiah 8:10–12   **Rejoicing in the Word**

Day 5: Nehemiah 8:13–18   **Remembering the Word**

DAY 1

Reading the Word

Lift Up ...

Dear Lord, ignite my heart to receive the Word of God with joy and excitement. Let it fall fresh on my mind and in my spirit. Like rain to parched ground, I pray to soak up Your Word. In Jesus' name. Amen.

Look At ...

Last week, we saw how important it was for the returning Jews to find their names written in the genealogical records of the first coming to Jerusalem. This was especially critical for returning priests, because without proof of their lineage rooted in Aaron, they were deemed unfit to serve in the holy functions of the priesthood in the temple. Only those men whose names were found were qualified to serve.

Today, we find the people gathered to listen to the reading of the Law of Moses. They stood in the hot sun and in the midst of a crowd, hungry for God's guidance as they listened to the prophet Ezra read to them for hours. They listened with ready hearts and understood what they heard.

Read Nehemiah 8:1–3.

Now all the people gathered together as one man in the open square that was in front of the Water Gate; and they told Ezra the scribe to bring the Book of the Law of Moses, which the LORD had commanded Israel. So Ezra the priest brought the Law before the assembly of men and women and all who could hear with understanding on the first day of the seventh month. Then he read from it in the open square that was in front of the Water Gate from morning until

midday, before the men and women and those who could understand; and the ears of all the people were attentive to the Book of the Law. Nehemiah 8:1–3

1. Where did the people gather?

2. What do you think was the significance of gathering there?

3. a. How is Ezra described?

   b. What did the people ask him to do?

4. Who gathered to hear the Law?

5. When did they gather?

6. According to verse 3:

   a. How long did Ezra read from God's Word?

   b. Who listened to God's Word? Who do you think "those who could understand" refers to?

7. How did the people respond to the book of the law?

Live Out ...

8. On a regular basis, we need to gather at our own "Water Gate" to hear God's Word and be cleansed by it. Write a prayer in your journal asking God to cleanse you of the impurities that have recently contaminated you.

9. The people of Israel wisely decided to start the year not with revelry but by reading God's Word. Think about how you could

2 Washed by the Word

In the Bible, water is a symbol of purification. Ephesians 5:26 refers to the reason Jesus gave His life for His bride: "that He might sanctify and cleanse her with the washing of water by the word." Water can also represent the Holy Spirit (see John 7:37–39).

3 Led by the Word

Scribes were members of a learned class in ancient Israel who studied the Scriptures and served as copyists, editors, and teachers of God's Word. Priests officiated worship by making offerings, leading the people in confession, and acting as mediators between man and God. Ezra served in both functions.

5 Celebrate the Word

The first day of each month was considered a holy day marked by special sacrifices. *Tishri* was the seventh month (September/October), which occurred during the rainy season. In this month, the first day was known as the Feast of Trumpets, and it brought in the New Year.

incorporate God's Word into your next New Year's Day. After giving it some thought, memorialize it on your calendar.

10. Today's lesson revealed that the men, women, and children who were gathered understood God's Word. Write in your journal about something that this Bible study has clarified that you didn't understand before.

8 Cleansed by the Word

Jesus pronounced the disciples clean "because of the word" (John 15:3). Cleansing from sin is possible through the blood of Jesus for all who confess their sins. *Sanctification* is the process of God's grace by which the believer is separated from sin and becomes dedicated to God's righteousness.

10 The Word Understood

God has offered to give us understanding when it comes to His Word. James advised us to ask for wisdom, and God will generously provide it (see James 1:5). After all, "God is not the author of confusion but of peace" (1 Cor. 14:33).

———————

The March on Washington was more than a rise against discrimination. Some of the primary goals included improving housing, employment, and living wages for African Americans. Not all of the objectives were achieved, but Martin Luther King's speech helped galvanize the civil rights movement.

The march forced the United States government to take action on those pressing issues, and the Civil Rights Act was passed in 1964, a year after the march. The act outlawed discrimination based on race, color, religion, sex, or national origin and ended racial segregation in public places. The following year, the Voting Rights Act of 1965 banned racial discrimination in voting.[2]

The political climate finally reached a point when these issues were taken seriously. There was a national understanding and mainstream acceptance that laws had to change. The road from ignorance to understanding can be long and filled with pain, fear, and sacrifice.

Today, we learned that the Israelites finally reached a point of understanding and embraced their position in God's eyes. They were finally home, secure inside their walls, and ready to hear from God. Their understanding of Ezra's reading sparked a national movement.

Listen To ...

It ain't those parts of the Bible that I can't understand that bother me, it is the parts that I do understand.

—*Mark Twain*

Responding to the Word

Most people can hear, but not everyone listens. The website wikiHow.com provides a tutorial for anyone interested in learning how to listen. The article contends that relationships will improve and the world will be enriched when we give one another our full attention. Here are some suggestions:

- Remove distractions. Eliminate anything that distracts you from focusing on what is being said. This means no glancing at screens, reading, or engaging in other activities.
- Stay focused. Listen to the speaker's words and look at his or her expressions and body language. Avoid letting your mind wander, and don't formulate an argument or response while he or she is speaking.
- Be unselfconscious. Stop thinking about yourself.
- Be empathetic. Put yourself in the other person's shoes and look at the situation from his or her point of view.
- Become a better hearer. Tune in to the other person's tone, and let that help you interpret and understand.[3]

There are times when we are ready to listen and other times when it is a disciplined decision. The Israelites didn't need wikiHow.com to give them tips; they were ready to actively listen. They had just seen God's protection and were enjoying the completion of the wall. Now they were hungry for spiritual nourishment. Their hearts, bodies, and minds were ready to engage and listen.

Lift Up ...

Dear Lord, there are times when I hear Your Word, but I am not tuned in to listen with my heart and my mind. Prepare me to hear, listen, and respond as You would like. In Jesus' name. Amen.

Look At ...

Yesterday, we found the Israelites gathered at the Water Gate to hear Ezra read the book of the Law of Moses. The people were on a precipice of change as they came into the city of Jerusalem, surrounded by its restored wall. They were eager to hear, and they stood out of respect and reverence.

Today, we see the speaker on the specially made platform. Everything about this event was significant and dignified. Respected men stood on either side of Ezra. The Israelites who had been of a mind to work were now of a mind and heart to listen. Everything about their actions confirmed a worshipful attitude, a humble response, and a listening ear.

Read Nehemiah 8:4–6.

So Ezra the scribe stood on a platform of wood which they had made for the purpose; and beside him, at his right hand, stood Mattithiah, Shema, Anaiah, Urijah, Hilkiah, and Maaseiah; and at his left hand Pedaiah, Mishael, Malchijah, Hashum, Hashbadana, Zechariah, and Meshullam. And Ezra opened the book in the sight of all the people, for he was standing above all the people; and when he opened it, all the people stood up. And Ezra blessed the LORD, the great God. Then all the people answered, "Amen, Amen!" while lifting up their hands. And they bowed their heads and worshiped the LORD with their faces to the ground. Nehemiah 8:4–6

1. Where did Ezra stand to read the book of the law?

2. What practical purpose did this serve?

3. How many men stood on Ezra's right? How many on his left?

4. What sign of respect did the people show toward God's Word?

5. How did Ezra begin the Bible study?

6. What was the people's verbal response, and what did it signify?

7. What three physical positions did they assume to worship the Lord?

    1.

    2.

    3.

Live Out ...

8. Thirteen men stood beside Ezra as he began to read God's Word. Your pastor is one of the people entrusted with the responsibility to teach God's Word to you. Stand beside him or her today by writing a prayer in your journal, asking God to give your pastor strength and wisdom to boldly proclaim the Word to the people.

9. Today we saw three different positions for worshiping God: lifting hands, bowing heads, and faces to the ground. Which of these positions have you observed in worship? Which, if any, have you *never* used to worship the Lord?

10. Ezra blessed his great God. Now it's your turn. Choose one of the postures for worship listed above (try a new one if there's one you haven't experienced) and recite this psalm as a blessing to *your* great God.

2 Above the Crowd

Ezra stood on a wooden platform—a pulpit—above the people so they could better see and hear him. He faced the public square where the people stood, and the wall and gate behind him may have served as a sounding board to help project his voice to the vast assembly.[4]

3 At His Side

Leaders need people to stand by them for support. When Moses got weary during the battle against the Amalekites, Aaron and Hur "supported his hands, one on one side, and the other on the other side" (Ex. 17:12). Standing or sitting beside a leader is also an honor: James and John's mother asked that her two sons sit at Jesus' right and left in His kingdom (see Matt. 20:21).

6 Active Agreement

Amen means "so be it." It reinforces a statement or indicates agreement. The people agreed with Ezra as he blessed their great God. In Nehemiah 5:13, the people also said "amen" as they agreed that God would rebuke any Jew who exploited another for money.

Let us come before His presence with thanksgiving;

Let us shout joyfully to Him with psalms.

For the LORD is the great God,

And the great King above all gods. (Ps. 95:2–3)

----

8 A Few Good Men

The Bible gives examples of able men chosen to support a leader. Jesus chose twelve disciples to help Him. Moses, on the advice of his father-in-law, appointed worthy men to help him judge the people (see Ex. 18). David also had his mighty men of valor (see 1 Chron. 12:21).

9 A Posture of Worship

David lifted his hands in supplication (see Ps. 28:2). Jehoshaphat bowed his head with his face to the ground on the eve of battle and worshiped the Lord. The people of Judah also followed his example as they were given assurance of victory (see 2 Chron. 20:18).

In addition to giving undivided attention, the next part of wikiHow.com advises using open body language:

- Lean forward a little. This posture demonstrates that you are interested in what the speaker is saying.
- Make eye contact, but not too much. This indicates that the speaker has your attention. Be careful not to make the other person uncomfortable.
- Nod in acknowledgement. This shows that you are tracking with the conversation. A nod indicates you agree or want the other person to say more.
- Don't fidget or slouch. Show you are engaged by sitting up straight. Don't check your nails, tap your feet, or cross your arms.
- Use appropriate facial expressions. Demonstrate you are listening by reacting appropriately with your expressions, such as by smiling, laughing, frowning, or shaking your head.[5]

Everything about the Israelites' response to Ezra's reading of the Word indicated they were listening intently. They stood in respect, raised their hands in worship, and bowed in humility. There was no doubt that the message got through to them. They needed no lessons on showing their interest and agreement.

Listen To ...

Listen to God with a broken heart. He is not only the doctor who mends it, but also the father who wipes away the tears.

—Criss Jami

Restoration by the Word

The Getty Conservation Institute in Los Angeles has a mission to preserve the world's cultural heritage in the form of all types of visual arts. Toward this end, the institute publishes books that give instructions on the proper solvents to use when restoring various mediums of artistic works, such as tapestries, books, etchings, and paintings: "The cleaning of a work of art often involves removing not only dirt and grime but also unwanted layers of varnish, gilding, and paint from the work's surface. The challenge for conservators lies in finding a cleaning agent that will act on one layer without affecting the layer being preserved and without leaving any harmful residues on the cleaned work."[6]

These people care enough to preserve and restore works of art so that future generations can enjoy their beauty and impact. The first people to view and admire the original works were privileged to see them in their initial state. The rest of us rely on the help of experts who restore the works as closely as possible to the original so we can appreciate what the artist intended.

Today, we see the Levites as conservators of the Law of God. One thousand years had passed since the Law of Moses was given. The children of Israel in Nehemiah's time had undergone cultural, language, and social changes. The Levites removed the "layers" that kept them from appreciating the beauty of God's original words.

Lift Up ...

Dear Lord, nothing is as beautiful as Your unvarnished Word. Allow me to see Your pure intent and discover and enjoy this fascinating passage. In Jesus' name. Amen.

Look At ...

In yesterday's lesson, Ezra read the Law of Moses to spiritually hungry Israelites. The Word humbled them to submissive worship and inspired them to corporately agree with what they heard. We determined the difference between hearing and listening and saw the impact on their behavior.

1 Holy Teachers

The Levites were not to drink wine, were to distinguish between holy and unholy, and were to discern the difference between clean and unclean. In addition, they were to "teach the children of Israel all the statutes which the LORD [had] spoken to them by the hand of Moses" (Lev. 10:11).

In today's lesson, we find the names of men who helped the people understand the Word of God. There was cooperation between Nehemiah, the priests, and the Levites—all were united with the same purpose: to impart deeper understanding. These men looked solely to the book of the law as they instructed and guided the Jews. Although convicted by the Word, the people were encouraged to delight in God and respect the holy joy of the day.

Read Nehemiah 8:7–9.

Also Jeshua, Bani, Sherebiah, Jamin, Akkub, Shabbethai, Hodijah, Maaseiah, Kelita, Azariah, Jozabad, Hanan, Pelaiah, and the Levites, helped the people to understand the Law; and the people stood in their place. So they read distinctly from the book, in the Law of God; and they gave the sense, and helped them to understand the reading. And Nehemiah, who was the governor, Ezra the priest and scribe, and the Levites who taught the people said to all the people, "This day is holy to the LORD your God; do not mourn nor weep." For all the people wept, when they heard the words of the Law. Nehemiah 8:7–9

1. What specific group of men helped the people understand the Law? Why do you think God made sure their names were recorded?

2 Avid Learners

The Levites were probably scattered among the crowd. When there was a pause, these men interpreted what Ezra had read. This is a good formula for any Bible study: Discover: "What does it say?" Learn: "What does it mean?" Apply: "What does it mean to me?"

6 Joyful Worshipers

God wants us to experience balance in our spiritual lives—He wants us to be grieved over sin, but He also wants us to rejoice that we have been forgiven. "To everything there is a season ... a time to weep, and a time to laugh; a time to mourn, and a time to dance" (Eccl. 3:1, 4).

7 Simply God

The teaching of God's Word is a sacred and serious undertaking. It is the teacher's responsibility to make God's Word understandable and applicable. The late Chuck Smith advised teachers to "simply teach the Word of God simply."[7] Otherwise, it benefits no one.

2. What three steps did the Levites take to help the people comprehend the Law?

    1.

    2.

    3.

3. How do you know that hearing God's Word touched the people's heart?

4. Why do you think they wept and mourned?

5. Read James 4:8–10. Why was mourning an appropriate response to their sinful condition?

6. Who joined together to convince the people that the time for mourning was over?

Live Out ...

7. Today we saw that the Levites went out among the people to help them understand and apply God's Word to their lives.

    a. Name some of the people who come alongside you to bring understanding of God's Word.

    b. Write one of them a note, telling that person how he or she helped you. Deliver that note this week.

8. We also discovered that Nehemiah and the spiritual leaders comforted the people who mourned because of their failure to keep God's Law. Read Matthew 5:4.

    a. What did Jesus promise believers who mourn?

b. Do you accept comfort or do you find it hard to let go of guilt or blame?

9. a. Fill in the following chart to discover what God uses to comfort His people.

Scripture	Comforted By
Psalm 23:4	
Romans 15:4	
2 Corinthians 1:3–4	
Philippians 2:1	
1 Thessalonians 5:11	

8 A Time to Feast

According to verse 2, it was the beginning of the seventh month. This marked the Feast of Trumpets, which was celebrated by eating, drinking, and sharing. This was yet another reason why the Israelites were discouraged from mourning.

b. Write in your journal about how God has used one or more of the above to comfort you during the study of Nehemiah.

———————————

The restoration of fine works of art is a skill achieved only through experience and hard work. The craft is learned primarily through apprenticeship and a dedication to precision and patience. Good restorers study the artist's other work and learn the nuances of his or her style. There is no room for personal interpretation or inserting their personal preference—art restorers are technicians, not artists. Their purpose is to reveal what the artist originally intended to convey.

The Levites' right and privilege was to study the Law and lead the people in their understanding. Before teaching others, many years of studying were required. Clearly, the Spirit of God was also at work in their efforts.

Not only were the Levites able to explain what God was saying through the Law, but they also cleared a path for the people to have an encounter with the Master Creator Himself. In the same way some people react emotionally to a work of art, the Israelites' hearts were penetrated by the Holy Spirit, and they were brought to repentance. The highest aim of any restorer is to connect artists and their audience in the way the artists originally intended.

Listen To ...

Restoration and hope is available each time you return to God.

—*Jim George*

Rejoicing in the Word

In 1858 in Bologna, Italy, a Catholic housekeeper secretly baptized a sickly Jewish child named Edgardo Mortara, fearing he was about to die. When the story reached the Bologna inquisitor, an order was issued to kidnap the child and put him in a special monastery for Jews who were converted to Catholicism.

Edgardo was not returned to his family because it was believed that a Catholic child could not be raised in a Jewish home. News of the kidnapped child reached the attention of powerful people in Britain, France, and America. At the age of eighteen, Edgardo became an Augustinian priest.[8] He never returned to his heartbroken family, and he came to symbolize the dominance of the Catholic Church and, ultimately, the need for reform.

Like Edgardo Mortara, some kidnapped people are never allowed to return to their home and country. But this was not the case for the nation of Israel in Nehemiah's time. Almost 150 years earlier, the Babylonians had taken Judah captive. After many years in captivity, Ezra led the first group of returnees to Jerusalem, and Nehemiah led the second group that rebuilt the wall. During that time, much had changed and the people became disconnected from their God. Today, we see the continuation of this emotional reacquaintance with their identity as Jews, the Law, and God's joy.

Lift Up ...

Dear Lord, I am so joyful that You have promised to return for Your children—Your church. That is cause for celebration. In the meantime, I pray that in my weak, human life, others will see the strength and joy of my heavenly Father. In Jesus' name. Amen.

3 A New Start

New Year's Day was a holy day in God's eyes. The Law of Moses directed that this holiday should be observed by blowing the trumpets. Today, this event is known as *Rosh Hashanah*, literally "beginning of the year." It is a time of introspection and planning for the New Year.⁹

4 A Deep Joy

Joy depends not on circumstances but on fellowship with God. The joy of the Lord taps into the deepest springs of human emotion, providing supernatural strength. Ezra wanted the people to rejoice not in the strength of the walls but in God, the true source of strength.

Look At ...

Yesterday, we found a holy collaboration of people gathered for the purposes of studying the book of the law, understanding what they heard, rejoicing in their loving God, and being encouraged to do so with confidence and assurance. Following the conviction that came from understanding God's Word, they were led to gratefully and joyfully celebrate.

Today, we find the Jews in a blessed time of celebration and feasting. Coming together in their restored homeland was an event worthy of celebration, yet the people needed guidance in these activities. Ezra, Nehemiah, and the Levites told the people to be joyful, to eat and drink, and then to be thoughtful, worshipful, and at peace. With understanding came even greater joy.

Read Nehemiah 8:10–12.

Then he said to them, "Go your way, eat the fat, drink the sweet, and send portions to those for whom nothing is prepared; for this day is holy to our Lord. Do not sorrow, for the joy of the LORD is your strength." So the Levites quieted all the people, saying, "Be still, for the day is holy; do not be grieved." And all the people went their way to eat and drink, to send portions and rejoice greatly, because they understood the words that were declared to them. Nehemiah 8:10–12

1. How did Ezra instruct the people to celebrate?

2. How did he encourage them to be generous to those who could not afford to celebrate?

3. How did Ezra describe the day to the people?

4. What reason did he give for the people to celebrate rather than feel sorrowful?

5. Why do you think the Levites needed to quiet the people?

6. a. What was the first thing they told the people to do?

b. What reason did they give?

7. Why were they able to celebrate, share, and rejoice?

Live Out ...

8. Ezra encouraged the people to celebrate God's holy day, the Feast of Trumpets.

a. Which of the holy days centering on Christ do you celebrate?

b. How do you celebrate?

9. In this passage, we learned that one of the characteristics of true celebration is generosity to those in need. How will you be generous to the less fortunate during the next holy day you celebrate?

10. The Levites encouraged the people to be quiet and still. Now it's your turn. Turn off the TV or radio, take the phone off the hook, and be still for five to ten minutes (more if possible). Dwell on what you have learned from God and about God today. After your time of stillness, write in your journal about its impact on you.

_____

6 A Quiet Response

The human response to trouble is to *do* something about it. However, biblical wisdom tells us to wait on God, who will comfort and direct us. "Be still, and know that I am God" (Ps. 46:10) is one of the simplest commands yet one of the most difficult to carry out.

8 A Time of Reflection

The Jewish High Holy Days are the ten days between the holiday of Rosh Hashanah (Jewish New Year) and Yom Kippur (Day of Atonement). Jews are required to focus on repentance and atonement during this period. They mark the holiday with festive meals and prayer services.

10 A Godly Conduit

God bestows joy and spiritual strength and wants us to do likewise for others. Support those you know and love: (1) be a good listener, (2) offer sincere appreciation, (3) openly express love, (4) remind them that victory over adversity is possible, and (5) talk about heaven and the hope God offers.

On April 26, 2005, Jennifer Carol Wilbanks ran away from home and claimed that she had been kidnapped and assaulted. It was later revealed she was running away from her own wedding, and the media dubbed her the Runaway Bride. Her false claims could have led to jail time, but she was sentenced to two years of probation and 120 hours of community service instead. This bride-to-be went to a lot of trouble to avoid her wedding. The ensuing media circus spiraled out of control, causing frustration, pain, and embarrassment for everyone involved. What a waste. What should have been a time of joy and celebration turned into a national debacle.[10]

The nation of Israel had a completely different experience. They were, in essence, a kidnapped bride who was finally returning home to her groom. Ezra and Nehemiah called for the time of mourning to come to an end. Celebration was ushered in. What a relief it must have been for all these captives to finally be home.

Listen To ...

There is not one blade of grass, there is no color in this world
that is not intended to make us rejoice.

—*John Calvin*

Remembering the Word

On speaking of revival, James I. Packer stated:

> Revival is the visitation of God which brings to life Christians who have been sleeping and restores a deep sense of God's near presence and holiness. Thence springs a vivid sense of sin and a profound exercise of heart in repentance, praise, and love, with an evangelistic outflow. Each revival movement has its own distinctive features, but the pattern is the same every time. First God comes. On New Year's Eve 1739, John Wesley, George Whitefield, and some of their friends held a "love feast" which became a watch night of prayer to see the New Year in. At about three a.m., Wesley wrote, "The power of God came mightily upon us, insomuch that many cried for exceeding joy, and many fell to the ground."[11]

The first sign of revival is a sense of the Holy One's closeness, and the second is a love for the gospel as never before. The sense of God's nearness creates an overwhelming awareness of one's own sinfulness; therefore, the power of the cleansing blood of Christ is greatly appreciated, and repentance deepens.

During the Ulster Revival of the 1920s, shipyard workers brought back so many stolen tools that new sheds had to be built to house the recovered property! Repentance results in restitution. The final sign of a revival is that godliness multiplies, Christians mature, and converts emerge.

Paul was at Thessalonica for less than three weeks, but God worked quickly, and Paul left behind a dynamic church. In today's study, we see how the children of Israel experienced a revival as they hungered for God's Word and chose to obey His commands.

Lift Up ...

Dear Lord, I am seeking greater understanding of Your Word and deeper love for Your Son. I pray to be willing to always make my time with You a priority. In Jesus' name. Amen.

Look At ...

Yesterday, we pondered the Jews as they were tutored in the ways of celebration and feasting in a manner that propagated joy and pleased God. The leaders and teachers did not leave them to their old ways but led them in thankful worship. Almost in the same breath, the Jews were reminded that corporate celebration must be accompanied with private periods of calm reflection. As they grew in understanding, their joy was magnified.

Today, we see the Jews seeking out greater understanding of the Law. The traditions and admonitions that God established had fallen so far from their culture that Ezra had to read from the Law to reeducate them. They were to leave their normal comforts and dwell in structures made for this significant, reflective time. Resuming their lives as children of God required more than building new walls and gates; it required understanding and obeying God's Law.

Read Nehemiah 8:13–18.

Now on the second day the heads of the fathers' houses of all the people, with the priests and Levites, were gathered to Ezra the scribe, in order to understand the words of the Law. And they found written in the Law, which the LORD had commanded by Moses, that the children of Israel should dwell in booths during the feast of the seventh month, and that they should announce and proclaim in all their cities and in Jerusalem, saying, "Go out to the mountain, and bring olive branches, branches of oil trees, myrtle branches, palm branches, and branches of leafy trees, to make booths, as it is written." Then the people went out and brought them and made themselves booths, each one on the roof of his house, or in their courtyards or the courts of the house of God, and in the open square of the Water Gate and in the open square of the Gate of Ephraim. So the whole assembly of those who had returned from the captivity made booths and sat under the booths; for since the days of Joshua the son of Nun until that day the children of Israel had not done so. And there was very great gladness. Also day by day, from the first day until the last day, he read from the Book of the Law of God. And they kept the feast seven days; and on the eighth day there was a sacred assembly, according to the prescribed manner. Nehemiah 8:13–18

1. Who gathered on the day after Ezra's great assembly? What was their goal?

2. a. What did the Israelites find written in the Law?

b. How did it apply specifically to their circumstances?

3. How did the people obey what they had discovered in God's Law?

4. How many of the people participated?

5. When was the last time the Israelites celebrated this festival?

6. Do some research and find out how much time had elapsed between the days of Joshua and Ezra and Nehemiah's time. (*Hint: study Bibles often include timelines.*)

7. How did the Israelites respond to the reinstitution of this festival?

Live Out ...

8. If we fail to stay in God's Word consistently, we might forget to obey some of His commands. The word *remember* is mentioned over 160 times in the Bible. Fill in the chart below to discover some of the things believers are commanded to remember.

1 Spiritual Craving

A taste of God's Word brings a craving for more. One day of Bible study is not enough; it must become a part of our daily routine. Just as we eat and drink for physical nourishment, we must partake of God's Word for spiritual suste-nance (see Matt. 5:6).

2 Wanderings Remembered

Following the New Year's celebration, the next festival on the Jewish calendar was the Feast of Booths or Tabernacles. This festival was observed in the seventh month to commemorate the Israelites' wandering in the wilderness. The Israelites were to live outdoors in booths made of palm and willow trees.

6 A Neglected Festival

This feast had been cel-ebrated in King Solomon's day (see 2 Chron. 8:13) and in Ezra's (see Ezra 3:1–4), but apparently not all participated fully by constructing the booths and living in them for the duration of the feast. The joyful participation by every family had not been seen since Joshua's time.

Scripture   **Remember**

Exodus 20:8

Psalm 105:5

Malachi 4:4

Acts 20:29–31

Romans 11:18

Ephesians 2:11–12

2 Timothy 2:8

Jude 17

9 Deliberately Forgotten

God asks you to remember His Word and obey it. When you remember Him and follow His ways, He chooses to forget your sin: "For I will be merciful to their unrighteousness, and their sins and their lawless deeds I will remember no more" (Heb. 8:12).

10 Reconciled to Righteousness

It is God's desire to reconcile His people to Himself: "Thus says the LORD of hosts: 'Return to Me,' says the LORD of hosts, 'and I will return to you,' says the LORD of hosts" (Zech. 1:3).

9.   a. Which of the above have you forgotten?

b. How will you respond now that you have been reminded?

10. This week, we discovered that hearing or reading God's Word results in worship, repentance, rejoicing, and remembrance. With this in mind, complete the following exercise in your journal.

I respond in worship to God because He is:

His Word has shown me that I must repent of:

I rejoice because God has:

I desire to always remember:

———————————

A woman reportedly asked American evangelist Billy Sunday, "Why do you keep having revivals when it doesn't last?" Sunday responded by asking, "Why do you keep taking baths?"

We keep seeking God because our hunger for Him can never be completely sated and we long for more. That is part of the wonder and beauty of living our lives for God. It is true that no celebration can last forever, but revival, an awakening to the character and holiness of God, is something we can keep alive in our lives and in the body of Christ around us.

Billy Graham once said, "If we ever needed guidance, if we ever needed stability, if we ever needed strength, if we ever needed faith, if we ever needed integrity, if we ever needed righteousness, if we ever needed a Heaven-sent revival it is at this present hour."[12] The Israelites were at the hour of revival and they hungered for more of God's Word. They demonstrated obedience by celebrating as God had originally intended.

There is so much we can do to ignite a passion in our own lives; it starts with prayer and God's Word. Time spent pursuing these two activities will never be wasted. Be a passionate woman of God of whom it can be said, "She lives her life in obedience to God."

Listen To ...

A true revival means nothing less than a revolution, casting out the spirit of worldliness and selfishness, and making God and His love triumph in the heart and life.

—Andrew Murray

Confession Is Good for the Soul

Nehemiah 9

In 1737 America saw a great revival led by George Whitefield. Over a period of only six weeks, Whitefield preached over 175 sermons to tens of thousands of people, sparking an overwhelming spiritual revival. Even now it is considered one of the most remarkable periods of American Christianity.

His approach was simple: he preached the Word of God. On many occasions, he said, "When the Word is proclaimed, lives change! When true repentance takes place, it will entirely change you. The bias of your souls will be changed, then you will delight in God, in Christ, in His law, and in His people."[1] George Whitefield was a preacher of extraordinary power who relied solely on God's Word and the work of the Holy Spirit to attract people from every rank and station in life to confess their sin and repent.

In the ninth chapter of Nehemiah, we see the nation of Israel respond to God's Word through the confession of sin and repentance, which resulted in a great revival among God's people. This week we have the opportunity to come with open hearts and open minds to see who God is, what He has done, and what He desires for our lives. Maybe, like the Israelites, we will experience a personal revival that will spread to those around us.

Day 1

We Bless His Name

Lift Up ...

Dear Lord, help me make an honest appraisal of my life. If I am doing anything that is not pleasing to You, lead me to prompt and sincere repentance. In Jesus' name. Amen.

Look At ...

We come to this chapter from a high point in the book of Nehemiah. The people had heard the Law read to them and gained a deeper, stronger understanding of it. They reinstituted long-neglected festivals and celebrations, giving themselves over to God's will and Word. The Israelites were reconnecting to their heritage and faith and, more importantly, to obedience. They had just observed the Feast of Tabernacles.

Now we see the people embark on a sacred assembly. They did not come to celebrate—far from it. Convicted of their sins, they came for the solemn purpose of repenting. They made confession not only for themselves but also for their fathers before them. The result was tears. Regret. Personal cleansing. And the kind of worship that comes from broken hearts fully aware of a holy God.

Read Nehemiah 9:1–6.

Now on the twenty-fourth day of this month the children of Israel were assembled with fasting, in sackcloth, and with dust on their heads. Then those of Israelite lineage separated themselves from all foreigners; and they stood and confessed their sins and the iniquities of their fathers. And they stood up in their place and read from the Book of the Law of the LORD their God for one-fourth of the day; and for another fourth they confessed and worshiped the Lord their God. Then Jeshua, Bani,

1 A Humbled Gathering

This great, humble gathering took place two days after the end of the celebration of the Feast of Tabernacles, a time to commemorate the years of wandering in the wilderness before the children of Israel occupied the Promised Land. As we've learned, the seventh month of *Tishri* corresponds to September/October and was the time for harvesting.

2 A Denial of Comfort

Wearing sackcloth indicated an individual's penitence for his or her sin. The garments were itchy, miserable, and self-afflicting. Fasting was observed as a denial of the flesh. The Israelites separated themselves and confessed their sins. Reading the Law had revealed their failure.

4 An Epic Prayer

The stairs of the Levites probably led to the elevated platform mentioned in Nehemiah 8:4, where Ezra stood when he read from the book of the law. According to tradition, Ezra stood again before the people to pray a great prayer, the longest prayer in the Bible (see Neh. 9:5–38).

Kadmiel, Shebaniah, Bunni, Sherebiah, Bani, and Chenani stood on the stairs of the Levites and cried out with a loud voice to the LORD their God. And the Levites, Jeshua, Kadmiel, Bani, Hashabniah, Sherebiah, Hodijah, Shebaniah, and Pethahiah, said: "Stand up and bless the LORD your God forever and ever! Blessed be Your glorious name, which is exalted above all blessing and praise! You alone are the LORD; You have made heaven, the heaven of heavens, with all their host, the earth and everything on it, the seas and all that is in them, and You preserve them all. The host of heaven worships You." Nehemiah 9:1–6

1. On what day of the month did the Israelites assemble? Refer again to Nehemiah 8:2 to learn which month this was, and record it here.

2. a. How was the physical state of the people described?
   b. Which group of people separated themselves to confess their sin?

3. a. How many hours of the day did they listen to the reading of the Law?
   b. How many hours were spent confessing and worshiping God?

4. a. Who are those named as standing on the stairs of the Levites?
   b. What did they do?

5. Of the groups of men named in verse 5, which ones are the same as those named in verse 4?

6. For what reasons did the people bless God?

7. Using your own words, rephrase the praise and adoration the people gave to the Lord.

Live Out ...

8. In response to God's Word, the Israelites realized and admitted they had sinned and confessed their sin before God. Is there any sin you need to confess before God today? Remember, God shows us our sin not just so we can humbly confess it but so that we can walk in a way that pleases Him. Confess and walk in obedience before Him today!

9. After confessing their sin, the people of Israel stood up and blessed the Lord. The word *bless* is recorded in the Bible 331 Times. Look up the word *bless* in a Bible dictionary, and record the definition. Search your Bible concordance for the word *bless*, and write out your favorite verse blessing God.

10. The doxology sung in many Protestant churches around the world praises God in this way:

> Praise God from whom all blessings flow.
> Praise Him, all creatures here below.
> Praise Him above all heavenly host.
> Praise Father, Son, and Holy Ghost.

    a. What does the doxology praise God for?

    b. Who should praise Him?

    c. Praise Him in the fullness of the Father, Son, and Holy Ghost. What other characteristics can you think of that would expand your worship? List them in your journal.

8 A Missed Mark

The word *sin* is an Old English archery term that conveys the idea of missing the mark.[2] If one did not hit the bull's-eye, whether missed by an inch or a foot, that person would say he or she *sinned*. We sin when we miss God's target for our lives.

10 A Blessed God

What a beautiful blessing the people offered to God. First, His name was blessed and raised up above all things. He was blessed because He was and is the only God; He is the Creator of all, and all heaven worships Him. Recognize Him today as your God above all gods.

———————

Through the ministry of George Whitefield, many in America responded to the Word of God. Benjamin Franklin estimated that Whitefield's booming voice could be heard clearly, without amplification, by up to thirty thousand people at one time. He wrote about Whitefield's impact on society:

> From being thoughtless and indifferent about religion, it seemed as if all the world were growing religious, so that one could not walk through Philadelphia in the evening without hearing Psalms sung in different families of every street.[3]

As with the Israelites, confession of sin, repentance, and salvation resulted in praise and worship to God due to Whitefield's efforts and God's ever-inspiring Word. The same is true today. God can use one person to achieve His purposes. People still crave truth; they still crave God.

Listen To ...

We need a broken heart to mourn our own sins, but a whole heart to praise the Lord's perfections.
—*Charles H. Spurgeon*

We Hear His Call

Consider this scenario: Sarah cautiously opened her email, hoping to see the notice that would reveal whether she had passed her teaching credential exams. Had the years of study paid off? Her eyes fell on one word: *pass*. She jumped up from her chair and rejoiced in her hard-earned new title. Now she was officially an educator. She finally felt noticed, validated, and respected. She had a new identity. But was it enough?

Our identities can be wrapped up in many different things. Our names and our professions speak loudly to others and to ourselves about who we are and how we live. Just as God gave Abraham in the Old Testament, He has given you a new name and a new identity. You are His. As a believer, you have been called by a new name. You are now called beloved, daughter, forgiven, redeemed, blessed, holy, and a treasure. He has called you to Himself for a glorious purpose. Remember how God sees you today, and let this beautiful truth define who you are.

Lift Up ...

Dear Lord, I thank You for calling me to be Your child. With that, I became a new person with a new standing in Your eyes. Whatever my worldly identity, it will not last forever, but my life hidden with Christ in God will endure for eternity. In Jesus' name. Amen.

Look At ...

Yesterday, we considered the Israelites' sacred assembly and their holy purpose. They were not gathered for a celebration; instead, they were united by their sinful nature that brought confession. They realized sinfulness had been present in the lives of their ancestors and that they were no better than those who had come before. In tears, acutely aware of their sin and the holiness of God, they asked for cleansing.

1 A Change of Name

When God chose Abram
and revealed Himself
to him, it was an act of
absolute grace, for Abram
was once an idolater in a
foreign land. God changed
his name from Abram to
Abraham, which means
"father of a multitude."
His new name matched
God's promise to make
him a great nation.

Today, we review the time when God found Abraham to be faithful and so made a covenant with him. In this lesson we find the people remembering their ever-faithful God who kept His promises, often miraculously. He was aware of the enemies in hot pursuit of His children. He heard their cries and provided a way. He bowed to no obstacle, and He made His presence known—both day and night. In the darkest of times, He shed His light to guide them to safety.

Read Nehemiah 9:7–12.

You are the LORD *God, who chose Abram, and brought him out of Ur of the Chaldeans, and gave him the name Abraham; You found his heart faithful before You, and made a covenant with him to give the land of the Canaanites, the Hittites, the Amorites, the Perizzites, the Jebusites, and the Girgashites—to give it to his descendants. You have performed Your words, for You are righteous. You saw the affliction of our fathers in Egypt, and heard their cry by the Red Sea. You showed signs and wonders against Pharaoh, against all his servants, and against all the people of his land. For You knew that they acted proudly against them. So You made a name for Yourself, as it is this day. And You divided the sea before them, so that they went through the midst of the sea on the dry land; and their persecutors You threw into the deep, as a stone into the mighty waters. Moreover You led them by day with a cloudy pillar, and by night with a pillar of fire, to give them light on the road which they should travel.* Nehemiah 9:7–12

1. a. From what country did God choose Abram?

    b. What was it about Abram that caused God to choose him?

2. In the covenant God made, the lands of which tribes were given to Abraham?

3. What things did the Levites praise God for in regard to His dealings with Abraham?

4. What did God know about Pharaoh and the Egyptians?

5. What do you think it means that God "made a name for" Himself?

6. a. What did God do to enable Moses and the Israelites to pass through the Red Sea?
    b. What was His punishment for their pursuers?

7. God used wondrous means to lead His people.
    a. How did He lead them during the day?
    b. How did He lead them at night?
    c. Can you sense how He is leading you through life?

Live Out ...

8. Through the testimony of these verses, we see God's faithfulness and display of power in Israel's history. From Abraham forward, it had been all about Him every step of the way. It was His story. Looking back at your own life, think of key moments of God's faithfulness. God is working out His story in you too.

9. Psalms 105–107 provide another look at the same ground covered in Nehemiah 9:7–12.

3 An Unconditional Covenant

God gave His people the land through an unconditional covenant He made with Abraham (see Gen. 15:9–20). In other words, God required nothing of Abraham to receive the land. "You have performed your words" (Neh. 9:8) conveys the sense that God's promise was made solely upon God's character.

5 A Reputation of Strength

God made such a name for Himself that during the time of Rahab and the spies, His reputation spread all the way to Jericho. The people of that day were fearful of what He might do to them. Kings, warriors, and nations knew to fear the God of Abraham, Isaac, and Jacob.

8 Prayers for a Nation

Three of Israel's great national prayers are recorded in Ezra 9; Nehemiah 9; and Daniel 9. The promise of 2 Chronicles 7:14 and Moses' intercession for the people in Exodus 32:31–33 are two other prominent national prayers.

10 Singled Out

The word *chosen* means specially selected or singled out from others for a special service or station. Believers are chosen people set apart to receive His Word and worship Him. God has chosen you purely because of His love and grace. "You did not choose me, but I chose you" (John 15:16 NIV).

a. Read the following Scripture verses and complete the table, showing how the Psalms are related specifically to Nehemiah 9:7–12.

Scripture	How the Verses Are Related
Psalm 105:7–10	
Psalm 105:44	
Psalm 106:9–11	

b. Which passage ministers to you today and why?

10. Like Abraham, you were chosen by God to be His own. Read 1 Peter 2:9.

a. What does this passage say about who you are?

b. What have you been called out of?

c. What are you called into?

d. In light of this passage, how should you be living?

———————————

As a child, Queen Victoria of England was feisty and noncompliant. Unaware that she was next in line for the throne, Victoria would slack off in her studies, pull pranks on others, and simply be naughty. Distraught by their daughter's behavior, Victoria's parents sat her down and explained her royal heritage. They told her that she was next in line to be the queen of England. After a lengthy explanation, Victoria stood up and humbly replied, "I understand. From now on, I shall be good." Upon recognition that she was of royal lineage, her behavior forever changed.[4]

As we reflect on our identity in Christ, we too should respond to the royal calling we have been given. We are a chosen people, called out of darkness and into God's light. Allow His light to shine through your life.

Listen To ...

The true calling of a Christian is not to do extraordinary things,
but to do ordinary things in an extraordinary way.

—*Dean Stanley*

We Remember His Faithfulness

When God's people crossed the Jordan River into the Promised Land, God told Joshua to choose twelve men. Each one took a stone from the middle of the river, and Joshua placed them together as a tangible reminder of what God had done that day. When future generations asked, "What do these stones mean?" they would be told about God's faithfulness, both to hold back the waters while the children of Israel crossed the Jordan River and to defeat their enemies.

As believers, we often keep tangible items that help remind us of what God has done. Maybe it's a card from someone who prayed for us during a trial or a flower pressed in the Bible at a special time of worship. When we see those simple things, we remember God's faithfulness, and we are encouraged.

Our mementos can also help our children and friends see that God's hand has been mighty in our lives, and, therefore, they serve as faith-builders to others.

Lift Up ...

Dear Lord, help me always remember the glorious things You have done for me. In the small and the great, open my understanding to Your overriding presence in my life. More than all else, make me mindful of how You gave Your Son, Jesus, so I could gain eternal life. In Jesus' name. Amen.

Look At ...

Yesterday, we studied the Israelites' remembrances of their remarkable God. They recalled the relationship between God and Abraham—the man found worthy of a covenant-promise from the God of the universe. Then, as the Israelites were being pursued by the Egyptians, God enabled His children to pass on dry land by temporarily stacking the waters of the Red Sea. Once they had safely passed through the Red Sea, He unstacked the waters and subsequently drowned the Egyptians. The memories of God's faithfulness were glorious and miraculous and brought the Israelites to a place of worship.

Today, we study the period when God gave the Israelites the Law and the commandments. This passage is rich with the history of God's faithfulness and patience in contrast with the people's hard and prideful responses. In the afterglow of a miraculous rescue, they were forgetful and stubborn. Yet God was there day and night for forty years—a visible, loving presence. He met all of their physical needs—feeding and clothing them and giving them water to drink.

Read Nehemiah 9:13–21.

You came down also on Mount Sinai, and spoke with them from heaven, and gave them just ordinances and true laws, good statutes and commandments. You made known to them Your holy Sabbath, and commanded them precepts, statutes and laws, by the hand of Moses Your servant. You gave them bread from heaven for their hunger, and brought them water out of the rock for their thirst, and told them to go in to possess the land which You had sworn to give them. But they and our fathers acted proudly, hardened their necks, and did not heed Your commandments. They refused to obey, and they were not mindful of Your wonders that You did among them. But they hardened their necks, and in their rebellion they appointed a leader to return to their bondage. But You are God, ready to pardon, gracious and merciful, slow to anger, abundant in kindness, and did not forsake them. Even when they made a molded calf for themselves, and said, "This is your god that brought you up out of Egypt," and worked great provocations, yet in Your manifold mercies You did not forsake them in the wilderness. The pillar of the cloud did not depart from them by day, to lead them on the road; nor the pillar of fire by night, to show them light, and the way they should go. You also gave Your good Spirit to instruct them, and did not withhold Your manna from their mouth, and gave them water for their thirst. Forty years You sustained them in the wilderness; they lacked nothing; their clothes did not wear out and their feet did not swell. Nehemiah 9:13–21

1. a. From which mountain did God speak?

    b. What was His primary purpose for speaking to the Israelites?

2 A Day for the Lord

Before Moses' encounter with God, there had never been a command to remember this day in any special way. "The Sabbath is a means by which our living pattern imitates God's. Work is followed by rest and is a time for God's people to think about and enjoy what God has accomplished."[5]

6 A Glorious Pardon

We can see the disparity between God's merciful nature and the Israelites' stubbornness. God's gracious answer to Israel's rebellion was a glorious readiness to pardon. Even now, God is ready to pardon those who are ready to repent and receive Him.

7 A Faithful Guide

Despite their disobedience, God did not abandon His people but continued to give them signs and wonders revealing the way they should go. He has given us the Bible and the power of the Holy Spirit within us to lead and guide our every step.

2. God made known a commandment about the Sabbath. Read Deuteronomy 5:12. Which commandment was this?

3. The other name for bread from heaven is _____. Read about the water from the rock in Exodus 17:6. What was Moses required to do with the rock?

4. a. What were the people told to do?
    b. What did God swear to give them?

5. List the ways the people showed their disdain for God and His commands.

6. What attributes of God kept Him from forsaking His people?

7. a. What "god" did the people make for themselves?
    b. What did they say about this "god"?

Live Out ...

8. God never failed His rebellious people. In the face of their hard hearts, God continued to lead and guide them every day. This brings us to an analysis of our own behavior.

a. Has your heart become hardened in some area?

b. Are you acting out in rebellion or disobedience?

c. Before you begin this portion of the day's lesson, pray that God will reveal how He wants you to change.

9. Although today a pillar of fire does not lead us, we have been given something far greater: the Holy Spirit's constant presence in our lives.

    a. Have you ever heard God's still, small voice?

    b. How does God communicate with you?

    c. How do you know when you have grieved Him by your actions?

10. After repeatedly experiencing God's deliverance and mercy, the children of Israel finally offered their gratitude and devotion to God.

    a. What are some ways you can express your gratitude for what God has done for you?

    b. Who would be blessed to hear your testimony?

8 A Grieved Lord

A hardened heart can be defined as a feeling of destitution and insensitivity to spiritual things, stubbornness, or self-willed behavior. The Pharisees' hard hearts grieved Jesus. They esteemed religion over compassion (see Mark 3:5).

9 Glorious Signs

From this pillar of cloud and fire, Jehovah was visibly present with Israel. This fire was the same as that in which the Lord revealed Himself in the burning bush and afterward descended upon Sinai amid thunder and lightning in a thick cloud (see Ex. 19:16–18).[6]

You've probably heard the expression "Tie a string around your finger so you won't forget!" In our busy lives, it is easy to forget things, but God doesn't want us to forget what He has done for us. The prayer in Nehemiah 9 called the children of Israel to remember the great and mighty things God had done for His people.

Often in Scripture, we too are called to remember. As believers, we take the Lord's Supper as a reminder of what Christ accomplished at the cross. Jesus said, "Do this in remembrance of Me" (Luke 22:19). As we take time in Communion to remember what it cost Him to accomplish the forgiveness of our sin, let's rejoice in the sweet sacrifice of Jesus, and may our remembrance shine through in a life of gratitude and joy.

Listen To ...

We should take all occasions to tell one another of the great
and kind things which God has done for us.

—Matthew Henry

DAY 4

We Disobey Him

In December 2004, a mighty tsunami brought devastation to Indonesia. But on the small island closest to the epicenter of the earthquake, a remarkable series of events unfolded that resulted in a high survival rate.

When a great earthquake shook the ground beneath them, the residents of Simeulue Island remembered stories they had heard from their grandparents. Growing up, they were told of the 1907 earthquake and the subsequent tsunami that killed thousands of people. The memory of those tales now served as an alarm to the current inhabitants. They knew they must take the earthquake seriously and quickly flee to higher ground before they were struck by the inevitable tsunami. Of the seventy-five thousand inhabitants of Simeulue Island, only seven lost their lives that day when thirty-foot waves hit the island only thirty minutes after the earthquake.[7]

In our reading this week, Israel was reminded of the disobedience of previous generations. Stories of their history were read as a needed reminder for the people to learn from and avoid making the same mistakes.

The lesson remains for us: if we hear or see warning signs in our lives today, it's time to run from our sin to the higher ground of obedience and God's forgiving grace.

Lift Up ...

Dear Lord, give me Your eyes to see the disobedience in my life. If I am deluding myself with a false sense of security, remind me of the dire consequences of disobedience. If I am grieving the Holy Spirit, make me grieved about it in my own spirit. In Jesus' name. Amen.

Look At ...

Yesterday, we saw God in all His grace and justice. He gave His people the Law and the commandments. In characteristic fashion, the Israelites exhibited their inclination to wander away from God and forget His faithful presence. In spite of His visible presence, His miraculous salvation from their enemies, and His constancy to meet their needs for food, water, and clothing, they were stubbornly disobedient.

Today, we see a litany of God's grace and mercy and the Israelites' continual pride and disobedience. It seemed that the more mercy and love God granted, the more the Israelites determined to shrug their shoulders, stiffen their necks, and turn deaf ears. On the heels of punishment, there were only brief periods of insight and joy.

Read Nehemiah 9:22–31.

Moreover You gave them kingdoms and nations, and divided them into districts. So they took possession of the land of Sihon, the land of the king of Heshbon, and the land of Og king of Bashan. You also multiplied their children as the stars of heaven, and brought them into the land which You had told their fathers to go in and possess. So the people went in and possessed the land; You subdued before them the inhabitants of the land, the Canaanites, and gave them into their hands, with their kings and the people of the land, that they might do with them as they wished. And they took strong cities and a rich land, and possessed houses full of all goods, cisterns already dug, vineyards, olive groves, and fruit trees in abundance. So they ate and were filled and grew fat, and delighted themselves in Your great goodness. Nevertheless they were disobedient and rebelled against You, cast Your law behind their backs and killed Your prophets, who testified against them to turn them to Yourself; and they worked great provocations. Therefore You delivered them into the hand of their enemies, who oppressed them; and in the time of their trouble, when they cried to You, You heard from heaven; and according to Your abundant mercies You gave them deliverers who saved them from the hand of their enemies. But after they had rest, they again did evil before You. Therefore You left them in the hand of their enemies, so that they had dominion over them; yet when they returned and cried out to You, You heard from heaven; and many times You delivered them according to Your mercies, and testified against them, that You might bring them back to Your law. Yet they acted proudly, and did not heed Your commandments, but sinned against Your judgments, "Which if a man does, he shall live by them." And they shrugged their shoulders, stiffened their necks, and would not hear. Yet for many years You had patience with them, and testified against them by Your Spirit in Your prophets. Yet they would not listen; therefore You gave them into the hand of the peoples of the lands. Nevertheless in Your great mercy You did not utterly consume them nor forsake them; for You are God, gracious and merciful. Nehemiah 9:22–31

1. a. What were the children given?

    b. What lands did they possess?

2. What analogy was used to illustrate the phrase *multiplied their children?*

3. a. What were the Israelites told to do next?

    b. What did God do to the Canaanites?

4. What seven things did God provide for His people in the land of Canaan?

    1.

    2.

    3.

    4.

    5.

    6.

    7.

5. How did the people respond to God's provision?

1 The Land of God

Around 1405 BC, the Israelites entered Canaan to claim the land that had been promised to them. Although promised to the children of Israel for an everlasting possession, their retention of it was conditional on their faithful fulfillment of its covenant obligations.[8] They were fully aware that the land, first and foremost, belonged to God.

3 The Children of Privilege

In the verses above, the conquest of these two kingdoms is named first because they preceded the possession of Canaan (see Num. 21:21–35). After this, the multiplication of the children of the Israelites is mentioned because the fathers had died in the wilderness and only their children were allowed to come into the land of Canaan.

6 The Pride of Prosperity

The Israelites remembered their vicious cycle of sin and rebellion. They enjoyed prosperity, became prideful, and lapsed into apostasy. God judged them and gave them over to the enemy. In desperation, they became repentant and cried out to God, who once again redeemed them. This cycle would be repeated many times over several hundred years.

6. a. The people exhibited five behaviors that angered God. What were they?

    1.

    2.

    3.

    4.

    5.

    b. How did God respond to their rebellion?

7. What parts of Israel's sin cycle do you see being repeated in today's passage? Record the phrases from the above passage that correspond to the portion of the sin cycle they were in.

❑ They enjoyed prosperity:

❑ They became prideful:

❑ They lapsed into apostasy:

❑ God judged and gave them to the enemy:

❑ They repented and cried out for a deliverer:

❑ God redeemed them:

Live Out ...

8. In Proverbs 30:8–9, Agur prayed, "Give me neither poverty nor riches—feed me with the food allotted to me; lest I be full and deny You, and say, 'Who is the LORD?'" The Israelites turned their backs on God during times of prosperity. Have you noticed in your own life that when things are going well, you become less prayerful and dependent on God? How can you change this dangerous pattern?

9. God's mercy abounded toward Israel, as seen in the prayer of Nehemiah 9. Verse 31 states, "In Your great mercy You did not

utterly consume them nor forsake them; for You are God, gracious and merciful."

a. Have you ever struggled with the sense that your sin is so great you could never be fully forgiven?

b. What hope do you find in God's grace and mercy?

c. On what basis can you plead for and claim God's mercy and forgiveness for your sin?

9 Ministry of Mercy

In Scripture, the word *mercy* carries the meaning of kindness and compassion. It could be described as not getting what you deserve, yet it is much more than that. Mercy is said to be a kindly ministry of love to bring relief from one's suffering and need.

10. Read 1 John 1:9.

a. How important is confession leading to repentance in your walk with God? How often do you confess to God?

❑ Immediately after sinning

❑ Daily

❑ Weekly

❑ Once a month

b. When you confess, is your heart repentant? Read Psalm 51. David wrote this psalm when reminded of his sin with Bathsheba. What is the main point of verses 3 and 4?

c. In your journal, write a prayer that incorporates your own confession to God.

10 Acknowledgement of Guilt

Confession describes the acknowledgment of sin. It implies yielding or changing convictions. Real confession recognizes that God is right and I am wrong. It admits that one is guilty of what he is accused. Confession is agreeing with God on these counts.

Around the time of the Civil War, Joseph Dixon began designing and producing the pencil. The only meaningful change that has been made to the pencil since that time has been the addition of the eraser.[9] A whole new world opened up with this small rubber tip added to the other end of the black lead point. Now, not only can we scribble, compose, sketch, and write with this instrument, but we can also quickly correct an error, change a figure, or start all over.

Every day, Christians write words and deeds on the record of their own lives. But as we seek the Lord and reflect on His Word, we become aware that some of our attitudes, thoughts, and actions are not pleasing to the Lord. Graciously, these sins are forgiven and fellowship with God is restored through honest confession and repentance. First John 1:9 is the eraser that gives us a new beginning!

Listen To ...

To be a Christian means to forgive the inexcusable, because
God has forgiven the inexcusable in you.

—C. S. Lewis

DAY 5

We Confess and Repent of Sin

Before the Civil War, America was in need of change. Abraham Lincoln brought to light the truth that all men are created equal and that no man should be enslaved. At the same time, Harriet Beecher Stowe wrote *Uncle Tom's Cabin*. Her words showed the cruelty and injustice that African Americans bore upon their backs. The book influenced the country and aided in the abolition of slavery after the Civil War.

On one occasion, Abraham Lincoln stated that Stowe was "the little woman who wrote the book that started this great war."[10] People like Lincoln and Stowe helped to change our nation's moral compass.

After the prayer of Nehemiah 9, Israel recognized their need to reset their national moral compass. God had previously spoken to them in 2 Chronicles 7:14 and showed them the way to change. He declared to King Solomon, "If My people who are called by My name will humble themselves, and pray and seek My face, and turn from their wicked ways, then I will hear from heaven, and will forgive their sin and heal their land."

Today, we must humbly come to the Lord in prayer, confession, and repentance. He sees us and hears our prayers whether we come to Him individually, corporately, or as a nation.

Lift Up ...

Dear Lord, I want to recognize my own sin and repent before I have to deal with long-term consequences. I know I am susceptible to the temptations of the world, the flesh, and the Devil. But I pray that my heart is always openly vulnerable to You, Your Word, and Your love. Make me stronger than I am without You. In Jesus' name. Amen.

Look At ...

Yesterday, we studied the Lord's astonishing grace and mercy in light of the Israelites' recurrent disobedience. We found that continual rejection of God results in apathy, pride, and selective hearing. Even in the rare moments of obedience and the resulting joy, the children of Israel were quick to turn to their rebellious ways.

Today, we see what happened as a result of having the Law read to them. The Israelites recognized their sins, confessed, and repented. They spent time memorializing all the things their great God had done for them. They knew He was a covenant-keeper, a merciful judge, a listener, a lawgiver, a generous rewarder, and a bountiful King of Kings. Today we see them at the point of making and sealing their covenant with God.

Read Nehemiah 9:32–38.

Now therefore, our God, the great, the mighty, and awesome God, who keeps covenant and mercy: do not let all the trouble seem small before You that has come upon us, our kings and our princes, our priests and our prophets, our fathers and on all Your people, from the days of the kings of Assyria until this day. However You are just in all that has befallen us; for You have dealt faithfully, but we have done wickedly. Neither our kings nor our princes, our priests nor our fathers, have kept Your law, nor heeded Your commandments and Your testimonies, with which You testified against them. For they have not served You in their kingdom, or in the many good things that You gave them, or in the large and rich land which You set before them; nor did they turn from their wicked works. Here we are, servants today! And the land that You gave to our fathers, to eat its fruit and its bounty, here we are, servants in it! And it yields much increase to the kings You have set over us, because of our sins; also they have dominion over our bodies and our cattle at their pleasure; and we are in great distress. And because of all this, we make a sure covenant and write it; our leaders, our Levites, and our priests seal it. Nehemiah 9:32–38

1. What title was given to God? Look back at Nehemiah 1:5 to see what attributes God demonstrated that resulted in the same title.

2. The people didn't want God to regard the troubles they were dealing with as _____.

3. a. How is God described here?

b. How had He previously dealt with the Israelites?

4. God dealt faithfully, but His people confessed, "But we have done _____." What had they failed to do?

5. What word did the Israelites use twice to describe themselves?

6. What was responsible for yielding the increase?

7. What were the three groups of people who sealed the covenant?
1.
2.
3.

Live Out ...

8. Read 2 Chronicles 7:14. Restate the verse in your own words, and tell how God expects believers to live and what He will do for us when we obey.

9. a. Do you think it is still true to say, "Neither our president nor our elected officials, our pastors nor our fathers, have served You with their whole hearts in Your kingdom, or in the many good things that You have given us, or in this large and rich land which You set before us; nor have we turned from our own wicked ways"?

1 A Recovered Life

Through the humility depicted in verse 32, it is evident that revival in the heart of Israel had begun. The word *revival* means to recover life and vigor and to return to consciousness. It also refers to one who has life, dies, and then is revived.

4 Sins of the Nation

Every level of society was mentioned twice in two verses. It was vital to remember that from the king down to the commoner, the people had neglected to do what they should have done. They identified with the sin of the nation and also acknowledged their own personal guilt.

7 A Future Commitment

Israel came to make a covenant with God—even writing it down to commit themselves to His ways. They had reached a point of decision, so this work of God would not be just a wonderful experience but something that would shape their future."

9 Prayers for Our Nation

As Christians, it is imperative that we be good citizens. First Timothy 2 instructs us to pray for the leaders of our government. We are to pray that they hold their offices in godliness and honor. Pray for revival in our leaders and our nation.

10 Between God and Man

A *covenant* is a transaction between God and man, a promise on the part of God to arrange His providences for the welfare of those who should render obedience to Him.

b. Read Deuteronomy 6:5. What are we to do with our whole heart? In what ways would you be able to overcome wickedness if you were to follow this command?

c. How can you pray for our elected officials and for our nation as a whole?

10. Make your own promise to the Lord. Begin with praises, then include your own history of the ways you have failed God. Thank Him for your many blessings. Finally, tell Him how you intend to change your life and what you will forsake to follow Him more closely.

This week in Nehemiah 9, we have seen who God is, what He has done, and how He wants us to respond. Warren Wiersbe put it this way: "We have seen that our God is a glorious God. He is powerful, faithful and concerned about the needs of His people. He is a pardoning God, who is long suffering when we sin but who chastens us when we rebel. He is a generous God, who gives us far more than we deserve. He is a God who keeps His promises even if we are unfaithful. Surely this God deserves our loving obedience!"[12]

It may be tempting to shake our heads at the rebellious and disobedient Israelites, but we often exhibit the same attitudes and actions. There is much for us to learn and remember from this week's account of the Israelites and their actions and reactions.

We read that the people gathered together in awareness of their sins and the sins of their fathers; we reviewed God's covenant with Abraham and His miraculous protection from their enemies; we considered God's faithfulness to a forgetful and stubborn people; and then we studied the pride and apathy that seemed even more pronounced in the light of God's generous mercy. In today's final lesson, we joyfully found a repentant Israel ready to renew their covenant and remember their astonishing and loving God.

Studying the roller-coaster history of the Israelites' emotions, repentance, awareness, forgetfulness, and remorse should put us on high alert to recognize and quickly alter our own stubborn tendencies. It was so easy for them to lose awareness of God.

Let each of us pray for a deep and loving God-awareness in our lives.

Listen To ...

No man ever repented of being a Christian on his death bed.

—*Hannah More*

Promises, Promises ...

Nehemiah 10

The human race is the only species on earth that is able to make promises. A *promise* can be defined as an oral or written agreement to do or not to do something, and it comes in the form of a vow, an oath, or a pledge. We have no problem establishing our intentions and committing ourselves to actions, but along with the ability to make promises comes a capacity to break them.

From an early age, we are taught that if we keep a promise, we can expect a good outcome. In childhood, this might mean writing a letter to Santa Claus, promising to be good so he will bring us presents. During our school years, we might promise a friend to keep secrets and not "tell." A scout makes a pledge that defines her goal to develop good character. Teens promise to be home on time in order to keep their curfew. Married couples make vows when they wed and promise to love each other forever. In a court of law, we take an oath to tell the truth when we are questioned. And then there are the promises we make to ourselves on New Year's Day. We call them resolutions, which may make them a little easier to break after the first week of good intentions.

We make—and break—a lot of promises! Thankfully, although we are promise breakers, God is a promise keeper.

Day 1: Nehemiah 10:1–27   **Set-Apart People**

Day 2: Nehemiah 10:28–30   **Set Apart from Others**

Day 3: Nehemiah 10:31   **Set-Apart Sabbath**

Day 4: Nehemiah 10:32–34   **Set-Apart Finances**

Day 5: Nehemiah 10:35–39   **Set-Apart Offerings**

Set-Apart People

Lift Up ...

Dear Lord, I am grateful that You keep Your word. With You, a promise made is a promise kept. Thank You for sealing me in our covenant relationship and allowing me to become set apart for You. In Jesus' name. Amen.

Look At ...

Last week we learned about the promise that tied the Lord to His people. Known as a *covenant*, it is central to the biblical perspective of the world. It is the basis of all relationships as well as a way to define and assign authority. We also studied the longest prayer in the Bible, wherein the Levites publicly reviewed God's faithfulness to the Israelites from the time of creation to the present. This reminder of their close and long-lasting connection to God inspired the Israelites to reestablish their covenant with Him. Looking back encouraged the people to look ahead to a new life of holiness where they would again live as people set apart for God.

This week, we find a list of names of those individuals who recommitted themselves to God and country. In so doing, they signed their names and verified their signatures with a seal. A solemn oath is a serious matter. God was seeking a commitment from those He loved that He would be their God and they would be His people.

Read Nehemiah 10:1–27.

Now those who placed their seal on the document were: Nehemiah the governor, the son of Hacaliah, and Zedekiah, Seraiah, Azariah, Jeremiah, Pashhur, Amariah, Malchijah, Hattush, Shebaniah, Malluch, Harim, Meremoth, Obadiah, Daniel, Ginnethon, Baruch, Meshullam,

Abijah, Mijamin, Maaziah, Bilgai, and Shemaiah. These were the priests. The Levites: Jeshua the son of Azaniah, Binnui of the sons of Henadad, and Kadmiel. Their brethren: Shebaniah, Hodijah, Kelita, Pelaiah, Hanan, Micha, Rehob, Hashabiah, Zaccur, Sherebiah, Shebaniah, Hodijah, Bani, and Beninu. The leaders of the people: Parosh, Pahath-Moab, Elam, Zattu, Bani, Bunni, Azgad, Bebai, Adonijah, Bigvai, Adin, Ater, Hezekiah, Azzur, Hodijah, Hashum, Bezai, Hariph, Anathoth, Nebai, Magpiash, Meshullam, Hezir, Meshezabel, Zadok, Jaddua, Pelatiah, Hanan, Anaiah, Hoshea, Hananiah, Hasshub, Hallohesh, Pilha, Shobek, Rehum, Hashabnah, Maaseiah, Ahijah, Hanan, Anan, Malluch, Harim, and Baanah. Nehemiah 10:1–27

1. Previously, in Nehemiah 9, the Levites cried out to God, praising His mercies, confessing their sin, and establishing a renewed relationship with the Lord. They chose to commemorate this moment by creating what kind of document?

2. What did the leaders, Levites, and priests place on the covenant document?

3. a. Who was the first to place his seal on the document?
    b. Why do you think he wanted to be first?

4. What group affixed their seals after Nehemiah and the other city leaders?

5. Who was the next group of signees?

6. The final category includes two groups from the noble families of Israel. How were these groups named?

2 Security Seals

A *seal* is the personalized identifier of an individual. Often in the form of a stamp or signet ring, each seal was applied by stamping a specific impression into soft clay. A person's seal was a mark of genuineness and authenticity. It secured the contents of a message.

4 Dependent Priests

Priests were of the line of Aaron, Moses' brother, and were in charge of sacrifices and offerings at worship places, particularly the tabernacle and temple. Of the tribe of Levi, Aaron and his descendants were landless and dependent on the offerings of God's people.

5 Landless Levites

The Levites were members of the tribe of Levi who were not related to Aaron. They assisted the priests and maintained the holiness of the temple but did not offer sacrifices. Like priests, they were landless, and their support came from the tithes of God's people.

8 An Exclusive Relationship

Through Abraham, the Lord established a covenant relationship with the Israelites. The Israelites promised to be His people, and He promised to be their God. They swore they would follow His rules while continuing their relationship with and fear of Him (see Gen. 17:7–8).

9 A High Calling

Being set apart for God was a high honor for the Israelites, and it came with a high calling—holiness: "And you shall be holy to Me, for I the LORD am holy, and have separated you from the peoples, that you should be Mine" (Lev. 20:26).

7. In total, how many men applied their seals to this covenant document?

Live Out ...

8. God takes His covenants seriously, and making a promise to God should not be taken lightly. Search your heart before doing so, and ask Him to bless your desire to please Him.

a. Lord, I promise I will:

b. Which part of your promise do you think will be the most difficult to maintain?

c. Write a prayer to God, asking for the ability to keep your promise.

9. Due to their covenant relationship with God, the Israelites were separated from the other tribes who were living in their area.

a. Explain how you feel set apart in your living environment.

I sense I am set apart because:

b. Describe how being set apart feels. Is it a blessing or a curse?

_____

In 1947 on her twenty-first birthday, Princess Elizabeth addressed a group of citizens of the British Commonwealth. She famously promised, "My whole life, whether it be long or short, shall be devoted to your service." Now, sixty-seven years into service for her country, Queen Elizabeth II continues to keep the promise she made so long ago. The queen is an example of someone who works to fulfill promises she has made.

According to Charles Moore's article in the *Daily Telegraph*, the queen demonstrates at least four character traits that support her ability to stay true to her promise. First, doing her duty does not equal misery, because she is good at her work. Second, her community senses her devotion to duty, so they trust and confide in her, for they realize she will never gossip. Third, in a dignified way, she makes people behave without stooping to lose her temper. Fourth, she is religious, attending church weekly and saying her prayers at night so she ends each day at peace.[1]

In Genesis, our Lord said, "I am with you and will watch over you wherever you go, and I will bring you back to this land. I will not leave you until I have done what I have promised you" (Gen. 28:15 NIV). Our Lord continues to do His duty and be the ultimate promise keeper.

Listen To ...

We must not promise what we ought not, lest we be called on to perform what we cannot.
—*Abraham Lincoln*

Set Apart from Others

What is the most recent promise you remember making? Did you promise to get to work early? To have lunches prepared for each of your children? To create a special dinner to entertain your husband's boss? We frequently make commitments to other people, but we have to ask ourselves, *How often do we break these promises?*

When we don't keep a promise we have made to someone, we are basically saying we don't value him or her. We have made a choice to put something else ahead of that promise and that person. This leads people to stop counting on us to follow through. It also reveals that we don't value our own word. We start to believe it's okay to let someone down or to say something we don't mean. This can harm our image and ourselves.

During the time of Nehemiah, the Israelites went through great changes. Their connection to and respect for God had diminished to the point that they were no longer following the Mosaic law. Nehemiah not only helped the people rebuild the walls of Jerusalem, but he also helped them keep their promise to return to loving the Lord and following His laws.

Lift Up ...

Dear Lord, I know that You tell me to be holy as You are holy. Help me set myself apart from those things that displease You. In Jesus' name. Amen.

Look At ...

Yesterday, we observed Nehemiah, the other city leaders, the Levites, the priests, the brethren, and assorted others as they each placed their seal upon the recovenant document. In doing so, the Israelites confirmed their promise to the Lord. Name by name, the document was signed and verified. By solemnly signing their names, their intentions became known to their compatriots.

This week, we discover more about what the signed covenant instructed the people to do. They made a promise to keep God's whole Law while keeping themselves apart from the ungodly. We find out that obedience brought a blessing, while disobedience resulted in a curse. Being set apart, whether in marriage or in departure from the ways of the world, requires a firm outlook based on personal integrity and love.

Read Nehemiah 10:28–30.

Now the rest of the people—the priests, the Levites, the gatekeepers, the singers, the Nethinim, and all those who had separated themselves from the peoples of the lands to the Law of God, their wives, their sons, and their daughters, everyone who had knowledge and understanding—these joined with their brethren, their nobles, and entered into a curse and an oath to walk in God's Law, which was given by Moses the servant of God, and to observe and do all the commandments of the LORD our Lord, and His ordinances and His statutes: We would not give our daughters as wives to the peoples of the land, nor take their daughters for our sons. Nehemiah 10:28–30

1. The rest of the people then entered into the covenant with God. What twelve groups were represented?

     1.

     2.

     3.

     4.

     5.

     6.

     7.

     8.

     9.

     10.

     11.

     12.

3 The Peoples of the Lands

The peoples of the lands worshiped idols. In Ezekiel 44:23, the Jewish priests were told to "teach My people the difference between the holy and the unholy, and cause them to discern between the unclean and the clean." Separation from nearby inhabitants would help conform the Jews to God's plan.

4 The Law of God

The commandments, ordinances, and statutes refer to all of the laws God gave to Moses for the Israelites to obey. These included the Ten Commandments as well as the many rules and regulations found in the Pentateuch: Genesis through Deuteronomy.

5 Curses and Oaths

A *curse* was a prayer for misfortune to befall someone. Putting a curse on themselves should they break the law meant that the people knew they deserved punishment for disobedience. An *oath* was a solemn statement to validate a promise and could be accompanied by protective curses to guarantee the oaths were kept.

2. What two characteristics did they have in common?

1.

2.

3. What did they separate themselves *from*?

4. What did they separate themselves *to*?

5. What two things did these people join their brethren and nobles in entering?

1.

2.

6. What things did the people promise concerning the Law?

7. What promise was made regarding future marriages?

Live Out ...

8. The Jewish people were described as having knowledge and understanding that presumably would set them apart from the peoples of the lands.

a. What knowledge and understanding do you have that sets you apart from non-Christians?

b. From what source have you gained your special knowledge and understanding?

c. If you feel that you are no longer comprehending or properly interpreting the Bible, what three steps can you take to remedy this situation?

1.

2.

3.

9. Take a few moments to review the Ten Commandments, recorded in Deuteronomy 5:7–21.

    a. Now turn to Matthew 22:37–40, and write out the commandments Jesus said were the basis for all of God's laws.

    b. How have you specifically kept these two commandments this week?

10. Why do you think the first commitment made after the sealing of the covenant concerned intermarriage with other peoples of the land?

———————————

Many situations in modern society call for the act of taking an oath. An *oath* is a ritualistic declaration, typically based on an appeal to God, that one will speak the truth, keep a promise, or remain faithful. Every four years in our country, we elect a president who takes the oath of office after the election but before assuming the office. During the inauguration ceremony, the president-elect raises his right hand, places his left hand on a Bible, and says, "I do solemnly swear that I will faithfully execute the office of president of the United States and will, to the best of my ability, preserve, protect, and defend the Constitution of the United States."

The framers of the Constitution mandated this oath because the president's office lacked the internal checks that were present in the other branches of government. It was necessary to tie the president's duty to "preserve, protect, and defend" to his obligations to God.[2]

The children of Israel entered into an oath when they reestablished their covenant relationship with their Lord. They tied their

8 Knowledge and Understanding

Proverbs 9:10 sums up the need for knowledge and understanding: "The fear of the LORD is the beginning of wisdom, and the knowledge of the Holy One is understanding." Knowledge of God is the greatest knowledge; it is also our chief duty (see Hos. 6:6).

9 Ten Commandments

The Ten Commandments are the ten fundamental principles of the covenant relationship. They call on the saved to respond to the unearned grace they have experienced by committing first to God and then to others. "With my whole heart I have sought You; oh, let me not wander from Your commandments!" (Ps. 119:10).

commitment to Him to the necessity of following His Law. They promised to follow His ordinances and His statutes. This oath invoked the name and possible judgment of the Lord. It was not to be taken lightly.

Listen To ...

It is not the oath that makes us believe the man, but the man the oath.

—*Aeschylus*

Set-Apart Sabbath

Maybe you've heard the often-told joke about asking for a day off. You go to your boss and ask for a day off. Your boss responds by suggesting you consider this request from his or her point of view and gives you the following information.

There are 365 days per year available for work. There are fifty-two weeks per year in which you already have two days off per week, leaving 261 days available for work. Since you spend sixteen hours each day away from work, you have used up 170 days, leaving only ninety-one days.

You spend thirty minutes each day on coffee breaks, which counts for twenty-three days each year, leaving only sixty-eight days. With a one-hour lunch each day, another forty-six days are used, leaving only twenty-two days for work.

You normally spend two days per year on sick leave. This leaves only twenty days per year for work. There are five holidays per year, so your available working time is down to fifteen days. The company generously gives fourteen days' vacation per year, which leaves only one day available for work.

Your boss concludes, "There's no way I'll let you take that day off!"

The above is an embellished representation of how our time is divided, but it makes the point that there can be many reasons why we feel we can't schedule a day off. Like the Israelites, we have to choose to follow the Lord's schedule, not humankind's, and to abide by His command to keep the Sabbath holy, set apart for Him.

Lift Up ...

Dear Lord, thank You for faithfully caring for me, knowing that having a day off every week allows me to spend time strengthening my relationship with You. Your provision of this day of rest refreshes me through You. I worship You. In Jesus' name. Amen.

1 Day of Rest

The principle of keeping one day out of seven for rest is as old as creation, when God Himself rested on the seventh day (see Gen. 2:2). The Lord followed this up with the eighth commandment, which mandates that all our work must cease on the blessed Sabbath day (see Ex. 20:8–11; Deut. 5:12–15).

Look At ...

Yesterday, we studied the steps God's people took to separate themselves from their tribal neighbors. To the Israelites, making an oath and standing by it was of solemn importance. It not only brought blessings; it prevented a curse. The Lord's people joined together and promised to walk in God's Law by observing all the commandments, ordinances, and statutes God had given them. Specifically, they promised not to intermarry with outsiders.

Today, we review their next promise, which was to keep the laws concerning the Sabbath. We find that God ordained the Sabbath as yet another way to set His people apart from the masses. It was a means of stepping away from the day-to-day demands of life to focus their hearts and minds on God. The Jews were a special people with special rewards and requirements.

Read Nehemiah 10:31.

If the peoples of the land brought wares or any grain to sell on the Sabbath day, we would not buy it from them on the Sabbath, or on a holy day; and we would forego the seventh year's produce and the exacting of every debt. Nehemiah 10:31

1. What did God's people expect the peoples of the land to do on the Sabbath?

2. What were the peoples of the land selling?

3. How did God's people choose to respond to the sales offers?

4. What other days were considered nonpurchasing days?

5. What was the next thing they promised to forego?

6. What else would they forego?

7. How do you think keeping the Sabbath and sabbatical year affected the Israelites? Did the observance build their faith or require a sacrifice on their part? Explain your thoughts.

Live Out ...

8. To learn more about the Sabbath, read Exodus 31:13–17.

a. What did the Sabbath signify (see v. 13)?

b. What was the penalty for failing to keep this command (see vv. 14–15)?

c. How long were the Israelites to keep this covenant command (see v. 16)?

d. What was the model for the establishment of the Sabbath (see v. 17)?

9. a. Describe your usual Sunday routine.

b. Now, circle the activities you regularly give up for the Sabbath.

Working

Shopping

Socializing

Other: _____

c. Circle the activities you choose to observe on the Sabbath.

Worship

Christian service

Community duties

5 Year of Renewal

The fallowing of the land every seventh year renewed both the land and the people of Israel. The land could reenergize, the people would survive off what grew wild, and the peasants would be allowed to eat from the untended fields.[3]

6 Year of Release

Because Israel had a history of suffering and deliverance, the people cared for the oppressed. Loans were to be an act of generosity, for lending was the sharing of God's gifts. The Sabbath year was a year of releasing debt, returning family property, and freeing slaves.[4]

9 Sabbath Shift

It's not clear exactly when the Saturday Sabbath transitioned to Sunday worship. Some believe this happened right after the resurrection, which took place on Easter Sunday. The disciples perhaps gathered on subsequent Sundays to remember Jesus and take the Lord's Supper together, creating the tradition of Sunday being the Lord's Day.[5]

10 Supernatural Supply

God's provision isn't dependent on the current economy, nor does He rely on a bank. Believers can put their entire trust in the Lord, because God promises to provide for His children: "And my God shall supply all your need according to His riches in glory by Christ Jesus" (Phil. 4:19).

Witnessing to unbelievers

Other: _____

d. What part of your Sabbath routine are you inspired to change?

10. The Israelites were commanded to let their land lie fallow and forgo collecting debts, relying on God to provide for their needs. Describe an experience you have had when you trusted only the Lord to provide for you.

    a. I had only God to help me when:

    b. How did the Lord take care of your needs?

_____

We learned that during the time Nehemiah walked the earth, the Sabbath had devolved from a day of worship to a day of acquisition and consumption. The Israelites recognized their folly and promised their activities during the Sabbath year would conform to God's commands for the Sabbath.

In our present-day, complicated world, many family or community activities can take place on Sunday. As children of the Lord, we must trust that He will lead us to an understanding of how we should spend our day of rest. Feeling His love in our hearts and understanding His desires through His Word, we will come to comprehend that we need to fulfill what He intends for us. In this way, we can spend our Sabbath, or Lord's Day, the way He means it to be spent.

James Montgomery Boice asked, "Why don't you make a commitment to make Sunday a day when you focus on Christian concerns specifically?" Continuing on, he quoted a friend who said, "If you want to grow in the Christian life, determine to come to church more than once a week, witness to your friends, ask your pastor for a job, and then get busy serving Jesus."[6] Think about it!

Listen To ...

> *Whatever You promise is too small and insufficient when I do not see and fully enjoy You alone. For my heart cannot rest or be fully content until, rising above all gifts and every created thing, it rests in You.*
>
> *—Thomas à Kempis*

Set-Apart Finances

John Greenleaf Whittier, an American poet and editor, was born in Massachusetts in 1807. The son of devout Quakers, he grew up on the family farm and had little formal schooling. He developed an interest in poetry, and by the time he was twenty, he had published enough verse to bring him to the attention of those interested in the antislavery cause. As a Quaker devoted to social causes and reform, Whittier worked passionately for a series of abolitionist newspapers and magazines. Others viewed him as a kind man whose verse gave unique expression to ideas they valued. Expressed in the poem that follows is a belief that meant a lot to him: the act of giving.

> Somehow, not only for Christmas,
> But all the long year through,
> The joy that you give to others,
> Is the joy that comes back to you.
> And the more you spend in blessing
> The poor and lonely and sad,
> The more of your heart's possessing
> Returns to you glad.

Giving back to God that which He has given to you is an ongoing part of religious life. Understanding that "the earth is the LORD's, and everything in it, the world, and all who live in it" (Ps. 24:1 NIV) frees us to be more generous with what God has provided. We are only caretakers.

Lift Up ...

Dear Lord, I know You promise to "render to each one according to his deeds" (Rom. 2:6). May You see me as Your child who gives generously to those things that are dear to Your heart. Help me know and understand what You treasure. In Jesus' name. Amen.

Look At ...

Yesterday, we investigated the importance of the Sabbath day and the Sabbath year during Nehemiah's time. We also had an opportunity to think about keeping one day a week holy and set apart for communion with the Lord. When we consider the heart behind the command, we see God desires fellowship and honor from the people He loves.

Today, we learn about how the people set up ordinances to take care of the Lord's official servants, resulting in blessings for everyone. Their commitment and care of the temple was a reflection of the esteem and priority of God in their lives. "An altar of earth you shall make for Me, and you shall sacrifice on it your burnt offerings and your peace offerings, your sheep and your oxen. In every place where I record My name I will come to you, and I will bless you" (Ex. 20:24).

Read Nehemiah 10:32–34.

Also we made ordinances for ourselves, to exact from ourselves yearly one-third of a shekel for the service of the house of our God: for the showbread, for the regular grain offering, for the regular burnt offering of the Sabbaths, the New Moons, and the set feasts; for the holy things, for the sin offerings to make atonement for Israel, and all the work of the house of our God. We cast lots among the priests, the Levites, and the people, for bringing the wood offering into the house of our God, according to our fathers' houses, at the appointed times year by year, to burn on the altar of the LORD *our God as it is written in the Law.* Nehemiah 10:32–34

1. What did the Israelites choose to make for themselves?

1 An Ordinance of Support

An *ordinance* is a command of an authoritative nature. The Israelites realized that the way they cared for the temple indicated what they thought of their God, so they passed their own temple tax law to stipulate how support would be obtained to maintain the house of their God.

2 A Tax for the Temple

The cash-based economy developed during this period necessitated giving cash to support the operations of the temple. At this time, ten shekels were about a year's wages.[7] This tax also served to remind the people that God had paid a price to set them free at the time of their redemption.

4 A Provision for Ministries

The money was to be used to provide what was needed for the work of the house of God, including the regular and special ministries performed in the temple. For Israel to be in a right relationship with God, the priests had to faithfully carry out their duties.[8]

2. How much and how often were the people required to pay the temple tax?

3. There is a list of services that would be provided or purchased for the house of God. Which three categories are listed first?

1.

2.

3.

4. What else would be obtained so all of the duties of the house of God would be covered?

5. Who would cast lots?

6. Why did they use this method?

7. Why were the wood offerings to burn on the altar of God brought at specific times?

Live Out ...

8. The Israelites saw a need and regulated themselves to fill it by providing funds that could be used to purchase materials for offerings or for religious feasts. We no longer have a large central temple where everyone worships, but those who attend services are still expected to share in the support of their church.

a. Check which of the following statements best describes your attitude toward supporting the work your church does on behalf of the Lord.

❑ It is my responsibility and privilege to give regularly.

❑ I give when I feel like it.

❑ I give when I have extra.

❑ Others have more; let them be the givers.

❑ I'm not sure what the church does with its money, so I don't want to give.

b. Witnessing the Israelites' efforts to set ordinances for their own giving, how might you change your attitude toward doing the same?

9. If funds are scarce, you can contribute in other ways, such as by giving your time. Check which of the following possibilities might work for you.

❑ Helping the needy by donating food or no longer needed items

❑ Helping the elderly by visiting nursing homes

❑ Helping youth in need by spending time at facilities for juvenile delinquents

❑ Helping women by working in the women's ministry

❑ Helping the church solve problems or achieve goals by offering your expertise

10. a. What Christian traditions and celebrations do you think warrant similar financial support of the church like the Israelites provided for the temple?

b. How can we keep our traditions alive?

_____

8 The Blessing of Giving

Giving can be a touchy subject among churchgoers, but we must "remember the words of the Lord Jesus, that He said, 'It is more blessed to give than to receive'" (Acts 20:35).

10 Cherished Traditions

A tradition is a teaching or ritual that is handed down. Some traditions that we hold dear include decorating and hiding Easter eggs, displaying an Advent calendar, preparing a holiday meal, saying grace, and giving gifts. Traditions celebrate our faith.

It would not have been smart for the Israelites, with their self-imposed laws, to make giving a responsibility rather than a choice. Charles Swindoll gave an illustration that helps us understand why:

> An older brother received a special little truck he loved to play with. In fact, he played with it until the paint was worn off. One day, the truck was sitting ignored on the coffee table. Up walked the little sister, who reached her tiny hand over to the well-worn truck, only to have her brother snatch it away from her. "It's my truck!" he exclaimed. "Mine! Mine!" Even though he didn't play with the truck, he didn't want to let go of the old toy, especially to his little sister. His parents, of course, told him to share, but that only compelled him to grip the truck even tighter. Finally, under threat of punishment, the boy tossed the toy to his little sister.
>
> This is an illustration of "giving grudgingly." When you are compelled to do something, as the big brother was, you are all the more reluctant to give it up.[9]

Most of us are happy to receive a gift from someone who is motivated by love rather than a sense of duty or obligation. Let's make a commitment to practice 2 Corinthians 9:7 and "give as he purposes in his heart, not grudgingly or of necessity; for God loves a cheerful giver."

Listen To ...

Not the maker of plans and promises, but rather the one who offers faithful service in small matters. This is the person who is most likely to achieve what is good and lasting.
—*Johann Wolfgang von Goethe*

Set-Apart Offerings

Psychiatrist Karl Menninger once asked a wealthy patient, "What on earth are you going to do with all of that money?" The patient replied, a bit reluctantly, "Just worry about it, I suppose." Menninger went on, "Do you get that much pleasure out of worrying about it?" "No," replied the patient, "but I get such terror when I think of giving some of it to somebody else."[10]

Does this story resonate with you? Do you hold onto your money out of fear? David Murray of Christianity.com listed ten reasons why giving is a blessing. One was that it demonstrates the giver's trust in God's provision. We might fear that if we give away too much, we won't have enough to meet our own needs. However, when we give above and beyond what is comfortable, we show our faith in God to provide for us. It's a joy to see God fulfill His promise of provision when we obey Him in this way.[11]

When we fix our eyes on things, we are guaranteed to be dissatisfied. The billionaire John D. Rockefeller was once asked, "How much does it take to satisfy a man completely?" He replied, "It takes a little bit more than he has."[12]

Lift Up ...

Dear Lord, nothing I give back to You can compare to all You have already given to me. Anything You ask of me I freely give to You, in Your service and for Your glory. Help me keep a light grasp on that which You have entrusted to me. In Jesus' name. Amen.

Look At ...

Yesterday, we studied the self-imposed system of ordinances that the Israelites established in order to involve the people in providing for the upkeep of the temple. Each was to annually pay one-third of a shekel to the religious leaders so they could purchase items needed for

1 Gifts of Life

The *firstfruits* are the first harvest of any crop and the firstborn of any mother. Generally, first-born sons were bought back by their families; this practice reminded the people that all life is a gift from God and is owed to Him.[13]

services, feast days, and sin offerings. In addition, everyone was given an appointed time at which they were to bring wood to burn on the altar. Care of the temple was an indicator of how highly the Jews regarded God, His Word, His temple, and His reputation to outsiders.

Today, we complete our study of Nehemiah 10 by learning about the offerings that provided for those who served in the temple: the priests and the Levites. The house of God was not to be neglected. The temple was a priority, deserving the very best of the Israelites and their crops.

Read Nehemiah 10:35–39.

And we made ordinances to bring the firstfruits of our ground and the firstfruits of all fruit of all trees, year by year, to the house of the LORD; to bring the firstborn of our sons and our cattle, as it is written in the Law, and the firstborn of our herds and our flocks, to the house of our God, to the priests who minister in the house of our God; to bring the firstfruits of our dough, our offerings, the fruit from all kinds of trees, the new wine and oil, to the priests, to the storerooms of the house of our God; and to bring the tithes of our land to the Levites, for the Levites should receive the tithes in all our farming communities. And the priest, the descendant of Aaron, shall be with the Levites when the Levites receive tithes; and the Levites shall bring up a tenth of the tithes to the house of our God, to the rooms of the storehouse. For the children of Israel and the children of Levi shall bring the offering of the grain, of the new wine and the oil, to the storerooms where the articles of the sanctuary are, where the priests who minister and the gatekeepers and the singers are; and we will not neglect the house of our God. Nehemiah 10:35–39

1. The next set of ordinances covers the delivery of what items?

2. What specific natural firstfruits did the people bring to the house of the Lord every year?

3. a. Where was the first set of the firstfruits to be taken?

   b. To whom were they given?

4. A second group of more prepared firstfruits was also taken to the temple and given to the priests. What categories of items did this group include?

5. What item did the people add as their next delivery item?

6. Who received the tithes?

7. How much of the tithe did the Levites bring to the storerooms of the house of God?

Live Out ...

8. a. What is an example of a firstfruit you might offer your Lord today?

   b. When you obediently give as God instructed us to give, how do you feel?

9. Today, we studied about how the people were to give of their first fruits and firstborn to the house of God.

   a. Read 1 Corinthians 15:20 and Colossians 1:15. Who did God offer as a firstfruit and firstborn to redeem humankind?

5 Gifts of Tenths

The word *tithe* means *a tenth*. By law, the Jews were to bring a tenth of their product to the temple each year to support the Levites. The Levites would then give a tithe of the tithe to the priests who oversaw the collection.[14]

7 Gifts of Support

The practice of designating one-tenth of all produce as wages for the priesthood was necessary because the Levites and priests owned no land of their own and were solely supported by all the people through the tithe.[15]

8 Gifts from the Heart

The New Testament contains no specific passage that obligates Christians to tithe. However, generous and cheerful giving is a pleasure to God (see 2 Cor. 9:7). Ask yourself not how much you are required to give but how much is appropriate to keep for your own maintenance.[16]

10 Gifts of Care

Webster's tells us that to *neglect* is to fail to care for or attend to sufficiently or properly. The Lord chastised the Israelites for neglect in the time of Haggai (see Hag. 1:3–4). Let us be as the recovenanted people were, promising not to neglect the house of God.

b. Phillip E. Howard Jr. wrote, "But if God was faithful and merciful to Israel, whom He chose not because of their righteousness, but only because of His love for them, how much more reason today to rest on the faithfulness of Him who gave His beloved Son for us! In that faithfulness is assured our right to God's promises."[17] How do you plan to take ownership of God's promises?

10. a. At the end of today's Scripture passage, what proclamation did the people make concerning the house of God?

b. In what ways can you be mindful not to neglect the needs of the house of God?

_____

We have been blessed by the opportunity to learn from the people of long ago. They have taught us about the importance of keeping our covenant promise to obey the commandments God has given us. We have also learned about our responsibility to our place of worship as well as to those who serve there.

The second verse of Russell Carter's 1886 hymn "Standing on the Promises" says:

Standing on the promises that cannot fail,
When the howling storms of doubt and fear assail,
By the living Word of God I shall prevail,
Standing on the promises of God.[18]

God's greatest promise to us came through our salvation, when we accepted Christ as our Lord and Savior and were promised eternal life. Titus 1:2 tells us that faith and knowledge rest "in the hope of eternal life, which God, who does not lie, promised before the beginning of time" (NIV). We are to "hold fast the confession of our hope without wavering, for He who promised is faithful" (Heb. 10:23) and to recognize that "the Lord is not slow in keeping his promise, as some understand slowness. Instead he is patient with you, not wanting anyone to perish, but everyone to come to repentance" (2 Pet. 3:9 NIV). Our God is a promise keeper, and we are to model ourselves after Him, as we remember that godly choices lead to godly changes. Stand firm on the promises of your God.

Listen To ...

God's promises are like the stars; the darker the night the brighter they shine.
—David Nicholas

The Holy City Sees ...

Nehemiah 11-12

In 2013 a quietly monumental occurrence began to unfold. In fact, some are calling this event the fulfillment of biblical prophecy in Israel. A small group of Jews believed to be of a "lost tribe" from northern Israel slowly began returning to the Holy Land. In a diminutive area of land between India, Myanmar (formerly Burma), and Bangladesh, this tribe, the Bnei Menashe, was found. They are believed to be descendants of the tribe of Manasseh.

The tribe's history goes like this: In 721 BC the Assyrians invaded the northern kingdom of Israel and enslaved ten tribes, exiling them to Assyria. In 2011 the Israeli government granted permission for 7,300 members of this lost tribe to return to Israel.[1]

The Jewish nation believes this is a fulfillment of the Old Testament prophecy from Isaiah: "It shall come to pass in that day that the Lord shall set His hand again the second time to recover the remnant of His people who are left, from Assyria and Egypt" (Isa. 11:11). Once God draws His nation together, it will mark the beginning of the end, or the last days.

Just as the Bnei Menashe have been called back to the Holy Land, in Nehemiah 11, we find Nehemiah calling the Israelites back to Jerusalem. For 142 years, the defenseless city had been deserted. It was time for the Israelites to come home and begin restoring the nation.

This week, we see Nehemiah continue his leadership over the restoration of Israel. From his plan to populate the city with those who worked so hard to rebuild it to the worship and praise march dedicating the rebuilt wall to the Lord, Nehemiah continued as a true, godly leader of the nation.

Day 1: Nehemiah 11:1–9   **Men Casting Lots**

Day 2: Nehemiah 11:10–24   **Men Choosing to Stay**

Day 3: Nehemiah 11:25–36   **Men Dwelling in Nearby Towns**

Day 4: Nehemiah 12:1–26   **Men Working for God**

Day 5: Nehemiah 12:27–47   **Men Dedicating the Walls**

Men Casting Lots

Lift Up ...

Dear Lord, show me where You want me to dwell. I want to create a true home, whether in the center of a busy city or in the outskirts of a small town. May I grow roots and be planted firmly in the spot You have for me. In Jesus' name. Amen.

Look At ...

Last week, at the conclusion of Nehemiah 10, we studied how the Jews made provision for those who served in the temple. The house of God was to be a priority to every citizen; their offerings were to be the best of the best. Covenants with God were not to be entered into lightly or vaguely—the people did their part, and God did His. We cannot enter into a one-sided covenant with the living God.

Today, we see Nehemiah begin his efforts to repopulate Jerusalem. Now that the wall was built, he was tasked with filling the newly secured city. This meant the Israelites would once again have to go to work. Warren Wiersbe explains, "[Nehemiah] knew that the nation of Israel could never be strong as long as Jerusalem was weak. But Jerusalem could not be strong unless the people were willing to sacrifice."[2] The Israelites had to do their part to ensure their nation's reestablishment.

Read Nehemiah 11:1–9.

Now the leaders of the people dwelt at Jerusalem; the rest of the people cast lots to bring one out of ten to dwell in Jerusalem, the holy city, and nine-tenths were to dwell in other cities. And the people blessed all the men who willingly offered themselves to dwell at Jerusalem. These are the heads

2 Casting Lots

Commentators believe the sacred lots were determined by using the Urim and Thummim—a method of decision making that was directed by the Lord. "The lot is cast into the lap, but its every decision is from the LORD" (Prov. 16:33).

3 Blessing Others

The repopulation of Jerusalem was necessary to ensure a thriving nation. Empty cities do not prosper. According to the repopulation method the Jews used, an estimated five thousand people out of the surrounding population of fifty thousand went back to occupy Jerusalem.[3]

of the province who dwelt in Jerusalem. (But in the cities of Judah everyone dwelt in his own possession in their cities—Israelites, priests, Levites, Nethinim, and descendants of Solomon's servants.) Also in Jerusalem dwelt some of the children of Judah and of the children of Benjamin. The children of Judah: Athaiah the son of Uzziah, the son of Zechariah, the son of Amariah, the son of Shephatiah, the son of Mahalalel, of the children of Perez; and Maaseiah the son of Baruch, the son of Col-Hozeh, the son of Hazaiah, the son of Adaiah, the son of Joiarib, the son of Zechariah, the son of Shiloni. All the sons of Perez who dwelt at Jerusalem were four hundred and sixty-eight valiant men. And these are the sons of Benjamin: Sallu the son of Meshullam, the son of Joed, the son of Pedaiah, the son of Kolaiah, the son of Maaseiah, the son of Ithiel, the son of Jeshaiah; and after him Gabbai and Sallai, nine hundred and twenty-eight. Joel the son of Zichri was their overseer, and Judah the son of Senuah was second over the city. Nehemiah 11:1–9

1. Which people dwelt in Jerusalem?

2. What system was used to determine who returned to Jerusalem?

3. What was given to those who *willingly* offered to live in Jerusalem?

4. a. What offices did the people hold who lived in Jerusalem?

    b. Which people did *not* live in Jerusalem?

5. We know God has a purpose for including lists of names in the Bible. Study the lists of names in this passage, and answer the following questions:

a. Fill in the blanks to see the descendants of Judah:

Athaiah the son of _____, the son of Zechariah, the son of _____, the son of Shephatiah, the son of_____, of the children of _____; and _____ the son of Baruch, the son of _____-_____, the son of Hazaiah, the son of _____, the son of _____, the son of _____, the son of Shiloni.

b. How many sons of Perez were dwelling in Jerusalem?

c. Now review the descendants of Benjamin, and fill in his family tree:

Sallu the son of _____, the son of Joed, the son of _____, the son of Kolaiah, the son of _____, the son of _____, the son of Jeshaiah; and after him _____ and _____.

d. How many sons of Benjamin were dwelling in Jerusalem?

6. Who are the two men representing the tribe of Benjamin listed as first and second over the city?

7. We see Perez listed in the genealogy of Judah. Read Matthew 1:1–16. What is the importance of Perez in the line of Judah?

8. Read 1 Kings 11:34–36 and 12:21. Why are Judah and Benjamin the only tribes mentioned?

4 Leading Fathers

God is not just our fathers' God or our grandfathers' God; He is *our* God, and He knows each of us by name. As parents, we must direct our children to the Lord: "For I have chosen him, so that he will direct his children and his household after him to keep the way of the LORD by doing what is right and just" (Gen. 18:19 NIV).

9 Heading Home

"You are the L ORD God, who chose Abram, and brought him out of Ur of the Chaldeans, and gave him the name Abraham" (Neh. 9:7). The Israelites in Nehemiah's time were familiar with Abraham and God's call upon him, but they may not have expected God to call them back to Jerusalem in the same manner.

10 Finding Faith

God calls each of us in various ways: some into ministry, some to leave a comfortable job, some into a marriage or to parenthood. Regardless of our calling, God promises we will not go alone: "I will instruct you and teach you in the way you should go; I will guide you with My eye" (Ps. 32:8).

Live Out ...

9. In the same way God called Abraham, sometimes He calls us out of our "country." Here we see that God called the Israelites back to the Holy City of Jerusalem. Some came willingly, and others cast lots and were volunteered. Think about suddenly having to move to another city. Do you think it would be difficult or easy? What emotional and spiritual effects would it have? Record your thoughts below.

10. Hebrews 11 tells us that by faith Abraham obeyed and followed the Lord. Is there something God is calling you into or out of that is testing your faith? Write a prayer in your journal, confessing to the Lord any fears or concerns. Ask Him to give you a faith like Abraham's.[4]

The 1906 San Francisco earthquake and its subsequent fires destroyed over 80 percent of the city and claimed over 3,000 lives. In the early morning hours of Wednesday, April 18, 1906, a 7.8 magnitude earthquake struck, rupturing gas mains and causing fires believed to be responsible for 90 percent of the total damage to the city. More than thirty fires destroyed around 25,000 buildings in a 490-block radius.

At the time of this disaster, San Francisco was the ninth largest city in the United States, with a population of almost 410,000. The destruction left almost 300,000 people displaced from their homes. As a result, parks and beaches were soon covered with makeshift tent cities that would remain for almost two years. With property losses upwards of $400 million, it took nine years to rebuild the city of San Francisco.[4]

California's governor at the time, George C. Pardee, saw the need to rebuild quickly. "California is too great and her resources are too numerous to permit her chief city to long lie a waste of fire-scathed ruins," he said.[5]

Like Governor Pardee, Nehemiah knew that thriving would follow rebuilding. By gathering the Israelites back to the city of Jerusalem, the people made a stand of faith: they would not be conquered by adversity but would overcome adversity with trust.

Listen To ...

God loves with a great love the man whose heart is bursting with a passion for the impossible.
—*William Booth*

Men Choosing to Stay

In the summer of 2014, fires raged in Northern California. One hundred and eighty homes were evacuated. Many of the residents of a rural Napa County neighborhood left their homes on a day in July, never dreaming they would not be able to return.

While most people heeded the warning to leave, one man bravely stayed behind. John Hallman, who is a member of a neighborhood fire prevention team, stayed behind for the purpose of rescuing pets left in homes that were in the path of danger. One by one, he broke into his neighbors' homes to check on or rescue pets in harm's way.

"I've been doing my best to rescue cats and dogs and one pig, [and] chickens," Hallman noted. Due to the three-day length of the evacuation, most pets were without food or water. Hallman's efforts saved one neighbor's beloved Chihuahua.

Days later, the residents returned, not knowing the fate of their pets or that one man stayed behind to take care of them.[6]

People stay behind for various reasons. Sometimes it's an individual who feels it's his or her right to stay, but other times, it is for the greater good of the community, which eclipses individual needs.

In today's Scriptures, we see those who are servants—the workers for the temple, the Levites, the priests, and gatekeepers—all coming together to help Jerusalem thrive. Their desire was to stay and help build a strong foundation for the city to rise from the ashes.

Lift Up ...

Dear Lord, no matter the task set before me, help me realize that it's Your work, and I am but a minister of Your grace. Help me do my best in any task You have called me to. I pray I will never look down on any activity as being too insignificant for my efforts. In Jesus' name. Amen.

Look At ...

Yesterday, we saw that the Israelites cast lots to determine who would live within the Holy City of Jerusalem. Some residents willingly chose to stay, while God determined where others would dwell. All together, 10 percent of the population was needed to begin to repopulate Jerusalem. Many of the people came from the tribes of Judah and Benjamin.

Today, we learn about the workers God called to His purpose. We see the groups of Levites and priests who chose to live within the new Jerusalem walls. While lists of names can often be daunting, they are a beautiful reminder that God knows each of us by name and He knows the exact work He has called and equipped us to do. You may be a stay-at-home mom, a teacher, or a manager, but remember God knows *your* name and the tasks He has placed before you.

Read Nehemiah 11:10–24.

Of the priests: Jedaiah the son of Joiarib, and Jachin; Seraiah the son of Hilkiah, the son of Meshullam, the son of Zadok, the son of Meraioth, the son of Ahitub, was the leader of the house of God. Their brethren who did the work of the house were eight hundred and twenty-two; and Adaiah the son of Jeroham, the son of Pelaliah, the son of Amzi, the son of Zechariah, the son of Pashhur, the son of Malchijah, and his brethren, heads of the fathers' houses, were two hundred and forty-two; and Amashai the son of Azarel, the son of Ahzai, the son of Meshillemoth, the son of Immer, and their brethren, mighty men of valor, were one hundred and twenty-eight. Their overseer was Zabdiel the son of one of the great men. Also of the Levites: Shemaiah the son of Hasshub, the son of Azrikam, the son of Hashabiah, the son of Bunni; Shabbethai and Jozabad, of the heads of the Levites, had the oversight of the business outside of the house of God; Mattaniah the son of Micha, the son of Zabdi, the son of Asaph, the leader who began the thanksgiving with prayer; Bakbukiah, the second among his brethren; and Abda the son of Shammua, the son of Galal, the son of Jeduthun. All the Levites in the holy city were two hundred and eighty-four. Moreover the gatekeepers, Akkub, Talmon, and their brethren who kept the gates, were one hundred and seventy-two. And the rest of Israel, of the priests and Levites, were in all the cities of Judah, everyone in his inheritance. But the Nethinim dwelt in Ophel. And Ziha and Gishpa were over the Nethinim. Also the overseer of the Levites at Jerusalem was Uzzi the son of Bani, the son of Hashabiah, the son of Mattaniah, the son of Micha, of the sons

of Asaph, the singers in charge of the service of the house of God. For it was the king's command concerning them that a certain portion should be for the singers, a quota day by day. Pethahiah the son of Meshezabel, of the children of Zerah the son of Judah, was the king's deputy in all matters concerning the people. Nehemiah 11:10–24

2 Strong Leaders

Seraiah was a leader of the house of God after the captivity. The work of the house of God would refer to the regular labor of the temple—mainly, the daily sacrifices.[7]

5 Strong Businessmen

The areas of oversight likely included feeding the priests, providing sacrificial animals, cleaning up the used vessels, and other necessary enterprises.[8] As with any endeavor, workers of all varieties were needed for the temple. Each was necessary and each was vital.

7 Strong Defenders

Gatekeepers were Levites responsible for opening and closing the gates as well as helping to defend the city. Jesus referred to Himself as a gatekeeper: "I tell you the truth, I am the gate for the sheep.... Yes, I am the gate. Those who come in through me will be saved" (John 10:7, 9 NLT).

1. What is the first group mentioned?

2. a. What was Seraiah assigned to lead?
    b. How many were included in the work of the house?

3. a. What do you think the phrase *heads of the fathers' houses* means?
    b. How many were included in this category?

4. a. How many were numbered as mighty men of valor?
    b. Why would priests need to act with valor?

5. What areas did the next group oversee?

6. The prayer of thanksgiving was an important part of worship. Name the two Levites assigned this function.
    1.
    2.

7   a. What were the names of the two gatekeepers noted?
    b. What was the total number of gatekeepers?

8. a. What responsibilities did Uzzi have?
    b. What were the sons of Asaph responsible for?

Live Out ...

9. The Levites covered a multitude of jobs within the temple, from music to gatekeeping to temple business. Every job was necessary. In today's world, women juggle many duties every day.

a. Check the jobs you currently hold:

❑ Mother ❑ Wife ❑ Caregiver

❑ Volunteer ❑ Board member ❑ Mother

❑ Employee/ employer ❑ Worker/ coworker ❑ Daughter

❑ Friend ❑ Other: _____

b. Which jobs require the majority of your attention?

c. Are any priorities out of sync due to immediate needs?

d. Write a prayer in your journal, asking God to help you organize your activities according to His priorities.

10. Sometimes our work goes unnoticed by others, but God sees us. Knowing our work is unto God allows us the freedom to go about our business without fear or worry. Fill in the chart below to see what God says about our efforts:

Scripture	Our Part
Proverbs 13:4	
1 Corinthians 10:31	
Philippians 2:14–15	
Colossians 3:17	
Colossians 3:23	

_____

9 Strong Women

We can glorify God in all things, even in difficulty. "Therefore, whether you eat or drink, or whatever you do, do all to the glory of God" (1 Cor. 10:31).

10 Strong Treasures

God Himself will try our works. "Each one's work will become clear... because it will be revealed by fire.... If anyone's work which he has built on it endures, he will receive a reward. If anyone's work is burned, he will suffer loss; but he himself will be saved, yet so as through fire" (1 Cor. 3:13–15).

On September 11, 2001, Avremel Zelmanowitz hugged his brother Yankel for the last time and went to work on the twenty-seventh floor of One World Trade Center. He and his friend Edward Beyea, who was a quadriplegic, were program analysts at Empire Blue Cross and Blue Shield.

After the plane hit Tower One, Yankel spoke to his brother two more times. Avremel was waiting to evacuate with his friend Ed, who could not make it down the stairs with his wheelchair. Avremel didn't want to leave Ed until help came because he feared people would injure him if they moved him improperly.

Avremel's sister-in-law noted, "He didn't stay to die; he stayed to help. That was his intention." His brother noted, "Avremel's actions that day are what defined him. He lived his entire life that way, always caring about people, always anticipating people's needs. You wouldn't have to ask Avremel for something; he'd understand that it had to be done and he'd go and do it. This was who he was."[9]

Avremel stayed behind because he wanted to make sure his friend was safe. Even when lives are in danger, some would rather stay and ensure the safety of others than think of their own safety. The Levites were God's people, called to the work of the temple. They were resuming the positions they held before the walls came down and were persevering for the city they loved. Sometimes staying can be an act of obedience and love.

Listen To …

Pray as though everything depended on God. Work as though everything depended on you.

—*Augustine*

DAY 3

Men Dwelling in Nearby Towns

Lily MacLeod and Gillian Shaw live 250 miles apart in Ontario, Canada. Both were born in China, both were the same age, and both were adopted. Lily and Gillian are identical twins who were given up for adoption and adopted by two families who didn't know each other.

The two families had met once before in an Ottawa-based adoption agency through which they traveled together to China with three other families to pick up their children. Concern arose when both families saw pictures of their identical, soon-to-be adopted daughters. They feared a mix-up had resulted in both families adopting the same child.

When they arrived, however, they learned they were each adopting one of the identical twin girls. Although Lily and Gillian live 250 miles apart, the parents made a pact to raise them together as best as they could. They are growing up separately and yet together.[10]

Today, we see that while not all of the Israelites would be living in Jerusalem, some would be living nearby in the surrounding areas. Although they would miss the day-by-day life with their Jerusalem counterparts, they would still be close enough to dwell together.

Who we are is important to God, and He sets us in the perfect dwelling place for specific reasons, like putting twin girls from China in Canada. God cares about where we dwell!

Lift Up ...

Dear Lord, thank You for appointing a place for every one of Your children. Help me remember that even though I dwell on this earth, I am not home until the day I enter into Your presence. In Jesus' name. Amen.

1 Important Cities

Places are significant in the Bible, so they are important to us. The Lord knows where we are and where we will be at the times of our death or when we are raptured. "Since his days are determined, the number of his months is with You; You have appointed his limits, so that he cannot pass" (Job 14:5).

Look At ...

Yesterday, we reviewed the names of the priests and Levites who were responsible for the work of the temple. We saw that God had a specific place for each person, whether a leader in the house of God, a gatekeeper, or a singer. We learned that God has a niche for each person in the body of Christ. Every individual is important and accounted for in His Book of Life.

Today, we examine cities and villages inhabited by the returning Israelites. While we may not be able to pinpoint where these cities were located, they played an important part in Israel's history and in our study of the Bible. They were—and still are—important to God. Israel was expanding as many of the people returned to the homes they occupied before they were exiled. Just like Dorothy in the *Wizard of Oz*, these people might have been thinking, *There's no place like home!*

Read Nehemiah 11:25–36.

And as for the villages with their fields, some of the children of Judah dwelt in Kirjath Arba and its villages, Dibon and its villages, Jekabzeel and its villages; in Jeshua, Moladah, Beth Pelet, Hazar Shual, and Beersheba and its villages; in Ziklag and Meconah and its villages; in En Rimmon, Zorah, Jarmuth, Zanoah, Adullam, and their villages; in Lachish and its fields; in Azekah and its villages. They dwelt from Beersheba to the Valley of Hinnom. Also the children of Benjamin from Geba dwelt in Michmash, Aija, and Bethel, and their villages; in Anathoth, Nob, Ananiah; in Hazor, Ramah, Gittaim; in Hadid, Zeboim, Neballat; in Lod, Ono, and the Valley of Craftsmen. Some of the Judean divisions of Levites were in Benjamin. Nehemiah 11:25–36

1. According to Genesis 23:1–2, who died in Kirjath Arba?

2. According to Joshua 19:1–2, to whom was Moladah originally allotted?

3. According to 2 Samuel 1:1–4, what was reported to David in Ziklag?

4. According to Nehemiah 3:13, the inhabitants of Zanoah were responsible for what?

5. According to Genesis 35:15, what significant event happened to Jacob at Bethel?

6. According to Jeremiah 1:1, what Old Testament prophet was from Anathoth?

7. According to Joshua 11:11, what did Joshua do to Hazor?

8. According to 1 Samuel 1:19–20, who was from Ramah?

Live Out ...

9. Today we have discovered that each place, whether village or city, is important to God. Significant things happen in our lives in every place we dwell. What is important to us is important to God.

a. Fill in the chart below with places you have lived (cities, countries, specific addresses) and something significant that occurred in each place.

Where I Lived	Significant Event That Occurred

3 Important Memories

God is with us throughout our lives, from birth to death, and He draws near to us in those times when we hear devastating news. "The LORD is near to those who have a broken heart, and saves such as have a contrite spirit" (Ps. 34:18).

5 Important Meetings

When God speaks to us, we must take note. God tells us that if we call to Him, He will answer. "Call to Me, and I will answer you, and show you great and mighty things, which you do not know" (Jer. 33:3).

9 Important Places

God cares about even the smallest things in our lives, from life changes to the number of hairs on our heads! God is detail-oriented, and His knowledge of each one of His children is endless. "But the very hairs of your head are all numbered. Do not fear therefore; you are of more value than many sparrows" (Luke 12:7).

10 Important Spaces

God doesn't want you to come to Him with just your marriage or job worries. He wants *all* areas of your life to be surrendered to Him. "You shall love the Lord your God with all your heart, with all your soul, and with all your strength" (Deut. 6:5). *All* means *all*!

b. Write about one of these significant events and what it meant in your life.

10. God dwells in His children, in the heavens, and in buildings.

a. Fill in the chart below to see places God has dwelt:

Scripture	Where God Dwells
1 Kings 6:13	
1 Kings 8:49	
Ezekiel 36:27	
Matthew 6:9	
1 Corinthians 3:16	
Ephesians 2:19–22	
Revelation 21:3	

b. If God does not dwell in your heart, write a prayer in your journal, asking Him to come in and fill every space in your life.

———————————————

Twins may be especially inclined to separation anxiety. This disorder is a psychological condition in which individuals experience anxiety when separated from a place or a person with whom they have a strong emotional attachment. Emotions and behavior can range from uneasiness to full-blown anxiety.[11]

We don't see evidence that any of the Israelites experienced anxiety disorder when leaving their friends and family in Jerusalem to set out for the surrounding areas. Maybe after captivity and exile, they were happy to simply dwell together in the freedom of the Holy Land. Sometimes it's healthier to focus on what you have rather than what was lost.

Listen To ...

God dwells in His creation and is everywhere indivisibly present in all His works. He is transcendent above all His works even while He is immanent within them.

—A. W. Tozer

DAY 4

Men Working for God

Os Hillman tells the story of a man in the Philippines who was radically saved. Although Os had no formal ministry training, he had been taught that as a believer, he had the power of God in him to make a change in his community—and maybe in the world.

Os began to frequent a local bar to find sinners to minister to. He focused his energies on the bartender because the young believer thought that this gay, drug-addicted pimp to sixty-five prostitutes would probably be the biggest sinner around. Regularly, Os went to the bar, ordered a Coke, and eventually gained the trust and friendship of the bartender. Day after day, he drank his Coke while sharing the gospel with the bartender. Eventually, the man was saved and delivered from his sinful lifestyle. At that point, the bartender began sharing the gospel with the prostitutes, and all sixty-five of them became Christians. They soon began holding church in the bar![12]

Sometimes we think we don't have the power to change the lives of those around us—and we don't. But God does! He has the power needed to affect an individual, and that individual can have a huge effect on the community.

Like the Israelites, whether we are missionaries or marketing executives, waitresses or window washers, we can all work for God to build our community, each in the exact place He has for us.

Lift Up ...

Dear Lord, sometimes in the midst of a group of people, I feel invisible. I wonder if You really see or hear me. Reveal Yourself to me in a new and powerful way so You can use me to the fullest extent possible. Show me how to live for You, work for You, and die to myself. In Jesus' name. Amen.

Look At ...

Yesterday, we saw the Israelites begin something like an urban sprawl as they relocated to the surrounding areas of Jerusalem. While the Holy City had been repopulated with 10 percent of the nation, others were shifting to neighboring cities and villages. Though some of these cities no longer exist, we know each held importance to God, as He included them in the Bible.

Today, we continue with lists of people and places, including priests who sealed the covenant in Nehemiah 10 and priests who were heads of their houses in Judah and priestly houses.

While lists of names may be daunting to study, it's important to remember that only those who could prove their priestly lineage were able to serve in the temple. Because of the scattering of the nation, it was vital to keep accurate family records to ensure God's work was done in accordance with the law.

Read Nehemiah 12:1–26.

Now these are the priests and the Levites who came up with Zerubbabel the son of Shealtiel, and Jeshua: Seraiah, Jeremiah, Ezra, Amariah, Malluch, Hattush, Shechaniah, Rehum, Meremoth, Iddo, Ginnethoi, Abijah, Mijamin, Maadiah, Bilgah, Shemaiah, Joiarib, Jedaiah, Sallu, Amok, Hilkiah, and Jedaiah. These were the heads of the priests and their brethren in the days of Jeshua. Moreover the Levites were Jeshua, Binnui, Kadmiel, Sherebiah, Judah, and Mattaniah who led the thanksgiving psalms, he and his brethren. Also Bakbukiah and Unni, their brethren, stood across from them in their duties. Jeshua begot Joiakim, Joiakim begot Eliashib, Eliashib begot Joiada, Joiada begot Jonathan, and Jonathan begot Jaddua. Now in the days of Joiakim, the priests, the heads of the fathers' houses were: of Seraiah, Meraiah; of Jeremiah, Hananiah; of Ezra, Meshullam; of Amariah, Jehohanan; of Melichu, Jonathan; of Shebaniah, Joseph; of Harim, Adna; of Meraioth, Helkai; of Iddo, Zechariah; of Ginnethon, Meshullam; of Abijah, Zichri; the son of Minjamin; of Moadiah, Piltai; of Bilgah, Shammua; of Shemaiah, Jehonathan; of Joiarib, Mattenai; of Jedaiah, Uzzi; of Sallai, Kallai; of Amok, Eber; of Hilkiah, Hashabiah; and of Jedaiah, Nethanel. During the reign of Darius the Persian, a record was also kept of the Levites and priests who had been heads of their fathers' houses in the days of Eliashib, Joiada, Johanan, and Jaddua. The sons of

2 Priestly Names

These verses list the heads of the priests and Levites who returned from Babylon with Zerubbabel and Jeshua. The high priests of five generations are also mentioned by name.[13]

4 Priestly Lines

This appears to be a complete listing of the high priests' lineage beginning with Jeshua, who represented the first return of the captives, and ending with Jaddua, who probably continued as the high priest during the time of Alexander the Great, in 336 BC.

6 Priestly Records

The king mentioned in this passage could have been either Darius III, who reigned 335–331 BC, or Darius II, who reigned from 423–404 BC. The consensus is that Darius the Persian was probably Darius II. The Levites were keeping the commands given by King David to praise and thank God.

Levi, the heads of the fathers' houses until the days of Johanan the son of Eliashib, were written in the book of the chronicles. And the heads of the Levites were Hashabiah, Sherebiah, and Jeshua the son of Kadmiel, with their brothers across from them, to praise and give thanks, group alternating with group, according to the command of David the man of God. Mattaniah, Bakbukiah, Obadiah, Meshullam, Talmon, and Akkub were gatekeepers keeping the watch at the storerooms of the gates. These lived in the days of Joiakim the son of Jeshua, the son of Jozadak, and in the days of Nehemiah the governor, and of Ezra the priest, the scribe. Nehemiah 12:1–26

1. Who was the father of Zerubbabel?

2. What positions did these men hold?

3. Who led a part of the worship service with his brothers? What part did he lead?

4. How many of the priests were heads of the fathers' houses?

5. What reigning monarch is mentioned here? What country was he from?

6. What record was kept during his time?

7. Draw a diagram based on the Scripture above that represents how you think the worship service was set up.

8. What job were the gatekeepers responsible for?

9. According to verse 26, what approximate time period does the passage refer to?

Live Out ...

10. Today, we reviewed the genealogy of priests, leaders, and people in authority doing God's holy work.

> a. In the chart below, list men and women in your family tree who have made an impact for God in your life and the lives of others. List some of their godly attributes and accomplishments done in God's name.

10 Family Duties

God is specific in His instructions to families: children obey your parents; parents train up your children. "Children, obey your parents in the Lord, for this is right.... And you, fathers ... bring them up in the training and admonition of the Lord" (Eph. 6:1, 4).

Family Member Name	Attributes and Accomplishments

> b. Choose someone from your list who is still living, and write a prayer of thanksgiving for his or her faithfulness in your life and in the community.
>
> c. Contact this person to say how his or her walk has impacted you. Thank this person for being a wonderful example, and encourage him or her to continue on for the Lord!

11. The following Scripture passages speak about labor and work.

> a. Match the verse with the reference.

11 Job Duties

We should labor for God for His pleasure and glory, for it is from Him that our reward comes. "Whatever you do, do it heartily, as to the Lord and not to men, knowing that from the Lord you will receive the reward of the inheritance; for you serve the Lord Christ" (Col. 3:23–24).

Reference	Verse
A. Ecclesiastes 3:13	___ So then neither he who plants is anything, nor he who waters, but God who gives the increase. Now he who plants and he who waters are one, and each one will receive his own reward according to his own labor.
B. Ecclesiastes 3:22	___ This *is* a faithful saying and worthy of all acceptance. For to this *end* we both labor and suffer reproach, because we trust in the living God, who is the Savior of all men, especially of those who believe.
C. 1 Corinthians 3:7–8	___ That every man should eat and drink and enjoy the good of all his labor—it *is* the gift of God.
D. 1 Corinthians 15:58	___ So I perceived that nothing *is* better than that a man should rejoice in his own works, for that *is* his heritage.
E. 1 Timothy 4:9–10	___ Therefore, my beloved brethren, be steadfast, immovable, always abounding in the work of the Lord, knowing that your labor is not in vain in the Lord.
F. Revelation 14:13	___ Then I heard a voice from heaven saying to me, "Write: 'Blessed *are* the dead who die in the Lord from now on.'" "Yes," says the Spirit, "that they may rest from their labors, and their works follow them."

b. Summarize what you learn from these verses.

_____

Most of us are familiar with Mother Teresa, the nun who spent the majority of her life working in the slums of Calcutta, India. She was born Agnes Bojaxhiu in 1910 to an Albanian family. Upon taking her orders to become a nun at the Sisters of Loreto convent in Ireland, she changed her name to Teresa, after her patron saint.

From an early age, Teresa was fascinated by stories of missionaries around the world. At the age of eighteen, she left home to begin her life's work.

She spoke five languages: English, Albanian, Serbo-Croat, Bengali, and Hindi. In 1979 she won the Nobel Peace Prize, but insisted that the money intended for the honorary dinner instead be given to charities she was a part of to help the poor.[14]

Mother Teresa was known for her charity work, but she was best known for helping those deemed "untouchable" in the slums of Calcutta. She was once quoted as saying, "No, I wouldn't touch a leper for a thousand pounds, yet I willingly care for him for the love of God."[15]

She died in 1997 at the age of eighty-seven. She is credited with starting 610 missions in 123 countries, including hospices and homes for people with AIDS/HIV, leprosy, and tuberculosis. While others would cringe at the idea of "God's work" involving disease and death, Mother Teresa selflessly worked for God.

Listen To ...

Be faithful in small things because it is in them that your strength lies.

—Mother Teresa

Men Dedicating the Walls

The Western Wall, also known as the Wailing Wall, is located in Jerusalem at the foot of the western side of the Temple Mount. This site is considered the holiest in Judaism and is visited by millions of people on pilgrimage every year. The Wailing Wall is a 187-foot area of the wall facing the plaza. It is the only remaining portion of the holy temple. It is set aside specifically for prayer.

The name Wailing Wall stems from the Jewish practice of coming to the site to mourn the destruction of the temple. According to Jewish law, one is obligated to grieve and rend one's garments upon visiting the Western Wall and seeing the desolation of the temple.

The wall was originally built by King Solomon in the tenth century. Later, Herod the Great expanded it, and it is believed to have been completed by King Agrippa II. In 70 BC, the Romans destroyed it.[16]

Today, the Western Wall is a symbol of sorrow and destruction for the Jewish nation, but for the Israelites of Nehemiah's time, the wall was a symbol of rejoicing and completion. Jerusalem was once again whole, and it will be again. In the New Jerusalem, we will see all things made new.

Lift Up ...

Lord, I dedicate myself to You. I want You to march around the walls of my heart and occupy every inch of it. May I always remember the restoration You have done in my life. In Jesus' name. Amen.

Look At ...

Yesterday, we saw that God's work involves many people with various backgrounds, occupations, and talents. God uses anyone who is willing to further His kingdom. He keeps His eyes on His children. Although it's not clear why the lists are so exhaustive and sometimes repetitive, it's possible Nehemiah wanted to make sure the people responsible for the revival of Jerusalem were noted and remembered. Psalm 112:6 says, "The righteous will be in everlasting remembrance." We must never forget what the righteous have done.

Today, we finally arrive at the celebration of the completed wall. Amid threats from enemies and difficult circumstances, the wall was completed, and Jerusalem was on its way to restoration. This dedication is thought to have taken place more than seventeen years after the completion of the wall. This is based on the date that Nehemiah returned to Shushan to take up his duties once again for Artaxerxes.

Read Nehemiah 12:27–47.

Now at the dedication of the wall of Jerusalem they sought out the Levites in all their places, to bring them to Jerusalem to celebrate the dedication with gladness, both with thanksgivings and singing, with cymbals and stringed instruments and harps. And the sons of the singers gathered together from the countryside around Jerusalem, from the villages of the Netophathites, from the house of Gilgal, and from the fields of Geba and Azmaveth; for the singers had built themselves villages all around Jerusalem. Then the priests and Levites purified themselves, and purified the people, the gates, and the wall. So I brought the leaders of Judah up on the wall, and appointed two large thanksgiving choirs. One went to the right hand on the wall toward the Refuse Gate. After them went Hoshaiah and half of the leaders of Judah, and Azariah, Ezra, Meshullam, Judah, Benjamin, Shemaiah, Jeremiah, and some of the priests' sons with trumpets—Zechariah the son of Jonathan, the son of Shemaiah, the son of Mattaniah, the son of Michaiah, the son of Zaccur, the son of Asaph, and his brethren, Shemaiah, Azarel, Milalai, Gilalai, Maai, Nethanel, Judah, and Hanani, with the musical instruments of David the man of God. Ezra the scribe went before them. By the Fountain Gate, in front of them, they went up the stairs of the City of David, on the

1 Dedication

"The word *dedication* comes from the Latin verb do, dare, *dedi, datum*—Latin words which mean to offer and to give. When an object is dedicated to the Lord, it's given to Him for His control and use. When a person dedicates herself to God, it is for the same reasons."[17]

stairway of the wall, beyond the house of David, as far as the Water Gate eastward. The other thanksgiving choir went the opposite way, and I was behind them with half of the people on the wall, going past the Tower of the Ovens as far as the Broad Wall, and above the Gate of Ephraim, above the Old Gate, above the Fish Gate, the Tower of Hananel, the Tower of the Hundred, as far as the Sheep Gate; and they stopped by the Gate of the Prison. So the two thanksgiving choirs stood in the house of God, likewise I and the half of the rulers with me; and the priests, Eliakim, Maaseiah, Minjamin, Michaiah, Elioenai, Zechariah, and Hananiah, with trumpets; also Maaseiah, Shemaiah, Eleazar, Uzzi, Jehohanan, Malchijah, Elam, and Ezer. The singers sang loudly with Jezrahiah the director. Also that day they offered great sacrifices, and rejoiced, for God had made them rejoice with great joy; the women and the children also rejoiced, so that the joy of Jerusalem was heard afar off. And at the same time some were appointed over the rooms of the storehouse for the offerings, the firstfruits, and the tithes, to gather into them from the fields of the cities the portions specified by the Law for the priests and Levites; for Judah rejoiced over the priests and Levites who ministered. Both the singers and the gatekeepers kept the charge of their God and the charge of the purification, according to the command of David and Solomon his son. For in the days of David and Asaph of old there were chiefs of the singers, and songs of praise and thanksgiving to God. In the days of Zerubbabel and in the days of Nehemiah all Israel gave the portions for the singers and the gatekeepers, a portion for each day. They also consecrated holy things for the Levites, and the Levites consecrated them for the children of Aaron. Nehemiah 12:27–47

1. What event was taking place?

2.   a. What group was sought out to dedicate the wall?

     b. Where had they come from?

3. a. What was the overall feeling among the people?

b. What instruments were used to celebrate?

4. What four things were purified by the priests and Levites?

1.

2.

3.

4.

4 Purification

Seeking out the Levites was important because the dedication could not take place without their help. Purification was representative of moral purity and was always a part of any ritual in Jewish festivals. It likely included peace offerings, in which the people shared a meal. Everyone—men, women, and children—took part.

5. Answer the questions below about the thanksgiving choirs:

a. How many choirs were there?

b. Which gates did the first choir head toward? Who led them?

c. What did they take with them from the man of God?

6. The second choir went in the opposite direction.

a. Who led the second group?

b. Which gates did they pass?

c. Which towers did they pass as they marched?

d. What was the order of the march? In other words, what group was following what other group?

6 Unification

It is significant that Nehemiah assembled these two great groups of singers and started the march at what was most likely the Valley Gate. This is the same gate where he began his survey of the walls back in Nehemiah 1.

10 Gratification

Thanksgiving is a term commonly found in the book of Psalms. It is a public acknowledgement to declare aloud in public to another. This word, along with singing and instruments, suggests the use of the Psalms in musical settings with words of praise and instrumental accompaniment.[18]

7. Storerooms were appointed for what offerings? Why were the offerings necessary?

8. The songs that were sung were of _____ and _____.

9. a. Who rejoiced?

b. Why?

11 Fortification

The walls were fortified and the people were celebrating. Their enemies said that a fox wouldn't be able to walk on the walls, yet the Israelites were marching on them! This testifies that God is a promise-keeper. "Not a word failed of any good thing which the LORD had spoken to the house of Israel. All came to pass" (Josh. 21:45).

Live Out ...

10. The Israelites were celebrating with thanksgiving.

   a. Fill in the chart below to see what the Bible says about thanksgiving.

Scripture	Thanksgiving
1 Chronicles 16:8	
Jonah 2:9	
Psalm 7:17	
Psalm 100:4	
Philippians 4:6	

b. In your journal write a prayer of thanksgiving to God. Thank Him for the work He has done in your life while you have been studying the book of Nehemiah.

11. Nehemiah and the Israelites built the wall upward toward heaven. Throughout this study, you have been encouraged to build your own walls of restoration for the broken down areas in your life.

   a. On the bricks of the wall below, write some areas of your life that God has restored.

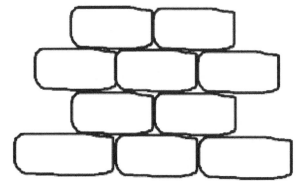

b. If there are still areas of your "wall" that God has not yet restored, ask Him for restoration in those areas now. Offer Him praise for the work He *will* do.

———————————

It is common practice at the Western Wall to write down prayers—deep requests from the heart entrusted to God—and squeeze the paper into the cracks of the wall. More than a million notes are placed in the wall each year. In this day of technology, there are companies that offer to receive your prayers through email, print them out, and place them in the wall. The notes come in different languages and handwriting. Some are long; some are short; some are written on scraps of paper like bubble gum wrappers; others are poetic verse and Bible verses. It is strictly forbidden to read a note that another has placed in the wall. Twice a year, the rabbi of the Western Wall collects all of the prayers and buries them in the Jewish cemetery on the Mount of Olives.[19]

Just as some people put their deepest desires into the cracks of the wall, the Israelites laid their hopes on the wall because it signified the promises of the Lord.

> Great is the LORD, and greatly to be praised
> In the city of our God,
> In His holy mountain.
> Beautiful in elevation,
> The joy of the whole earth,
> Is Mount Zion on the sides of the north,
> The city of the great King.
> —Psalm 48:1–2

Nehemiah promised the Jews that God would fight for them and see them through. Standing on the wall proclaiming and celebrating victory reminds us that we can put all of our expectations on God.

Listen To ...

The believer should undertake nothing which he does not dedicate to the Lord.

—*Matthew Henry*

Remember the Covenant

Nehemiah 13

In March of 1970, Vinko Bogataj, an outstanding ski jumper, competed in the "Ski-Flying World Championships" in West Germany. The snow began to fall as the competition commenced, and by the third-round jumps the weather conditions had greatly deteriorated. About halfway down the ramp, Bogataj realized that the heavy snow was making his approach too fast. He attempted to slow down and abort the jump, but he lost control and shot off the end of the ramp. He flipped until he crashed through a retaining fence. Although the accident was horrific, the ski champ escaped with only a minor concussion.[1]

The film crew for *The Wide World of Sports* television show captured Bogataj's dramatic wipeout. For years, this spectacular defeat was the show's opening scene, coupled with the tag line: "The thrill of victory and the agony of defeat."

In our study this week, we will recognize a similar scenario. After experiencing the great success of building both the wall and their faith, the residents of Jerusalem lost their spiritual balance and were headed for a fall. As we read Nehemiah 13, we will see that there is value in both the "thrill of victory and the agony of defeat."

Day 1: Nehemiah 13:1–3   **The Command to Be Separate**

Day 2: Nehemiah 13:4–9   **The Call to Be Cleansed**

Day 3: Nehemiah 13:10–14   **The Reminder to Be Restored**

Day 4: Nehemiah 13:15–22   **The Charge to Be Sanctified**

Day 5: Nehemiah 13:23–31   **The Need to Be Chastened**

The Command to Be Separate

Lift Up ...

Dear Lord, I live in this world, but Your Word tells me to "come out" from the world and be separate. Please give me the courage I need to be *in* the world but not *of* the world. In Jesus' name. Amen.

Look At ...

Last week we found Jerusalem in a phase of resettling. The wall had been restored but additional restoration was necessary: the restoration of the people. A well-deserved celebration was in progress following the completion of the wall, but the enemies' threats were a constant obstacle. The dedication of the wall would happen years after its completion.

Today we see the natural separation between God's people and unbelieving people. The purity of the Jews was essential to God, yet they were historically prone to violate and ignore His Word. Not only were God's "chosen people" stubborn and weak; they were feared and hated by others. We find that despite evil intentions and actions, God was in control. He was in control during Nehemiah's time, and He is in our time as well.

Read Nehemiah 13:1–3.

On that day they read from the Book of Moses in the hearing of the people, and in it was found written that no Ammonite or Moabite should ever come into the assembly of God, because they had not met the children of Israel with bread and water, but hired Balaam against them to curse them. However, our God turned the curse into a blessing. So it was, when they had heard the Law, that they separated all the mixed multitude from Israel. Nehemiah 13:1–3

1. What book was read in the hearing of the people? What instruction did they find written there?

2. From previous lessons in Nehemiah, we learned that a prominent Ammonite had come into the assembly of God. What was his name (Neh. 2:10)?

3. Deuteronomy 2 relates the story of Israel's journey through the lands of Ammon. Read Deuteronomy 2:25–30 then answer the following questions.

   a. In verse 27, what did Moses ask of the king of Heshbon?

   b. What was his request in verse 28?

   c. How did the king respond in verse 30?

4. Read Numbers 22:1–6. Why did Balak hire Balaam to curse the Israelites?

5. Numbers 22–24 recounts the narrative of Balak, Balaam, and the children of Israel. In summary, answer these questions:

   a. Read Numbers 22:35–38. How did Balaam decide what to say to the people?

   b. Read Numbers 23:19–20. Why did Balaam pronounce a blessing instead of a curse?

6. In Nehemiah 13:3, we see that the people obeyed God's command. What was their immediate response upon hearing the Law?

2 Separation

The Israelites were guilty of ignoring God's command to maintain the purity of their race. The Lord required total separation, knowing that only then would they resist idolatry. He desired holiness, just as He desires holiness from His people today (see Lev. 20:26).

3 Deprivation

The Ammonites and the Amorites refused the reasonable requests of God's people. Although the Israelites offered to pay for the provisions, the king refused to sell them the basic necessities needed to continue their journey. This act caused enmity between these nations for centuries to come.

5 Retaliation

The Moabites were terrified of the children of Israel and sought to bring a curse upon the nation. In Nehemiah 6:12–13, we learned that Shemaiah, like Balaam, was hired by enemies to prophesy against God's people. Both men's efforts were thwarted, however, by the sovereign Lord God of heaven. God was in control.

7 His Provision

God commands us to live separate from the world, and He gives us everything we need to accomplish this task. God never asks from us what He hasn't experienced (see Heb. 4:15). He doesn't allow us to be tempted beyond what we are capable of resisting (see 1 Cor. 10:13). He doesn't leave us alone (see Deut. 31:6).

8 Our Words

In His Word, God spends a great deal of time instructing and warning us about our words. Of all our enemies, our tongues can be the most deadly. "But no man can tame the tongue. It is an unruly evil, full of deadly poison" (James 3:8). "Death and life are in the power of the tongue" (Prov. 18:21).

Live Out ...

7. Today we saw the Lord call His chosen people to separate themselves from the defilement of the world. You and I must live in the world, but we are admonished to keep the world from living in us.

a. Check any boxes below that indicate ways the world can recognize that you are separate.

❑ by the books I read   ❑ by the conversations I have

❑ by the television shows I watch   ❑ by the places I go

❑ by the company I keep   ❑ by the words that I use

❑ by the way I spend my money   ❑ by the way I run my business

b. Examine any boxes you were unable to check. Is compromise with the world keeping you from being separate unto the Lord? Journal a prayer asking the Lord to help you make any changes necessary to live a life set apart for Him. Begin to make these changes today!

8. Balaam had a mighty encounter with the Angel of the Lord (see Num. 22:21–35). The angel admonished Balaam to speak only the words given to him by God. We also need to choose our words based upon approval from the Lord.

Read Ephesians 4:29 and answer the following questions concerning God's guidelines for your speech.

a. What should *not* come out of your mouth?

b. What *should* come out of your mouth?

c. What should your words *do*?

9. God often turns curses into blessings in the lives of His people. Read the following Scriptures to determine how God transformed evil in the sight of men into a blessing for His glory.

Character/Reference	The Curse	The Blessing
Joseph—Genesis 50:17–20		
Job—Job 1:13–22; 42:10		
Paul—2 Corinthians 12:7–9		
Jesus—Galatians 3:13–14		

Victor Bogataj's painful wipeout, captured by *The Wide World of Sports*, is forever associated with the "agony of defeat." Curiously, no single photograph has that kind of staying power to represent the "thrill of victory." The television show used various images—often a video of the most recent personal triumph or team victory.

This illustrates an interesting phenomenon in the sports world and life in general: our victories are short-lived but our failures haunt us indefinitely. Dr. Joel Fish, a reputable sports psychologist, stated, "A lot of athletes I have worked with compete not only to win, but to avoid losing, because the losing is so bitter. The highs are high, but the lows are really, really low."[2] We joyfully remember our victories, but when we recall the defeats, the old pain is still real and tangible. If we allow it, the agony of defeat may overshadow the thrill of victory.

The Israelites walked closely with God as they rebuilt both the wall and their faith. Clearly, their accomplishments were anointed. Yet how easily and quickly they fell from the joy of victory to the anguish of sin and defeat. As we continue our study, we learn that defeat is not the end of the Israelites' story, and defeat is never the end of a believer's story either.

Listen To ...

What God has chosen for my significant witness was not my triumph or victories, but my defeat.

—*Charles Colson*

The Call to Be Cleansed

We all love a clean home, but maintaining that fresh feel is an ongoing task. Even as we scrub and dust and sweep in one area, dirt and clutter have already begun gaining ground in others. Unfortunately, this can be the case in our Christian walk. When we ask Jesus to be the Lord of our lives, we want Him to clean things up, to make us pure before Him; but then almost imperceptibly, the clutter and filth of this world begins to edge back in.

Robert Boyd Munger wrote a story entitled *My Heart—Christ's Home* about a man who asked Jesus to live in his heart. Together they take a tour of Christ's new home. They step into the study, which represents the man's mind; the dining room, his appetites; the den, his entertainment; the work room, his time and talent. It became apparent that this new home needed to be cleaned up, and the man was willing to let Jesus transform him—until they came to one closet. The door was locked, and Jesus was not allowed access. Slowly, the stench from that closed closet permeated the rest of the clean house.[3]

Nehemiah and the people made great strides in cleaning up Jerusalem and rebuilding walls, gates, hearts, and faith, but when Nehemiah went away, sin once again gained ground. The people reverted to their old ways and broke their promises.

Restoration was possible in Nehemiah's time—just as it is today. No matter how dirty we get, it is never too much for God to clean up!

Lift Up ...

Dear Lord, You are pure, but I have allowed sin to stain my life. Forgive me for holding on to my sin. Please clean and restore my heart. In Jesus' name. Amen.

Look At ...

Yesterday we looked at the Israelites' tendency to ignore God's Word. No matter how closely He led the people, they persisted in stubborn and willful actions. They were God's "chosen." The Jews were feared because their enemies saw that God had His powerful hand on them. God required separation from "the world" to maintain the purity of the race, yet they were prone to disobey and wander from God.

Today, and for the remaining days of our study, we will see a pattern. The people of Israel broke every promise they made in chapter 10. Nehemiah confronted each sin and sought to restore a sense of law and order. Once our lives have been defiled by sin, there is a process to restoration. We find Nehemiah in the midst of that course.

Read Nehemiah 13:4–9.

Now before this, Eliashib the priest, having authority over the storerooms of the house of our God, was allied with Tobiah. And he had prepared for him a large room, where previously they had stored the grain offerings, the frankincense, the articles, the tithes of grain, the new wine and oil, which were commanded to be given to the Levites and singers and gatekeepers, and the offerings for the priests. But during all this I was not in Jerusalem, for in the thirty-second year of Artaxerxes king of Babylon I had returned to the king. Then after certain days I obtained leave from the king, and I came to Jerusalem and discovered the evil that Eliashib had done for Tobiah, in preparing a room for him in the courts of the house of God. And it grieved me bitterly; therefore I threw all the household goods of Tobiah out of the room. Then I commanded them to cleanse the rooms; and I brought back into them the articles of the house of God, with the grain offering and the frankincense. Nehemiah 13:4–9

1. Who had authority over the temple storerooms? Refer to Nehemiah 3:1. Who was this man, and what did he help construct?

2. With whom was Eliashib allied? How was Eliashib related to Sanballat, Tobiah's co-conspirator against Israel (v. 28)?

3 Abused Authority

Eliashib formed an alliance with Tobiah, an enemy of the people and the rebuilding project (Neh. 2:19). Eliashib was trusted by Nehemiah and given an important responsibility to supervise the storerooms in the temple. However, he abused his authority: "Eliashib seriously misused his office. He used a holy privilege for an unholy purpose."[4]

5 Refused Respect

The children of Israel broke their promise to the Lord. In Nehemiah 10, the people promised to bring the best of all they had to the temple storerooms. Here we find the storerooms empty. They pledged, "We will not neglect the house of our God" (Neh. 10:39). Yet they had total disregard for the sanctity of the temple.

6 Acquired Wives

There is no biblical record of how long Nehemiah was away from Jerusalem, but we can surmise that it was several years. This would allow for some of the Jewish men to marry foreign women and have children. They had time to learn languages other than the Hebrew (see Neh. 13:23–24).

3. What had Eliashib prepared for Tobiah?

4. List the six things previously stored in Tobiah's quarters.

   1.

   2.

   3.

   4.

   5.

   6.

5. These items were to be given to what groups of people? Who was to receive the offerings?

6. Where was Nehemiah during this time? If Nehemiah came to Jerusalem the first time in the twentieth year of King Artaxerxes, how long did he reside in the city before returning to the king?

7. When Nehemiah departed Persia and returned to Jerusalem, he discovered a grave situation. What immediate actions did he take?

Live Out ...

8. When Nehemiah learned of Eliashib's negligence, he was filled with emotion. Compare Nehemiah 13:8 in these four translations to better understand what he was feeling.

   NKJV: "grieved me bitterly"

   NIV:

   NLT:

   ESV:

Think about a time when you felt bitterly grieved.

9. We read in Nehemiah 13:8 that Nehemiah "threw all the household goods of Tobiah out of the room." Many years later, Jesus Christ responded similarly to unholy and sinful activity in the temple.

a. Read Matthew 21:12–13. What was Jesus upset about? What admonishment did Jesus give in this verse?

b. Jesus took seriously the sanctity of His Father's temple. Spend some time examining your own attitude and approach to God's house. Journal a prayer asking Jesus to instill in your heart the reverence due to God's house of prayer.

8 Justified Emotions

Scripture attributes emotion such as grief, displeasure, and anger to the Lord Jesus as He looks upon the sin of His people. These emotions are real and acceptable so long as we respond biblically, without sin, as both Jesus and Nehemiah did (Eph. 4:26; Ps. 4:4).

10. Nehemiah dealt with Eliashib's sin of harboring Tobiah in the temple in three ways. Look at each step and consider them personally. Journal through the steps Nehemiah took in dealing with sin.

Step One: He confronted the sin, although doing so brought him grief. Are you harboring sin in God's temple (your body) that should not be there (anger, bitterness, jealousy, selfishness, or worry)? Tell God of your grief over that sin and your desire for His promised forgiveness.

Step Two: He cleansed the rooms, ridding them of anything that was unclean. He removed the unholy items and then thoroughly cleaned the rooms. Humbly come before God telling Him of your desire for His cleansing touch.

Step Three: He restored the rooms by filling them with the articles and offerings that belonged there. Ask the Lord to restore you and fill you with His Spirit.

9 Cleansed Hearts

Once the temple was cleansed, the rooms were ready to be filled again. In the same way, our bodies are temples of God's Holy Spirit. We can grieve the Spirit by our acts of disobedience. Yet God stands ready to forgive us when we confess our sins and repent of our wicked ways.

———————

The homeowner who locked his closet in the book *My Heart—God's Home* eventually unlocked that filthy room and allowed Jesus to cleanse it. The stench of sin was replaced with an aroma of freedom and the fresh breeze of a new beginning. Once the man realized that he couldn't keep his life clean in his own strength, he admitted to Jesus, "I'm getting tired of trying to maintain a clean heart and an obedient life. I just am not up to it!" So he asked Jesus, "Lord, is there a possibility that you would be willing to manage the whole house and operate it for me? Could I give to you the responsibility of keeping my heart what it ought to be? … Lord you have been my guest and I have been trying to play the host. From now on you are going to be the owner and master of this house. I'm going to be the servant!"[5]

Jesus longs to be the Lord and Master of our hearts, but He won't demand it. He is waiting to be asked—to be given permission to do some housekeeping over every aspect of our lives.

Just as God worked with Nehemiah and the men of Judah, He will work with us to clean up our mistakes and restore our hearts and lives to Him.

Listen To ...

He who is completely sanctified, or cleansed from all sin, and dies in this state, is fit for glory.
—*Adam Clarke*

DAY 3

The Reminder to Be Restored

A young college student named Paul received a brand new automobile from his brother as an early Christmas gift. On Christmas Eve, when Paul came out of his office, he found an underprivileged young boy walking around the shiny new car, admiring it. "Is this your car, mister?" he asked.

Paul nodded and said, "My brother gave it to me for Christmas."

The boy looked astonished. "You mean your brother just gave it to you, and it didn't cost you nothin'? Boy, I wish …"

The young boy hesitated, and Paul expected him to say that he wished he had a brother like that. "I wish," the boy went on, "that I could be a brother like that."[6] Even in his own poverty, this boy wanted to give lavishly to his brother.

Nehemiah felt the same way. The people had stopped giving to support the needs of the temple; they had lost the desire to be a part of the blessing of God's work.

The demands of this human life can quickly overshadow the joy and privilege of giving ourselves to God's people. The Lord wants to restore that desire in us; and really, don't we all want to be a "brother like that?"

Lift Up ...

Dear Lord, some days I get so busy that I neglect to care for those around me. Help me be attentive to the needs of the people You place in my path. In Jesus' name. Amen.

Look At ...

Yesterday Nehemiah dealt with the cleansing and restoration of the temple storerooms. He was angry, and rightly so. He had turned his back for a moment, and the disobedient men of

1 Broken Promises

The children of Israel broke another promise made to the Lord. In Nehemiah 10:37, the people vowed "to bring the tithes of our land to the Levites, for the Levites should receive the tithes in all our farming communities." Ironically the Levites were now forced to work in those same farming communities!

Judah had contaminated the temple storeroom. Nehemiah, the leader of the monumental effort of the restoration of the walls and the city of Jerusalem, demonstrated the response of a godly man to ungodly actions.

Today we see that the temple hierarchy needed to be reestablished and restored as well. Responsibility exposed corruption in the leaders but simultaneously revealed the faithful. Nehemiah continued in his God-appointed role as the leader of the newly established Jerusalem. Once again, he prayerfully assessed the situation and appointed worthy men to lead, administer, and monitor.

Read Nehemiah 13:10–14.

I also realized that the portions for the Levites had not been given them; for each of the Levites and the singers who did the work had gone back to his field. So I contended with the rulers, and said, "Why is the house of God forsaken?" And I gathered them together and set them in their place. Then all Judah brought the tithe of the grain and the new wine and the oil to the storehouse. And I appointed as treasurers over the storehouse Shelemiah the priest and Zadok the scribe, and of the Levites, Pedaiah; and next to them was Hanan the son of Zaccur, the son of Mattaniah; for they were considered faithful, and their task was to distribute to their brethren. Remember me, O my God, concerning this, and do not wipe out my good deeds that I have done for the house of my God, and for its services! Nehemiah 13:10–14

1. How did Nehemiah know that provisions had not been made for the Levites and the singers?

2. What action did Nehemiah take with the rulers to deal with the "forsaken house of God"?

3. What three things did the people of Judah bring to the storehouse?

    1.

    2.

    3.

4. What step did Nehemiah take to ensure that no single individual would ever again have sole power over the provisions of the storehouse?

5. Why were these individual men chosen as treasurers?

6. What was their task?

7. What did Nehemiah want God to remember? What did he ask God *not* to do?

Live Out ...

8. Your body is a temple of the Holy Spirit living within you. Compare your mind to the temple's "storehouse."

    a. Based on Philippians 4:8, your "storehouse" should be filled with what?

      Whatever things are

      _____

      _____

      _____

      _____

      _____

      _____

      And if there is any _____

      Or anything _____

3 Renewed Promises

The people of Judah would fulfill the vow they made in Nehemiah 10:39 to "bring the offering of the grain, of the new wine and the oil, to the storerooms where the articles of the sanctuary are, where the priests who minister and the gatekeepers and the singers are; and we will not neglect the house of God."

7 Obedient Response

This is the first of four prayers recorded in chapter 13. Nehemiah begins this prayer with "Remember me," not in pride or self-exaltation, but in humility, expressing his desire to do God's work, God's way. Nehemiah did not want recognition or reward; he simply wanted to be obedient to the Lord.

8 Prayerful Response

Nehemiah's prayer habits are a wonderful example for us to follow. He prayed before he began his work (1:4); when facing obstacles (4:9); when things went well (5:19); when he needed strength (6:9); when he made decisions (13:14, 22, 29); and in all things (13:31).

10 Found Faithful

Faithfulness is a requirement for a servant of the Lord. Paul writes in 1 Corinthians 4:2, "Moreover it is required in stewards that one be found faithful." God is faithful to us and desires the same in return. We should all desire to hear these words from our Lord: "Well done, good and faithful servant" (Matt. 25:21).

b. Are you "storing" anything that doesn't abide by this criteria? Humbly ask the Lord to cleanse and restore your heart and mind.

9. In prayer, Nehemiah asked God to remember his attempts to do His will. Fill in the following chart to discover some other things God "remembers."

Scripture	What God Remembers
Psalm 9:12	the cry of the humble
Psalm 98:3	
Psalm 103:14	
Psalm 105:8	
Psalm 136:23	

10. Nehemiah appointed treasurers that he considered to be faithful. Below is a list of definitions for the Hebrew word *Aman*, which is translated "faithful" in this passage.

    a. Prayerfully consider each one and underline any in which you desire to grow stronger.

to believe	to be certain
to trust	to be steadfast
to be permanent	to be trustworthy
to be faithful	

b. Journal a prayer asking God to strengthen and grow you in these areas so that you will be "considered faithful" to serve God and His people.

_____

The people promised to support the temple and God's servants, but they had gone back on that promise. Nehemiah, although heartbroken, took action to rectify the situation. He knew that rebuilt walls were useless without restored hearts. Being willing to give freely and generously to God's work was one proof of a rebuilt and restored heart.

A modern-day example of this attitude is seen in the life of singer/songwriter Rich Mullins. He was a successful Christian artist who chose to live an unassuming lifestyle. After finishing his music education, Mullins moved to New Mexico and took up residency in a *hogan*, which is a traditional hut of logs and earth found on the Navajo Indian reservation. He lived there until his untimely death in 1997. During his life, all proceeds from his tours and album sales were funneled through his church. After paying Mullins a modest salary, the church would distribute the rest of his income to various charities. The following quote from Mullins explains his philosophy:

> Jesus said whatever you do to the least of these my brother you've done it to me. And this is what I have come to think. That if I want to identify fully with Jesus Christ, who I claim to be my Savior and Lord, the best way that I can do that is to identify with the poor. Christianity is not about building an absolutely secure little niche in the world … it is about learning to love like Jesus loved, and Jesus loved the poor and Jesus loved the broken-hearted.…[7]

Listen To ...

I do not believe one can settle how much we ought to give. I am afraid the only safe road is to give more than we can spare.

—*C. S. Lewis*

The Charge to Be Sanctified

Chuck Swindoll tells a story about a man who came across a place called "The Church of God Grill" while searching for a new restaurant. Intrigued, he phoned the establishment, and asked the friendly manager how the restaurant had gotten that unusual name. "Well," the man answered, "we had a little mission church downtown, and to help pay the bills we began selling chicken dinners after church on Sunday. People loved the chicken, and we did such a good business, we found ourselves needing to shorten up our church services in order to get enough dinners ready on time. Eventually, we closed down the church altogether and just served chicken. We kept our original name, 'The Church of God Grill.'"[8]

The management of the Church of God Grill and the leaders in Jerusalem were experiencing the same questions: Is it greed? Is it need? Is it priority? Is it compromise? Even as the people completed the wall, they began to reestablish their old rhythm of life. They were placing priority on physical rather than spiritual needs. They sacrificed the Sabbath, the day of rest and worship, to secure their financial well-being. This behavior is easy to recognize in the people of Judah and in the management decisions at the Church of God Grill. It is not nearly as recognizable in our own lives. Allow the Lord to work in your heart as you examine your priorities this week.

Lift Up ...

Dear Lord, in Your original design, You set one day apart as holy and separate so that Your people might rest from their toil and be devoted to You. Empower me by Your Spirit that I might devote myself to You every single day of the week. In Jesus' name. Amen.

Look At ...

Yesterday, we found Nehemiah in a clean-up role. He held the corrupt leaders accountable for their actions and the neglect of their responsibilities. Even in the refurbished environment, sin had entered and dirtied the temple. As a result, people suffered loss. Nehemiah cleaned house. He replaced the corrupt men with faithful men. Once again, he prayerfully assessed the situation and appointed worthy men to lead, administer, and monitor.

Today we will see the Jews as slaves to the "almighty dollar" and profaning the Sabbath in the process. Their true colors and greed undermined the community, the Sabbath, and the word of the law. Once again, Nehemiah confronted and contended with the nobles and hierarchy of Judah. He called their actions what they were: "evil." He asked if they were prepared to reap the same result their fathers had experienced when they had done such things.

Read Nehemiah 13:15–22.

In those days I saw people in Judah treading wine presses on the Sabbath, and bringing in sheaves, and loading donkeys with wine, grapes, figs, and all kinds of burdens, which they brought into Jerusalem on the Sabbath day. And I warned them about the day on which they were selling provisions. Men of Tyre dwelt there also, who brought in fish and all kinds of goods, and sold them on the Sabbath to the children of Judah, and in Jerusalem. Then I contended with the nobles of Judah, and said to them, "What evil thing is this that you do, by which you profane the Sabbath day? Did not your fathers do thus, and did not our God bring all this disaster on us and on this city? Yet you bring added wrath on Israel by profaning the Sabbath." So it was, at the gates of Jerusalem, as it began to be dark before the Sabbath, that I commanded the gates to be shut, and charged that they must not be opened till after the Sabbath. Then I posted some of my servants at the gates, so that no burdens would be brought in on the Sabbath day. Now the merchants and sellers of all kinds of wares lodged outside Jerusalem once or twice. Then I warned them, and said to them, "Why do you spend the night around the wall? If you do so again, I will lay hands on you!" From that time on they came no more on the Sabbath. And I commanded the Levites that they should cleanse themselves, and that they should go and guard the gates, to sanctify the Sabbath day. Remember me, O my God, concerning this also, and spare me according to the greatness of Your mercy! Nehemiah 13:15–22

3 Warped Priorities

In the Book of Moses, the admonition to refrain from work on the Sabbath was repeated over and over again (Gen. 2:2–3; Ex. 20:8; 23:12). As the Law was read and explained to the people, they could not avoid hearing this commandment. Yet they made personal gain a higher priority than obedience to God.

5 Short Memories

The children of Israel broke yet another promise. In Nehemiah 10:31, they had said, "If the peoples of the land brought wares or any grain to sell on the Sabbath day, we would not buy it from them on the Sabbath, or on a holy day." Once again, how quickly they forgot!

6 Rebuked Nobles

Nehemiah rebuked the nobles for allowing the Sabbath to be defiled on their watch (Neh. 13:17–18). He then took it upon himself to raise up the Levites to guard over the gates and to guard over the Sabbath. They were to cleanse themselves and therefore become examples of keeping the Sabbath holy.

1. What three things did Nehemiah observe the people doing on the Sabbath?

   1.

   2.

   3.

2. What other group of people dwelt in Judah? What did these men do with their goods?

3. When their forefathers broke the Sabbath laws, God brought disaster in the form of exile and oppression by their enemies. By profaning the Sabbath, what risks had the nobles introduced?

4. What did Nehemiah command to be done at sundown the day before the Sabbath?

5. What did Nehemiah threaten if the merchants and sellers continued to spend the night around the wall? Did the threat deter them? How do you know?

6. Nehemiah commanded the Levites to do several things:

   They should _____ themselves.

   They should go and _____ the _____.

   They were to do these things in order to _____ the Sabbath day.

7. What did Nehemiah ask God to remember? What attribute of God did Nehemiah rely on to be spared?

Live Out ...

8. The people of Jerusalem were defiling the Jewish law by conducting business and trade on the Sabbath. Nehemiah recognized that they were choosing financial security over spiritual security. Read the following verses and record what *should* take priority over wealth.

Scripture	Priority over Wealth
Psalm 19:9–10	
Psalm 119:127	
Psalm 119:162	
Matthew 19:21	

9. Examine your heart before God and answer these questions:

a. In your typical week, does the Lord receive as much consideration as do your physical needs?

b. Do you honestly believe that God is able to provide for you financially if you willingly relinquish control to Him?

c. Read Matthew 6:30–33 and then rewrite verse 33 into a prayer, asking the Lord to help you keep your priorities in order. "But seek first the kingdom of God and His righteousness, and all these things shall be added to you."

10. In verse 22, Nehemiah turns to the Lord in prayer: "Remember me, O my God, concerning this also, and spare me according to the greatness of Your mercy."

a. Look up a few verses pertaining to God's mercy and record one that is meaningful to you today.

8 Spoiled Witness

The Old Testament laws governing the Jewish Sabbath don't apply to the Christian's Lord's Day; however, keeping the day holy is still necessary. Warren Wiersbe said, "But I do know that many Christians have killed their joy, witness, and spiritual power by turning Sunday into an ordinary day and not putting Christ first in the week."[9]

10 Delivered from Judgment

The terms *mercy* and *grace* are often confused. *Mercy* is God choosing not to punish us as we truly deserve; *grace* is God bestowing blessings on us even though we are unworthy and underserving of them. In verse 22, Nehemiah is asking for deliverance from judgment—God's great mercy.[10]

b. Write a prayer asking God to "spare you according to His mercy" for a specific unrighteous behavior.

_____
,

When Eric Liddell announced that he would not run the hundred-meter race in the 1924 Paris Olympic Games, he made himself unpopular with his Scottish countrymen. The finals of that decisive race were scheduled on a Sunday. For Eric, Sunday was a day of worship and rest. He would not run. Although he was called a traitor, Eric Liddell stood firm. He had never run on Sunday and wouldn't start now.

With little time left before the opening ceremonies, Eric qualified for the four-hundred-meter race, which was not scheduled on Sunday. He knew his chances of winning the four hundred were slim, but he was encouraged by a note handed to him right before the race began. It read: "He who honors Him, He (God) will honor."

The race began and Eric Liddell took off with his head back, running in his own unusual style. When he rounded the track where the racers usually merge, he realized he was all alone. Eric ran with all he had and crossed the finish line first, winning the gold medal and setting a new world record in the four-hundred-meter race.[11]

Both Eric and his countrymen acknowledged that God had honored Eric Liddell's obedience to do it God's way. We don't always understand God's standards, but He has His reasons and they are always for our best and His highest. True victory comes when we do it God's way!

Listen To ...

When we put God first all other things fall into their proper place or drop out of our lives.
—*Ezra Taft Benson*

The Need to Be Chastened

As our study in Nehemiah draws to a close, we are keenly aware of how narrow the road is that runs between the thrill of victory and the agony of defeat. During the years covered by this book, we walked with Nehemiah and the people as they began in defeat, rose in amazing victory, plunged back into defeat, and were restored again to victory. Their journey is filled with important spiritual principles needed for our own spiritual journey:

- God wants our hearts to be broken by the things that break His heart and to bring those things to Him in prayer.
- God guides us to rebuild the walls and gates in our lives, then He asks us to stand guard to protect them.
- God wants us to be aware of the enemy's tactics, and He tells us to clothe ourselves daily with Him in order to stand protected against that enemy.
- God wants us to remember that it is He, the great and awesome God, who fights for us.
- God wants us to be aware of our tendency to trust in ourselves rather than in His mighty ability to guard and protect us.
- God desires a covenant relationship with us in which He will be our God and we will be His people.

Lift Up ...

Dear Lord, just as a father disciplines his children, so You, Father, chasten me at times. Thank You that You care enough to discipline me when I am disobedient. Soften my prideful heart that I might learn from Your correction. In Jesus' name. Amen.

Look At ...

Yesterday we saw the profound effect greed had on the rulers, the people, and the city. Not only was the Sabbath blatantly ignored; it was profaned by greed and selfishness. Sin is never private and greed always creates victims. Nehemiah must have been amazed that God's chosen people had once again followed the path of sin and evil done by their fathers before them. Nehemiah confronted the leaders with their blatant disregard of the Sabbath. Nehemiah drew a line in the sand with the nobles and he took action to ensure they would not cross it.

Nehemiah is the leading man in this true story. He has demonstrated undaunted courage, consistent work, patient prayerfulness, mighty determination, undisturbed hopefulness, righteous anger, and godly leadership. Today we see Nehemiah in a new light. He aggressively confronted a sin repeated again and again by God's people. He reacted in strength because He served a mighty God.

Read Nehemiah 13:23–31.

In those days I also saw Jews who had married women of Ashdod, Ammon, and Moab. And half of their children spoke the language of Ashdod, and could not speak the language of Judah, but spoke according to the language of one or the other people. So I contended with them and cursed them, struck some of them and pulled out their hair, and made them swear by God, saying, "You shall not give your daughters as wives to their sons, nor take their daughters for your sons or yourselves. Did not Solomon king of Israel sin by these things? Yet among many nations there was no king like him, who was beloved of his God; and God made him king over all Israel. Nevertheless pagan women caused even him to sin. Should we then hear of your doing all this great evil, transgressing against our God by marrying pagan women?" And one of the sons of Joiada, the son of Eliashib the high priest, was a son-in-law of Sanballat the Horonite; therefore I drove him from me. Remember them, O my God, because they have defiled the priesthood and the covenant of the priesthood and the Levites. Thus I cleansed them of everything pagan. I also assigned duties to the priests and the Levites, each to his service, and to bringing the wood offering and the firstfruits at appointed times. Remember me, O my God, for good! Nehemiah 13:23–31

1. Who had the Jewish men married?

2. How did this intermarriage affect the children born of the foreign women? Why was this language barrier such a serious problem (Neh. 8:2)?

3. Nehemiah had a strong reaction to this latest trespass by the people. List the five actions he took against (or required of) the people. What did he make them swear not to do?

    1.

    2.

    3.

    4.

    5.

4. Nehemiah drew a parallel between the people's sin and the sin of Solomon. Based on these verses, complete the following sentences about Solomon.

    a. He was king of _____.

    b. Among many _____ there was no _____ like him.

    c. He was _____ of his God.

    d. _____ made him king over Israel.

    e. _____ _____ caused him to sin.

5. The sin of intermarriage affected even the leadership. Eliashib's (the high priest's) grandson had married Sanballat's (local leader's) daughter. What was Nehemiah's attitude toward this leader's grandson?

6. What did Nehemiah first ask God to remember? What two things had the people defiled?

2 The Language of Sin

If the children did not know Hebrew, they would not be able to comprehend the reading of the Law. Therefore, their godly instruction would be greatly hindered. God's Word says, "Therefore you shall lay up these words of mine in your heart and in your soul.... You shall teach them to your children...." (Deut. 11:18–19).

3 Impact on Heritage

This was the latest in a string of broken promises by the people of Judah. In Nehemiah 10:30, the people vowed not to "give our daughters in marriage to the peoples of the land, nor take their daughters for our sons." Yet a few years later, their broken vow resulted in children of dual heritage.

4 Disloyal to God

In 1 Kings 11, we learn that Solomon loved many foreign women (11:1) from the nations that the Lord had told the children of Israel not to intermarry with (11:2). "For it was so, when Solomon was old, that his wives turned his heart after other gods; and his heart was not loyal to the LORD his God" (1 Kings 11:4).

7. In Nehemiah's final prayer, what did he ask God to remember?

Live Out ...

8. Nehemiah was a prayerful and godly leader.

a. Think back on his actions, and list some of the character traits and leadership qualities that he exhibited.

b. Examine your own heart and consider whether you possess and exhibit these qualities. Ask God to build and strengthen any areas you want to improve.

9. God is in the business of renewing and restoring hearts and lives. Look at the following verses and record what God will restore or renew.

Scripture	What God Will Restore or Renew
Psalm 23:3	
Psalm 51:10	
Psalm 51:12	
2 Corinthians 4:16	

10. The people had done good things: they rebuilt the walls and renewed the covenant with the Lord. As time passed, however, complacency crept in, and they sinned against God. The people needed to be reminded of their initial passion to obey God's Word.

In Revelation 2:4–5, Jesus spoke these words to the church at Ephesus (and to us): "I have this against you, that you have left your first love. Remember therefore from where you have fallen; repent and do the first works, or else I will come to you quickly and remove your lampstand from its place—unless you repent."

8 Bookends of Prayer

The book of Nehemiah opens and closes with prayer. Nehemiah regularly communicated with God, asking Him to remember his faithful service. "His conscience was clear, for he knew he had done everything for the good of the people and for the glory of God."[12]

9 People of God

God wants His best for us just as He wants the best from us. "Then I will give them one heart, and I will put a new spirit within them ... that they may walk in My statutes and keep My judgments and do them; and they shall be My people, and I will be their God" (Ezek. 11:19–20).

a. What does Christ have against those to whom He is speaking?

b. Pray through the steps presented in this passage to rekindle your love relationship with Jesus:

> 1. Remember your joy, passion, and commitment at salvation.
>
> 2. Repent of your current sinful habits or lifestyle.
>
> 3. Recall and recommit to some of your first works for the Lord.

c. Journal a prayer asking the Lord to bring you back to your first love—to overcome spiritual complacency—and to restore intimate fellowship with Him.

Here, at the end of our study of Nehemiah, we have seen that God, in His infinite grace and mercy, used Nehemiah to chasten, cleanse, and restore His city and His children. God's people walked closely with Him throughout the entire rebuilding and restoration process; however, when their faith was tested, they stumbled and fell back into their sinful ways.

The distance between the thrill of victory and the agony of defeat might be one small step. We can be sitting high on the mountain of a life victory and the very next moment find ourselves in the valley of failure and defeat: "Never is the believer in greater danger of a spiritual fall, than directly following a spiritual victory. We are prone to drop our guard and begin to trust in ourselves or in our past victories rather than in the Lord. One victory never ensures the next!"[13]

God's desire is to bring restoration to our lives. He was faithful to guide the people of Judah through the process of rebuilding the walls of Jerusalem. He was faithful to bring restoration to their crumbling spiritual lives. He is just as faithful to each of us as He rebuilds and restores us.

Hopefully, God, in His wisdom and grace, has used the book of Nehemiah to bring strength, victory, and restoration in your life so that you may be able to say, as Nehemiah did, "Remember me, O my God, for good" (Neh. 13:31).

Listen To ...

In reading the lives of great men, I found that the first victory they won was over themselves ... self-discipline with all came first.

—*Harry S. Truman*

With Gratitude

Heartfelt appreciation to my family, who enrich my life: thanks to my husband, Skip, for providing a latte each morning and a kiss each night; to my son, Nathan, for a sense of humor that provokes deep belly laughs; to my daughter-in-love, Janaé, for her throw-down loyalty in the face of opposition; to my grandchildren, Seth and Kaydence, for adding such joy to my life.

Special thanks to Misty Foster, Maria Guy, Vicki Perrigo, Trisha Petero, Laura Sowers, and Christy Willis, whose contribution to writing this book is priceless. I'm grateful for the incredible influence of these sisters.

Notes

Lesson One

1. "East Germany Begins Construction of the Berlin Wall," A&E Television Networks, accessed May 11, 2014, www.history.com/this-day-in-history/east-germany-begins-construction-of-the-berlin-wall.

2. Ronald F. Youngblood, F. F. Bruce, and R. K. Harrison, *Nelson's Illustrated Bible Dictionary* (Nashville: Thomas Nelson, 2014), 231.

3. Warren Wiersbe, *Be Determined* (Colorado Springs: David C Cook, 2009), 22.

4. "Berlin Wall," A&E Television Networks, accessed May 11, 2014, www.history.com/topics/cold-war/berlin-wall.

5. "D-Day, June 6, 1944," US Army, accessed May 14, 2014, www.army.mil/d-day.

6. "Prayers of the Presidents," BeliefNet, accessed May 17, 2014, www.beliefnet.com/Faiths/Faith-Tools/Meditation/2005/01/Prayers-Of-The-Presidents.aspx.

7. "Prayers of the Presidents," BeliefNet, accessed May 17, 2014, www.beliefnet.com/Faiths/Faith-Tools/Meditation/2005/01/Prayers-Of-The-Presidents.aspx.

8. Jamie Frater, "Top 10 Fascinating Deathbed Confessions," ListVerse, http://listverse.com/2009/09/29/top-10-fascinating-deathbed-confessions.

9. Raymond Brown, *The Message of Nehemiah* (Downers Grove, IL: InterVarsity Press, 1998), 38.

10. Jamie Frater, "Top 10 Fascinating Deathbed Confessions," ListVerse, September 29, 2009, http://listverse.com/2009/09/29/top-10-fascinating-deathbed-confessions.

11. "Schindler's List," SparkNotes, accessed May 29, 2014, www.sparknotes.com/film/schindlerslist/context.html.

12. "God's Promise to the Nations," BCFWorld, accessed June 3, 2014, www.bcfworld.org/bible_studies/gods_promise_lesson_08.htm.

13. David M. Crow, "Oskar Schindler: The Untold Story," *Forbes*, March 19, 2014, www.forbes.com/sites/stuartanderson/2014/03/19/oskar-schindler-the-untold-story-3.

14. "Nathan Hale Volunteers to Spy behind British Lines," A&E Television Networks, accessed June 4, 2014, www.history.com/this-day-in-history/nathan-hale-volunteers-to-spy-behind-british-lines.

15. Raymond Brown, *The Message of Nehemiah* (Downers Grove, IL: InterVarsity Press, 1998), 41.

16. "Nathan Hale Volunteers to Spy behind British Lines," A&E Television Networks, accessed June 6, 2014, www.history.com/this-day-in-history/nathan-hale-volunteers-to-spy-behind-british-lines.

Lesson Two

1. Eric Metaxas, *7 Men and the Secret of Their Greatness* (Nashville: Thomas Nelson, 2013), 43.

2. Ronald F. Youngblood , F. F. Bruce, and R. K. Harrison, *Nelson's Illustrated Bible Dictionary* (Nashville: Thomas Nelson, 2014), 213.

3. Franklin Graham with Jeanette Lockerbie, *Bob Pierce: This One Thing I Do* (Waco, TX: Word, 1983), 220.

4. Eric Metaxas, *7 Men and the Secret of Their Greatness* (Nashville: Thomas Nelson, 2013), 49–50.

5. Ronald F. Youngblood , F. F. Bruce, and R. K. Harrison, *Nelson's Illustrated Bible Dictionary* (Nashville: Thomas Nelson, 2014), 42.

6. Laurence Bergreen, *Marco Polo: From Venice to Xanadu* (New York: Vintage, 2007), 167.

7. Wikipedia, "1900 Galveston Hurricane," accessed July 17, 2017, https://en.wikipedia.org/wiki/1900_Galveston _hurricane.

8. Wikiquote, "Braveheart," accessed April 9, 2014, http://en.wikiquote.org/w/index.php?title=Special:Cite&page =Braveheart&id=1710683.

9. Wikipedia, "St Crispin's Day Speech," accessed May 21, 2014, https://en.wikipedia.org/wiki/St_Crispin%27s _Day_Speech.

10. Wikiquote, "The Lord of the Rings: The Return of the Kings (film)," accessed June 11, 2014, http://en.wikiquote.org/wiki/The_Lord_of_the_Rings:_The_Return_of_the_King_(film)#Aragorn.

Lesson Three

1. Eileen Flynn, *Why Believe? Foundations of Catholic Theology* (Franklin, WI: Sheed & Ward, 2000), 142.

2. Adapted from *Matthew Henry's Commentary in One Volume* (Grand Rapids, MI: Zondervan, 2000), 493.

3. Warren Wiersbe, *Be Determined* (Colorado Springs: David C Cook, 2009), 48.

4. Wikiquote, "James Hudson Taylor," accessed July 23, 2017, https://en.wikiquote.org/wiki/James_Hudson_Taylor.

5. David Guzik, "The Building of the Walls," Blue Letter Bible, accessed June 14, 2014, www.blueletterbible.org /Comm/guzik_david/StudyGuide_Neh/Neh_3.cfm?a=416001.

6. David Parsons, "Garbage Collectors," SearchSermon, accessed June 14, 2014, www.sermonsearch.com/sermon -illustrations/541/garbage-collectors.

7. "1968 New York and Memphis: Sanitation Workers on Strike," *Workers World*, January 8, 2011, www.workers .org/2011/us/1968_sanitation_workers_0113.

8. Warren Wiersbe, *Be Determined* (Colorado Springs: David C Cook, 2009), 51.

9. Warren Wiersbe, *Be Determined* (Colorado Springs: David C Cook, 2009), 52.

10. Gordon Johnson, "Every Instrument Is Necessary," *Christianity Today*, accessed June 14, 2014, www.preachingtoday.com/illustrations/2000/january/5014.html.

11. Warren Wiersbe, *Be Determined* (Colorado Springs: David C Cook, 2009), 52.

12. *The Nelson Study Bible* (Nashville: Thomas Nelson, 1997), 1293.

13. David Guzik, "The Building of the Walls," Blue Letter Bible, accessed June 14, 2014, www.blueletterbible.org /Comm/guzik_david/StudyGuide_Neh/Neh_3.cfm?a=416001.

14. "Vietnam Veterans Memorial," National Park Service, accessed June 19, 2014, www.nps.gov/vive/faqs.htm.

15. Warren Wiersbe, *Be Determined* (Colorado Springs: David C Cook, 2009), 53.

Lesson Four

1. Wikipedia, "The Screwtape Letters," accessed July 26, 2014, http://en.wikipedia.org/wiki/The_Screwtape_Letters.

2. "C. S. Lewis on 'The Screwtape Letters and Man in Space," CBN.com, accessed July 18, 2017, http://blogs.cbn .com/churchwatch/archive/2010/09/02/c.s.-lewis-on-the-screwtape-letters-and-man-in-space.aspx?mobile=false.

3. Jon Courson, *Jon Courson's Application Commentary* (Nashville: Thomas Nelson, 2005),1247.

4. Wikipedia, "Sticks and Stones," accessed July 18, 2017, https://en.wikipedia.org/wiki/Sticks_and_Stones.

5. "Cyber Bullying Statistics 2014," NoBullying, accessed July 26, 2014, http://nobullying.com/cyber-bullying -statistics-2014/.

6. Adapted from Warren W. Wiersbe, *The Bible Exposition Commentary: Old Testament* (Colorado Springs: Cook Communication Ministries, 2001), 63.

7. Aaron Elstein, "Partners in Crime: Gupta, Rajaratnam in Same Prison," Crain Communications, June 17, 2014, www.crainsnewyork.com/article/20140617/BLOGS02/140619877/partners-in-crime-gupta-rajaratnam-in -same-prison.

8. Matthew Henry, *Matthew Henry's Concise Commentary on the Whole Bible* (Nashville: Thomas Nelson, 1997), 399.

9. Katherina Hauner, "Why Do We Develop Certain Irrational Phobias?," *Scientific American*, December 19, 2013, www.scientificamerican.com/article/why-do-we-develop-certain-irrationa/.

10. Adapted from Warren W. Wiersbe, *The Bible Exposition Commentary: Old Testament* (Colorado Springs: Cook Communication Ministries, 2001), 64.

11. "Oprah Talks to Jaime Foxx," *Oprah*, December 2005, www.oprah.com/omagazine/Oprahs-Interview-with -Jamie-Foxx.

12. The Free Dictionary, "Caveat Emptor," accessed July 26, 2014, http://legal-dictionary.thefreedictionary.com /Buyer+beware.

13. "Woman Learns House Was Scene of Murder, Torture," Fox 6 News, July 8, 2014, http://ksn.com/2014/07/08 /woman-learns-home-was-scene-of-murder-torture/.

14. Wikipedia, "Louis Zamperini," accessed July 14, 2014, http://en.wikipedia.org/wiki/Louis_Zamperini.

15. Associated Press, "Louis Zamperini, World War II Hero and Olympian, Dies," *USA Today*, July 3, 2014, www.usatoday.com/story/sports/olympics/2014/07/03/louis-zamperini-olympic-runner-world-war-ii -veteran-dies/12132699.

16. Jon Courson, *Jon Courson's Application Commentary* (Nashville: Thomas Nelson, 2005), 1250.

17. Associated Press, "Louis Zamperini, World War II Hero and Olympian, Dies," *USA Today*, July 3, 2014, www.usatoday.com/story/sports/olympics/2014/07/03/louis-zamperini-olympic-runner-world-war-ii -veteran-dies/12132699.

18. Wikipedia, "Louis Zamperini," accessed July 14, 2014, http://en.wikipedia.org/wiki/Louis_Zamperini.

19. James Montgomery Boice, *Nehemiah* (Grand Rapids, MI: Baker, 2005), 57.

Lesson Five

1. dc Talk, *Jesus Freaks: Martyrs* (Minneapolis, MN: Bethany, 1999), 84.

2. Adapted from *Vine's Complete Expository Dictionary of Old and New Testament Words* (Nashville: Thomas Nelson, 1996), 25.

3. C. H. Spurgeon, *The Salt Cellars* (London: Alabaster, Passmore, and Sons, 1889), 165.

4. Khaled Hosseini, *The Kite Runner* (New York: Penguin, 2004), 27.

5. C. H. Spurgeon, "The Bed and Its Covering," January 9, 1859, www.sermonindex.net/modules/articles/index .php?view=article&aid=1371.

6. Adapted from Sermon Central Text Illustrators, Matthew Kray, Dec. 2007, www.sermoncentral.com/illustrations /sermon-illustration-matthew-kratz-stories-64094.

7. Jon Bloom, "Lay Aside the Fear of Man," Desiring God, July 23, 2017, www.desiringgod.org/articles/lay-aside -the-fear-of-man.

8. Raymond Brown, *The Message of Nehemiah* (Downers Grove, IL: InterVarsity Press, 1998), 95.

9. Warren Wiersbe, *Be Determined* (Colorado Springs: David C Cook, 2009), 76.

10. Joyce Cary, *Except the Lord* (New York: New Directions, 1953), 47.

11. C. Philip Green, "Moses Prayer: A Prayer for Mercy," February 3, 2015, www.sermoncentral.com/sermons /moses-prayer-a-prayer-for-mercy-c-philip-green-sermon-on-moses-intercedes-191264?page=5.

12. Adapted from *The Bible Knowledge Commentary: Old Testament* (Wheaton, IL: Victor Books, 1985), 684.

13. Evan Stretch, "British Prisoner of War Freed to Visit Dying Mother Kept His Promise and Returned to German Captors," *Mirror*, September 4, 2013, www.mirror.co.uk/news/real-life-stories/british-prisoner-war-freed -visit-2248453.

14. Adapted from Sermon Central Illustrations, "No Failure," Steve Shepherd, accessed July 19, 2017, www.sermoncentral.com/sermons/no-failure-steve-shepherd-sermon-on-faith-125967.

15. J. Oswald Sanders, *Spiritual Leadership* (Chicago, IL: Moody Press, 1994), 22.

16. Adapted from Sermon Central Text Illustrations, "Leadership Magazine Carried a Story about 4 Young Men," Melvin Newland, accessed July 5, 2014, https://sermoncentral.com/illustrations/sermon-illustration-melvin -newland-stories-giving-1397?ref=TextIllustrationSerps.

Lesson Six

1. Roy E. Plotnick, "In Search of Watty Piper: A Brief History of the 'Little Engine' Story," accessed July 1, 2014, http://tigger.uic.edu/~plotnick/littleng.htm.

2. Charles W. Draper, ed., *Holman Illustrated Bible Dictionary* (Nashville: Holman Bible Publishers, 2003), 641, 1443, 1603.

3. Wikiquote, "An Essay on Man," accessed July 19, 2017, https://en.wikiquote.org/wiki/An_Essay_on_Man.

4. Charles W. Draper, ed., *Holman Illustrated Bible Dictionary* (Nashville: Holman Bible Publishers, 2003), 1223.

5. James Montgomery Boice, *Nehemiah* (Grand Rapids, MI: Baker, 2005), 70.

6. Charles R. Swindoll, *The Tale of the Tardy Oxcart* (Nashville: Word, 1998), 438.

7. Warren Wiersbe, *Be Determined* (Colorado Springs: David C Cook, 1992), 87.

8. Brownie Marie, "Maya Angelou on Christian Faith: 'If God Loves Me, What Is It I Can't Do?,'" *Christianity Today*, May 29, 2014, www.christiantoday.com/article/maya.angelou.christian.faith.civil.rights.leader.passes .away.86/37748.htm.

9. Maya Angelou, "Still I Rise," PBS, June 5, 2014, www.pbs.org/wnet/americanmasters/blog/maya-angelou -still-rise/.

10. Adapted from Secret Angel, "Little Red Riding Hood … Beware of Wolves in Sheep's Clothing!," *The Christian Gazette*, June 18, 2014, http://thechristiangazette.wordpress.com/2014/06/18/little-red-riding-hood-beware -of-wolves-in-sheeps-clothing-acts-2029.

11. Charles W. Draper, ed., *Holman Illustrated Bible Dictionary* (Nashville, TN: Holman Bible Publishers, 2003), 1194.

12. "Aesop & Aesop's Fables," Greek Myths & Greek Mythology, accessed July 7, 2014, www.greekmyths-greekmythology.com/aesop-greek-aesops-fables.

13. Adapted from "The Tortoise and the Hare," Story Arts, accessed July 7, 2014, www.storyarts.org/library /aesops/stories/tortoise.html.

14. Charles W. Draper, ed., *Holman Illustrated Bible Dictionary* (Nashville: Holman Bible Publishers, 2003), 485.

15. James Montgomery Boice, *Nehemiah* (Grand Rapids, MI: Baker, 2005), 74–75.

16. Wikipedia, "Three Little Pigs," accessed July 8, 2014, http://en.wikipedia.org/wiki/Three_Little_Pigs.

17. John F. Walvoord and Roy B. Zuck, *The Bible Knowledge Commentary* (Colorado Springs: Cook Communications Ministries, 1985), 686–87.

18. Charles R. Swindoll, *The Tale of the Tardy Oxcart* (Nashville: Word, 1998), 440.

Lesson Seven

1. "Paul Revere: A Brief Biography," Paul Revere Memorial Association, accessed September 12, 2014, www.paulreverehouse.org/bio/bio.html.

2. "Billy Graham, Quotes," Good Reads, accessed July 19, 2017, www.goodreads.com/author/quotes/40328 .Billy_Graham.

3. Jamieson-Fausset-Brown, "Nehemiah 7:3," Bible Hub, accessed October 2, 2014, http://biblehub.com /commentaries/nehemiah/7-3.htm.

4. "Starting a Neighborhood Watch," National Crime Prevention Council, 2002, www.ncpc.org/resources/files /pdf/neighborhood-safety/nwstart.pdf.

5. "Paul Revere: A Brief Biography," Paul Revere Memorial Association, accessed September 12, 2014, www.paulreverehouse.org/bio/bio.html.

6. "Paul Revere: A Brief Biography," Paul Revere Memorial Association, accessed September 12, 2014, www.paulreverehouse.org/bio/bio.html.

7. Kristi Hedges, "The Five Best Tricks to Remember Names," *Forbes*, August 21, 2013, www.forbes.com /sites/work-in-progress/2013/08/21/the-best-five-tricks-to-remember-names.

8. Alicia Crane Williams, "Part 1: The Society of Mayflower Descendants," accessed September 12, 2014, www.americanancestors.org/staticcontent/articles?searchby=author&subquery=Alicia%20Crane %20Williams&id=256.

9. "Zerubbabel," Bible Hub, accessed October 6, 2014, http://biblehub.com/topical/z/zerubbabel.htm.

10. Alicia Crane Williams, "Part 1: The Society of Mayflower Descendants," accessed September 12, 2014, www.americanancestors.org/staticcontent/articles?searchby=author&subquery=Alicia%20Crane %20Williams&id=256.

11. "New American Stories," The National Partnership for New Americans, accessed September 22, 2014, www.partnershipfornewamericans.org/new-american-stories.

12. Ronald F. Youngblood, F. F. Bruce, R. K. Harrison, *Nelson's Illustrated Study Bible Dictionary* (Nashville: Thomas Nelson, 2014), 806.

13. "Citizenship Rights and Responsibilities," US Citizenship and Immigration Services, accessed September 20, 2014, www.uscis.gov/citizenship/learners/citizenship-rights-and-responsibilities.

14. "Citizenship Rights and Responsibilities," US Citizenship and Immigration Services, accessed September 20, 2014, www.uscis.gov/citizenship/learners/citizenship-rights-and-responsibilities.

15. Ryan Bonfiglio, "Priests and Priesthood in the Hebrew Bible," Oxford Biblical Studies Online, accessed October 11, 2014, www.oxfordbiblicalstudies.com/resource/priests.xhtml.

16. "Citizenship Rights and Responsibilities," US Citizenship and Immigration Services, accessed September 20, 2014, www.uscis.gov/citizenship/learners/citizenship-rights-and-responsibilities.

Lesson Eight

1. Wikipedia, "March on Washington for Jobs and Freedom," accessed July 18, 2014, http://en.wikipedia.org/w/index.php?title=March_on_Washington_for_Jobs_and_Freedom&oldid=617400152.

2. Wikipedia, "March on Washington for Jobs and Freedom," accessed July 18, 2014, http://en.wikipedia.org/w/index.php?title=March_on_Washington_for_Jobs_and_Freedom&oldid=617400152.

3. "How to Listen," WikiHow, accessed July 22, 2014, www.wikihow.com/Listen.

4. Warren Wiersbe, *Be Determined* (Colorado Springs: David C Cook, 2009), 110–19.

5. "How to Listen," WikiHow, accessed July 22, 2014, www.wikihow.com/Listen.

6. Ivan Lindsay, "Good as New—The Benefits and Dangers of Art Restoration," The Getty Conservation, December 4, 2012, www.getty.edu/conservation/publications_resources/books/solvent_gels_for_cleaning.html.

7. "Simply Teach Simply: Sermon Notes for Nehemiah 8:8," Blue Letter Bible, Chuck Smith, accessed July 19, 2017, www.blueletterbible.org/Comm/smith_chuck/SermonNotes_Neh/Neh_13.cfm.

8. David Kertzer, "The Kidnapping of Edgardo Mortara," accessed October 23, 2014, www.davidkertzer.com/books/kidnapping-edgardo-mortara.

9. Tracey Rich, "Judaism 101: Rosh Hashanah," accessed October 9, 2014, www.jewfaq.org/holiday2.htm.

10. Wikipedia, "Runaway Bride Case," accessed October 29, 2014, http://en.wikipedia.org/w/index.php?title=Runaway_bride_case&oldid=630116825.

11. J. I. Packer, "The Visitation of God," Bible.org, accessed July 23, 2017, https://bible.org/illustration/visitation-god.

12. "We Need a Heaven-Sent Revival: A Classic Message from Billy Graham," accessed July 20, 2017, https://billygraham.org/decision-magazine/july-2017/56832-2/.

Lesson Nine

1. Tony Cauchi, "The First Great Awakening in America—George Whitefield," Revival Library, May 2006, www.revival-library.org/index.php/pensketches-menu/historical-revivals/1st-great-awakening-g-whitefield-usa.

2. Bible Hub, "Hamartia," accessed July 20, 2017, http://biblehub.com/greek/266.htm.

3. Tony Cauchi, "The First Great Awakening—George Whitefield," Revival Library, May 2006, www.revival-library .org/index.php/pensketches-menu/historical-revivals/1st-great-awakening-g-whitefield-usa.

4. Herbert Vander Lugt, "I Will Be Good," Our Daily Bread, May 23, 2005, https://odb.org/2005/05/23/i-will -be-good/.

5. Ronald F. Youngblood , F. F. Bruce, and R. K. Harrison, *Nelson's Illustrated Bible Dictionary* (Nashville: Thomas Nelson, 2014), 1002.

6. Merrill F. Unger, *The New Unger's Bible Dictionary* (Chicago: Moody Press, 1988), 1012.

7. David C. McCasland, "Heed the Warning," Our Daily Bread, May 3, 2006, http://odb.org/2006/05/03/heed -the-warning.

8. Merrill F. Unger, *The New Unger's Bible Dictionary* (Chicago, IL: Moody Press, 1988), 754.

9. Dennis J. DeHaan, "The Eraser of Confession," Our Daily Bread, July 28, 2006, https://odb.org/2006/07/28/the -eraser-of-confession/.

10. Dennis Fisher, "Our Moral Compass," Our Daily Bread, August 4, 2009, https://odb.org/2009/08/04/our-moral -compass/.

11. David Guzik, "Israel Confesses Their Sin," Blue Letter Bible, accessed September 20, 2014, www.blueletterbible.org/Comm/guzik_david/StudyGuide_Neh/Neh_9.cfm.

12. Warren W. Wiersbe, *The Bible Exposition Commentary: Old Testament* (Colorado Springs: Cook Communication Ministries, 2001), 682.

Lesson Ten

1. Charles Moore, "The Young Princess Has Always Kept the Faith with Her People," *The Telegraph*, June 1, 2012, www.telegraph.co.uk/news/uknews/queen-elizabeth-II/9305673/The-young-Princess-has-always-kept-the -faith-with-her-people.html.

2. Vasan Kesavan, "Oath of Office," The Heritage Foundation, accessed August 5, 2014, www.heritage.org/constitution/#!/articles/2/essays/85/oath-of-office.

3. Charles W. Draper, ed., *Holman Illustrated Bible Dictionary* (Nashville: Holman Bible Publishers, 2003), 1427.

4. Charles W. Draper, ed., *Holman Illustrated Bible Dictionary* (Nashville: Holman Bible Publishers, 2003), 1043.

5. Mary Fairchild, "Why Do Christians Worship on Sunday?," ThoughtCo, accessed August 4, 2014, http://christianity.about.com/od/whatdoesthebiblesay/f/sundayworship.htm.

6. James Montgomery Boice, *Nehemiah* (Grand Rapids, MI: Baker, 2005), 111.

7. John H. Walton, Victor H. Matthews, and Mark W. Chavalas, *The IVP Background Commentary*, Old Testament (Madison, WI: Intervarsity Press, 2000), 480, 144.

8. Warren Wiersbe, *Be Determined* (Colorado Springs: David C Cook, 2009), 138–39.

9. Charles R. Swindoll, *The Tale of the Tardy Oxcart* (Nashville: Word Publishing Group, 1998), 230.

10. Charles R. Swindoll, *The Tale of the Tardy Oxcart* (Nashville: Word Publishing Group, 1998), 230.

11. David Murray, "10 Reasons Why It Is More Blessed to Give Than to Receive," Christianity, accessed August 8, 2014, www.christianity.com/church/tithing-and-giving/10-reasons-why-it-is-more-blessed-to-give-than-to -receive.html.

12. Charles R. Swindoll, *The Tale of the Tardy Oxcart* (Nashville: Word, 1998), 392.

13. James Montgomery Boice, *Nehemiah* (Grand Rapids, MI: Baker, 2005), 112.

14. Warren Wiersbe, *Be Determined* (Colorado Springs: David C Cook, 2009), 140.

15. John H. Walton, Victor H. Matthews, and Mark W. Chavalas, *The IVP Background Commentary*, Old Testament (Madison, WI: Intervarsity Press, 2000), 155.

16. James Montgomery Boice, *Nehemiah* (Grand Rapids, MI: Baker, 2005), 113.

17. Dorothy Valcarcel, Transformation Garden—June 20, 2012, accessed July 20, 2017, www.ibelieve.com /devotionals/transformation-garden/transformation-garden-june-20-2012.html.

18. Robert J. Morgan, *Then Sings My Soul* (Nashville: Thomas Nelson, 2003), 214–15.

Lesson Eleven

1. Jonathan Bernis, "Prophetic Fulfillment: Regathering the 'Lost Tribes' of Israel," Charisma News, October 13, 2014, www.charismanews.com/opinion/45733-prophetic-fulfillment-regathering-the-lost-tribes-of-israel.

2. Warren W. Wiersbe, *The Bible Exposition Commentary: Old Testament* (Colorado Springs: Cook Communication Ministries, 2001), 143.

3. Jon Courson, *Jon Courson's Application Commentary* (Nashville: Thomas Nelson, 2005), 1261.

4. Wikipedia, "1906 San Francisco Earthquake, " accessed November 22, 2014, http://en.wikipedia.org/wiki/1906 _San_Francisco_earthquake#cite_note-37.

5. "San Francisco History," *The New San Francisco Magazine*, accessed November 22, 2014, www.sfgenealogy.com/sf /history/1906/06nsfmart.htm.

6. Mark Matthews, "Butts Fire: Neighbors Evacuated, Napa County Man Stays Behind to Care for Neighbors' Pets," NBC Bay Area, July 3, 2014, http://www.nbcbayarea.com/news/local/Napa-County-Man-Stays-Behind-to -Care-for-Neighbors-Pets-265774271.html.

7. *The Nelson Study Bible* (Nashville: Thomas Nelson, 1997), 805.

8. *The Nelson Study Bible* (Nashville: Thomas Nelson, 1997), 805.

9. "9/11 Ten Years Later, Remembering Avremel (Abe) Zelmanowitz," Jewish Action, August 17, 2011, www.ou.org/jewish_action/08/2011/9_11_ten_years_later/.

10. Amy Dempsey, "Identical Twins Adopted from China by Two Different Ontario Families Grow Up 400 km Apart," *The Star*, March 3, 2012, www.thestar.com/news/insight/2012/03/03/identical_twins_adopted_from _china_by_two_different_ontario_families_grow_up_400_km_apart.html.

11. Wikipedia, "Separation Anxiety Disorder," accessed October 17, 2014, http://en.wikipedia.org/wiki /Separation_anxiety_disorder.

12. Os Hillman, *TGIF: Today God Is First* (Grand Rapids, MI: Baker, 2007).

13. *Keil & Delitzsch Commentary on the Old Testament: New Updated Edition* (Peabody, MA: Hendrickson, 1996).

14. Wikipedia, "Mother Teresa," accessed November 22, 2014, http://en.wikipedia.org/wiki/Mother_Teresa.

15. Harriet Heyman, "Teresa of the Slums," *Life Magazine*, July 1980, www.maryellenmark.com/text/magazines /life/905W-000-014.html.

16. Wikipedia, "The Western Wall, " accessed November 22, 2014, http://en.wikipedia.org/wiki/Western_Wall#cite
_ref-111.

17. James Montgomery Boice, *Nehemiah* (Grand Rapids, MI: Baker, 2005), 128.

18. *The Nelson Study Bible* (Nashville: Thomas Nelson, 1997), 806.

19. Wikipedia, "Placing Notes in the Western Wall," accessed July 20, 2017, https://en.wikipedia.org/wiki
/Placing_notes_in_the_Western_Wall.

Lesson Twelve

1. Wikipedia, "Vinko Bogataj," accessed September 18, 2014, https://en.wikipedia.org/wiki/Vinko_Bogataj.

2. Pat Forde, "Agony of Defeat Trumps Thrill of Victory," ESPN, August 2, 2010, http://sports.espn.go.com/ncf
/columns/story?id=5428166.

3. Robert Boyd Munger, *My Heart Christ's Home* (Minneapolis, MN: Billy Graham Evangelistic Association,
1955), 1.

4. Raymond Brown, *The Message of Nehemiah* (Downers Grove, IL: InterVarsity Press, 1998), 228.

5. Robert Boyd Munger, *My Heart Christ's Home* (Minneapolis, MN: Billy Graham Evangelistic Association,
1955), 12.

6. Adapted from Quick Verse Sermon Builder 4.0, 2005, "A Brother Like That."

7. Wikipedia, "Rich Mullins," accessed September 15, 2014, https://en.wikipedia.org/wiki/Rich_mullins.

8. Adapted from Davon Huss, "Man in a Hurry," Sermon Central Text Illustrators, January 7, 2014,
www.sermoncentral.com/illustrations/sermon-illustration-davon-huss-stories-trials-frustration-hurry-83574.asp.

9. Warren Wiersbe, *Be Determined* (Colorado Springs: David C Cook, 2009), 164.

10. "What Is the Difference between Mercy and Grace?," The GQ Network, accessed 12 Nov. 2014,
www.gotquestions.org/mercy-grace.html.

11. "Eric Liddell," Biography, accessed October 10, 2014, www.biography.com/people/eric-liddell-9381746.

12. Warren Wiersbe, *Be Determined* (Colorado Springs: David C Cook, 2009), 149.

13. "The Agony of Defeat (Joshua 7:1–26)," Bible.org, accessed August 26, 2014, https://bible.org/article
/agony-defeat-joshua-71-26.

About the Author

Born in a small town on the shores of Lake Michigan, Lenya Heitzig moved to beach cities in California and Hawaii before settling into the mountainous terrain of Albuquerque, New Mexico, where she now resides. Whether majoring in fashion merchandising, or serving as a missionary with YWAM, or being a cancer survivor, Lenya thrives on adventure. As executive director of *she* Ministries at Calvary Albuquerque and coauthor for two Bible study series—the Fresh Life series and the Pathway series.

Lenya delights in seeing God's Word do God's work in the lives of women. Her first book, *Pathway to God's Treasure: Ephesians*, received the Gold Medallion Award. She also contributed a number of devotionals to the *New Women's Devotional Bible*, which was a finalist in the 2007 Christian Book Awards. Her semi-biographical book, *Holy Moments*, published by Regal, enlightens readers to see God's hand of providence move miraculously in daily life. Her husband, Skip Heitzig, is senior pastor of a fourteen thousand-member congregation. Their son, Nathan, and his wife, Janaé, have two children, Seth Nathaniel and Kaydence Joy.

Fresh Life
20-Minutes-a-Day Studies

Designed with today's busy woman in mind,
each lesson can be completed in as little as 20 minutes per day,
but leave you with a lifetime of valuable insights.

Live Fearlessly
A Study in the Book of Joshua
ISBN 978-1-4347-9941-8

Live Hopefully
A Study in the Book of Nehemiah
ISBN 978-1-4347-1247-9

Live Deeply
A Study of the Parables of Jesus
ISBN 978-1-4347-9986-9

Live Brilliantly
A Study in the Book of 1 John
ISBN 978-1-4347-1248-6

Live Intimately
Lessons from the Upper Room
ISBN 978-1-4347-6790-5

Available wherever Christian books are sold

DAVID C COOK
transforming lives together